STUDIES IN PLAY AND GAMES

This is a volume in the Arno Press collection

STUDIES IN PLAY AND GAMES

Advisory Editor

Brian Sutton-Smith

Editorial Board

E.M. Avedon
Andreas Flitner
John W. Loy

*See last page of this volume
for a complete list of titles*

THE PSYCHOLOGY OF PLAY ACTIVITIES

BY

HARVEY C. LEHMAN

AND

PAUL A. WITTY

ARNO PRESS

A New York Times Company

New York — 1976

Editorial Supervision: SHEILA MEHLMAN

———◆———

Reprint Edition 1976 by Arno Press Inc.

Reprinted from a copy in the University
  of Virginia Library

STUDIES IN PLAY AND GAMES
ISBN for complete set: 0-405-07912-5
See last pages of this volume for titles.

Manufactured in the United States of America

———◆———

Library of Congress Cataloging in Publication Data

Lehman, Harvey Christian.
    The psychology of play activities.

    (Studies in play and games)
    Reprint of the 1927 ed. published by A. S. Barnes,
New York.
    Includes bibliographies.
    1. Play. 2. Child psychology. I. Witty, Paul
Andrew, 1898-   joint author. II. Title.
III. Series. [DNLM: 1. Play--Collected works.
WS105 P976]
BF717.L4 1976   155.4'1   75-35074
ISBN 0-405-07924-9

THE PSYCHOLOGY OF
PLAY ACTIVITIES

BY

HARVEY C. LEHMAN

AND

PAUL A. WITTY

School of Education, University of Kansas

NEW YORK

A. S. BARNES AND COMPANY

1927

PREFACE

One of the great contributions of psychology to education has been emphasis upon individual differences. Through extended research, we have learned much regarding what to expect of children of various stages of development. The intelligence test and its educational corollary, the standardized educational test, have effected a more intelligent and satisfactory adjustment of the child to his school life. Differentiated education is the result of the recognition of the variability of human beings in mental ability and consequent educational attainment. The dissemination of knowledge regarding individual differences gleaned from intelligence tests has been a potent factor in effecting reorganization of school practices.

Individual differences in mental development are, however, only a small portion of total human variation. Some insist that the more important variables conditioning individual adjustment are associated with certain personality traits. The temperamental traits constituting personality are not amenable to any psychological refinement of standardization. They depend upon the child's condition as a unit, resulting from his heredity and all of the environmental factors acting upon him during the growth period. Though not directly measurable through the tools now available, these personality traits are reflected in certain forms of *behavior*. One type of behavior of paramount significance in determining a child's adjustment is his play.

The activities to which children and adults spontaneously turn in their leisure are becoming increasingly significant features of present-day life. The present standard of living has resulted not only in greater material comfort and more leisure for the wealthy but it has made possible a diffusion of the gains of civilization providing greater material comfort and greater leisure for the masses.

Since the year 1889 the personnel required to produce a unit of manufactured product has decreased 33 per cent. This increased efficiency makes for a higher standard of living which in turn increases human efficiency. Thus an unending circle is produced, increased production resulting in a higher standard of living and the higher standard of living resulting in further increase of production. It is inevitable that the time and money devoted to leisure occupations will increase as time goes on.

It is felt by many that much present-day maladjustment results from the unwise choice of leisure-time activities. It is, of course, obvious that educators should assume the responsibility of training children for profitable use of leisure. The first step in such a procedure implies an accurate accounting of what children actually do in their leisure time. The second step implies an evaluation of the multitudinous activities of childhood in terms of their individual or social worth.

The play life of children constitutes a significant part of their leisure-time activity; detailed knowledge of play should form a salient feature of any thorough-going attempt to evaluate leisure-time activities.

The present writers have attempted to discover: (1) the games and other play activities most commonly engaged in by persons from five to twenty-two years of age residing in certain communities: (2) the games and other play activities these individuals liked best; (3) the games and other play activities on which these individuals thought they had spent the largest amount of time; and (4) the effect on play behavior of such variables as age, sex, race, season, intelligence, community, etc.

The modification or the elimination of unwholesome desires with provision for satisfying wholesome desires must be reserved until decision in reference to "wholesome" and "unwholesome" activities has been agreed upon. Popular opinion assumes a given activity either to be desirable or undesirable. It may be that the amount of time and energy devoted to a given activity is a fairly reliable criterion of the desirability of that activity. Practical observation seems to indicate that moderation is desirable in many activities. Similarly social activities are often assumed to be wholly desirable. Common sense would seem to support the thesis that though it is necessary for the child to mingle with other children in order to learn how to get along with other people, it is desirable that he be alone a part of the time in order that individuality may develop to its maximum.

Lack of adequate technique heretofore has militated against measurement of the extent to which a given child mingles with other children. Obviously there is need to account for the child's social contacts. Deviation from normal in respect to social participation will be intelligible to the student of education only when it is measured quantitatively. Qualitative expression of deviation is no longer satisfactory. The present study represents but a beginning of quantitative measurement of play behavior.

The present writers are under obligation to former teachers and colleagues who stimulated the series of investigations and subsequent interpretations. The first-named author wishes to acknowledge his indebtedness to Professor Charles H. Judd for suggestion of the initial study. He is greatly indebted also to Professor Frank H. Freeman for encouragement and valuable suggestions given during the time that he was engaged in working out a doctor's dissertation on this subject. The second-named author who collaborated in the last investigation and the interpretation of the data wishes to acknowledge his indebtedness to his former teachers of Educational Psychology at Columbia University whose opinions are reflected frequently throughout the book.

Both authors are indebted to Dean Raymond A. Schwegler of the University of Kansas for his frequent and helpful advice. They wish to express their sincere thanks to the various public school. officials who granted facilities for the researches. They are obligated especially to Mr. Lawson Wise of the Kansas City, Kansas, public schools, and to Mr. George Melcher of the Kansas City, Missouri, public schools for coöperation granted so willingly. The authors take pleasure in acknowledging the courtesy of the editors of the following publications for permission to reproduce material that has previously appeared in print: The Pedagogical Seminary, The Psychological Review, Supplementary Educational Monographs (Department of Education of The University of Chicago), Education, The High School Quarterly, The Playground, The Educational Review, The Journal of Educational

Method, Childhood Education, The Journal of Religious Education, The Journal of Educational Psychology, The Journal of Applied Psychology, The American Physical Education Review, and The Journal of Rural Education.

HARVEY C. LEHMAN.

PAUL A. WITTY.

THE UNIVERSITY OF KANSAS,
  January, 1927.

CONTENTS

LIST OF ILLUSTRATIONS

LIST OF TABLES

CHAPTER I

CHANGING ATTITUDES TOWARD PLAY *

The effort to discover what education should accomplish in the light of the contradictory and varied demands of present-day life constitutes the significant work of philosophers in education. As conditions and demands of life change, so too does the philosophy. The successive demands and the consequent changes in our philosophy of education are reflected in the changing attitudes toward various forms of human behavior. Conspicuous among such radically changed attitudes is that toward play. The attitude toward play which dominated the schools of America until very recently was the product of religious conviction; it was the result of an uncritical acceptance of customs brought from the old world. The following quotation gives evidence of the coercive measures of school discipline employed in Germany at the beginning of the 18th century:

" 'Play,' said Franke, 'must be forbidden in any and all of its forms. The children shall be instructed in this matter in such a way as to show them, through the presentation of religious principles, the wastefulness and folly of all play. They shall be led to see that play will distract their hearts and minds from God, the eternal Good, and will work nothing but harm to their spiritual lives. Their true joy and hearty devotion should be given to their blessed and holy Savior and not to earthly things, for the reward of those who seek earthly things is tears and sorrow.' " [1]

The Methodist Church in America in 1792 gave sanction to an educational system similar to that advocated by Franke. This scheme too resulted from deep-rooted religious convictions and squared with the prevailing doctrine of total depravity.

" . . . we prohibit *play* in the strongest terms. . . .

"The students shall rise at five o'clock . . . summer and winter. . . .

* Printed in *The Playground* for November, 1926, and here republished with the consent of the editors.

1

Their recreation shall be gardening, walking, riding, and bathing, without doors, and the carpenter's, joiner's, cabinet-maker's or turner's business within doors. . . . A person skilled in gardening shall be appointed to overlook the students . . . in this recreation. . . . A Master . . . shall always be present at the time of bathing. Only one shall bathe at a time; and no one shall remain in the water above a minute. No student shall be allowed to bathe in the river. A *Taberna Lignaria* (carpenter's shop) shall be provided . . . with all proper instruments and materials, and a skillful person . . . to overlook the students at this recreation. . . . The students shall be indulged with nothing which the world calls *play*. Let this rule be observed with the strictest nicety; for those who play when they are young, will play when they are old." Discipline of the M. E. Church. 1792.[2]

FOLLY OF TRYING TO SUPPRESS THE PLAY IMPULSE

The traditional attitude toward play was modified gradually. The change was occasioned largely by the stimulating discussions of foreign educational philosophies which American students of education brought home from the old world. The influence of Rousseau was a potent force in effecting this change.

The past 25 years have encompassed rapid changes in the philosophy of education. A variety of forces have caused educators to examine critically prevailing customs. Attempts have been made to codify experience and to develop a consistent system of thought and educational procedure. The various attempts have culminated in their highest form in the philosophy of John Dewey. His attitude toward play is expressed in the following:

"The idea that the need (for play) can be suppressed is absolutely fallacious, and the Puritanic tradition which disallows the need has entailed an enormous crop of evils. If education does not afford opportunity for wholesome recreation and train capacity for seeking and finding it, the suppressed instincts find all sorts of illicit outlets, sometimes overt, sometimes confined to indulgence of the imagination. Education has no more serious responsibility than making adequate provision for enjoyment of recreative leisure; not only for the sake of immediate health, but still more if possible for the sake of its lasting effect upon habits of mind." [3]

PLAY A DIRECT EDUCATIVE AGENT

Professor Dewey's insistence upon education as life and not a preparation therefor has resulted in the overthrow of many traditional doctrines. The school curriculum consists not of a preconceived body of dogma but of an abundance of experience vital to and part of the life of the developing child. The idea that subject matter is to be found in the experience of the child leads the educator to an evaluation of all experience in which the child takes part in and out of school. The play life of the child must therefore be treated as an educative agent.

"For years, play was looked upon merely as a sort of inevitable waste of time among children, but scientific study . . . has shown that play is in most respects the best, the ideal form of the exercise of the powers. Particularly is it true of younger children, but it is in a large measure true as they grow older. . . . The young child perhaps learns more and develops better through its play than through any other form of activity." [4]

Thorndike has pointed to the fact that all learning involves reacting and that without reaction nothing is learned. Since play activities afford children opportunities to react it follows that play activities afford them opportunities to learn. Inasmuch as play is a constituent of growth, it follows that play affords children an excellent opportunity for learning. Carr has summed up the value of play responses in child development as follows:

First, Play reactions are easier than those of work, because they involve the oldest and most used centers.

Second, Play brings a greater amount of activity, because it is easier, more pleasurable, and less fatiguing than work.

Third, The intensity of response is greater, because attention is undivided and spontaneous, and therefore interest is keener.

Fourth, Play is a better stimulant to growth and development than work because it meets nature's demands in a natural and timely way.

Fifth, Play is the most variable of all reactions, and thus provides constant and suitable exercise of all important physical and mental activities. [5]

PLAY A MECHANISM OF INDIVIDUAL ADJUSTMENT

Recent writers have emphasized the value of play as a mechanism of adjustment. Many writers have stressed the importance of play in obtaining well-rounded physical development. Others have pointed out that play forms an important instrument in developing mental balance.

Watson has stated that the growing boy is "straightened out" by the knocks received from other boys.

"The indulgent mother favors a certain child, allows it to eat what it wants, to play with what it calls for, puts no authority upon it, does everything for it and even anticipates its demands. . . . During boyhood he is petted and spoiled. His side is taken whenever the other boys attempt to give him the knocks that would straighten him out. . . . As long as the old favoring environment lasts he floats, but when a crisis occurs, when he is forced to face the world unaided, he has not the assets with which to do it. His equipment is inadequate." [6]

The importance of utilizing the play life of the child in effective well-balanced development is expressed in the following:

"In short, play is the principal instrument of growth. It is safe to conclude that, without play, there would be no normal adult cognitive life; without play, no healthful development of affective life; without play, no full development of the power of the will." [7]

PLAY A SOCIALIZING FORCE

To participate intelligently in group life, voluntary coöperation is necessary. The following quotations show the value of play in developing this ability.

"Growth through play is evident in the development of the social nature of the child, and is especially marked in the development of his consciousness of kinship with a group. . . . Child play reproduces on its level the struggles and achievements of developed social life . . . the child gradually approaches the stern adult realities, taught and trained, hardened and softened, warmed and cooled, roused and rationalized, through these very engagements in play, which without break or loss of their original character gradually blend into the duties, responsibilities, opportunities, and achievements of adult life." [8]

"Play is essentially social; it is, therefore, natural that one of its aims and rewards should be a sense of fellowship . . . the playing group fuses into a common consciousness on a plane of equality. . . . Play is the making of a social man. It is that which welds the bonds of fellowship in the social group. We become like those with whom we play. . . ." [9]

Again, McDougall stresses the value of play as a socializing force. Following is a summary of McDougall's position:

Play has a socializing influence, molding the individual, and preparing him for social life, for coöperation, for submission, and for leadership, for the postponement of individual to collective ends, playing no inconsiderable part in shaping the destinies of empires, encouraging friendly intercourse and rivalry between the widely scattered parts, and by keeping the various parts present to the consciousness of each other.

In so far as it is a principal root of artistic production, it has its share in the socializing influence of art. Works of art tend to increase mutual understanding and sympathy, furthering the homogeneity of the mind which is an essential condition of the development of the collective mental life of a people. Similarly, art tends to soften and socialize the relations between nations.[10]

The above quotations from modern educators are presented not as evidence of scientifically demonstrated truths, but simply as exemplification of the present-day attitude toward play. Taken collectively the quotations are illustrative of the profound change of attitude toward play that has occurred within two centuries.

REFERENCES

1. Quoted by Charles H. Judd in *Genetic Psychology for Teachers*. New York and London. D. Appleton and Company. 1911. Pp. xiii-329. (p. 72.)
2. Quoted by Williarm Heard Kilpatrick in *Source Book in the Philosophy of Education*. New York. The Macmillan Co. 1925. Pp. viii-365. (p. 4 f.)
3. Dewey, John. *Democracy and Education*. New York. The Macmillan Co. 1921. Pp. xii-434. (p. 241.)
4. Jennings, Herbert Spencer; John B. Watson; Adolph Meyer; and William I. Thomas. *Suggestions of Modern Science Concerning Education*. New York. The Macmillan Co. 1920. Pp. vii-211. (p. 46 f.)

5. Carr, Harvey A. "The Survival Values of Play." *Investigations of the Department of Psychology and Education of the University of Colorado.* Vol. I, No. 2. Pp. 1-47. (p. 27 ff.)

6. Watson, John B. *Psychology from the Standpoint of a Behaviorist.* Philadelphia and London. J. B. Lippincott and Co. 1924. Pp. xiii-448. (pp. 439-40.)

7. Seashore, Carl. *Psychology in Daily Life.* New York and London. D. Appleton and Company. 1916. Pp. xvii-225. (p. 8.)

8. Seashore, Carl. *op. cit.* p. 7.

9. Seashore, Carl. *op. cit.* p. 19 f.

10. McDougall, William. *Social Psychology.* Boston, John W. Luce & Co. 1918. 418 pp. (p. 352.)

CHAPTER II

THEORIES WHICH SEEK TO "EXPLAIN" PLAY

PLAY A COMPLEX PHENOMENON

Play is the result of so many variables, it appears so commonly and in such a variety of forms, it involves such a large number of those elements of which the ego is compounded, and its results are so subtle and so far-reaching, that any definition or explanation necessarily must be partial and incomplete. Play has an almost unlimited number of aspects. The better-known theories of play have been criticized not so much because of their lack of validity but because of their incompleteness. The whole truth regarding play cannot be known until the whole truth regarding life itself is known, for play is not an isolated phenomenon; it cannot be satisfactorily explained apart from its background, that is to say, apart from other life phenomena. Appreciation of the impossibility of formulating a wholly satisfactory theory of play should result in tolerance toward those theorists who have failed in this regard. It should bring also a willingness to accept such elements of truth as each of the various theories may contain.

THE SCHILLER-SPENCER SURPLUS ENERGY THEORY

Very well known among the modern theories of play is that which commonly is called "The Schiller-Spencer surplus energy theory." The principle which is set forth in this theory has been stated also by other writers. It seems probable that the prestige and the popularity of Schiller and Spencer have had much to do with the linking of their names with the principle. In the writings of Schiller the idea of surplus energy is incidental merely. With Spencer, it evidently is not original.[1]

In discussing this theory Bowen and Mitchell make the following comment:

7

"The original author of this theory is not definitely known. One writer says that it dates from the Stoic philosophers of ancient Greece, but this has not been verified. Many modern writers call it the 'Schiller-Spencer' theory, but this is not a good name for it. It was mentioned in educational literature long before the day of Schiller and Spencer; moreover, Spencer explains play in an entirely different manner. Schiller evidently accepted the theory and possibly expressed it more fully and plainly than any one before him." [2]

Schiller's statement regarding play is found in his letters "On the Æsthetic Education of Mankind." His words follow:

"No doubt nature has given more than is necessary to unreasoning beings; she has caused a gleam of freedom to shine even in the darkness of animal life. When the lion is not tormented by hunger, and when no wild beast challenges him to fight, his unemployed energy creates an object for himself; full of ardor, he fills the reëchoing desert with his terrible roars and his exuberant force rejoices in itself, showing itself without an object. The insect flits about rejoicing in the sunlight, and it is certainly not the cry of want that makes itself heard in the melodious song of the bird; there is undeniably freedom in these movements, though it is not emancipation from want in general, but from a determinate external necessity.

"The animal *works* when a privation is the motor of its activity, and it *plays* when the plenitude of force is this motor, when an exuberant life is excited to action." [3]

The above quotation certainly is largely spurious when examined from a scientific standpoint. Hobhouse has pointed out that the apparently aimless activities of birds and insects are frequently, if not always, for the fulfillment of nature's serious purposes.[4] Undoubtedly much of what seems to be random or aimless movement in the animal world is in reality search for food and mate. One is not justified in designating an activity as an end in itself merely because no ulterior end is clearly evident. Schiller's assertations that the roar of the lion is "without an object," that the melodious song of the bird is "certainly not the cry of want," and that "the insect flits about rejoicing in life in the sunlight," are therefore questionable.

A second part of the Schiller theory of play posits unhindered utilization of the excess of energy. In line with this conception are Schiller's statements regarding the play of imagination in man:

"The imagination, like the bodily organs, has in man its free movement and its material play, a play in which, without reference to form, it simply takes pleasure in its arbitrary power, and in the absence of all hindrance. These plays of fancy inasmuch as form is not mixed up with them, and because a free succession of images makes all their charm, though confined to man, belong exclusively to animal life, and only prove one thing . . . that he is delivered from all external sensuous constraint . . . without our being entitled to infer that there is in it an independent plastic form." [5]

Used in this sense, play has much in common with art. Indeed, Schiller considered art to be merely a higher form of play.[6]

Schiller's contention that in man the imagination enjoys "free movement," "arbitrary power," and "the absence of all hindrance" certainly needs validation. The imagination probably does not have free movement if these words are taken literally. Imagination is, of course, dependent upon the inner neural organization of the individual. This neural organization is determined in turn by definite antecedent causes.

Schiller wrote as a poet. It is perhaps needless to remark that hyperbole is permissible in the poet.

SPENCER

Herbert Spencer extended and qualified the "surplus energy" theory in a manner indicative of a profound comprehension of the complexity of the phenomenon of play.

Spencer's critics commonly leave one with the impression that Spencer's conception of play consisted exclusively of the idea of "surplus energy." In this connection it is to be noted that most of the criticism directed against Spencer's treatment of the subject of play is to the effect that the words "surplus energy" do not suffice to explain play.

Typical of such criticisms are the following:

(a) "The Spencer theory, therefore misses the whole point. It is true because it is a truism." [7]

(b) "Yes, the boy plays on account of surplus energy in the same way that Raphael painted the Sistine Madonna because of surplus paint." [8]

(c) "In one point only does Spencer go beyond Schiller's conception: he connects the idea of imitation with that of the overflow of energy." [9]

(d) "It (the surplus energy theory) does not sufficiently account for the forms the play activities take." [10]

(e) "Can a phenomenon that is of so great, so incalculable value possibly be simply a convenient method of dissipating superfluous accumulations of energy?" [11]

(f) "A further difficulty with Spencer's theory is that it does not apply to the play of children at all, for the reason that the child is not a working animal and does not provide his own maintenance." [12]

(g) "There can be no question but that surplus energy is a favorable condition to play. The animal or child that possesses it will play longer and harder, will feel a more insistent craving for activity than the animal or child without it; but no one to-day would accept the theory as an explanation." [13]

The sweeping manner in which Spencer's broad philosophy of play has been condensed and dismissed certainly is unjust. His discussion of play and art is so much more comprehensive than the two words "surplus energy" indicate that it ill becomes a critic to charge him with uttering a truism, or to imply that he considered "surplus energy" a satisfactory explanation of play. Spencer himself would have been the last to assert that a phenomenon so complex as play could be explained by so simple a formula. Indeed, he did not attempt to explain play at all. Regarding his own treatment of the æsthetic sentiments he wrote:

"To deal fully with the psychology of æsthetics is out of the question. Its phenomena are extremely involved, and to treat them adequately would require many chapters. Here, in addition to the above general conceptions, I will set down such hints as seem needful for rightly developing them." [14]

Like Schiller, Spencer looked upon art merely as one aspect of play. It is of interest that many other writers agree that there is a close relationship between play and art.

"Art and play, then, fulfill the same function, provide us the same refreshment. Moreover, they are both their own excuse for being." [15]

"And not only do we call the child's dearest interests by a name implying that they are of negligible importance, but we heighten the misunderstanding by (very properly) calling the same identical interests when they appear in grown people by a variety of high-sounding names,—such as work, art, science, patriotism, idealism, genius,—that we never think of applying to children's play." [16]

"The phrase 'Art for art's sake,' although it has become distorted from its original meaning, had this idea back of it, that any work worthy of being considered æsthetic must be done for the joy of the process." [17]

Unable to accept the theory of the identity of play and art Ebbinghaus has made what seems to be a valid distinction between the two behavior manifestations.

"But play is not identical with art, because it is still too serious a matter. The boy who plays robber and police is not like an actor playing the rôle of a robber. He really is the robber so far as the advantages, the freedom, and the power-of a robber are concerned; and he enjoys these advantages, while the actor does not even think of them. The actor, even while playing the rôle of a king, desires to play the king, not to be the king. Play, that is, the instinctive activity of play, is intermediate between art and life, a gateway to the former." [18]

Discussing the similarity between the play impulse and the art impulse, Spencer wrote:

"The activities we call play are united with the æsthetic activities, by the trait that neither subserve, in any direct way, the processes conducive to life. The bodily powers, the intellectual faculties, the instincts, appetites, passions, and even those highest feelings we have lately dealt with, have maintenance of the organic equilibrium of the individual, or else maintenance of the species, as their immediate or remote ends. . . . But while the primary actions of the faculties, bodily and mental, with their accompanying gratifications, are thus obviously related to proximate ends that imply ulterior benefits, those actions of them which constitute play, and those which yield the æsthetic gratifications, do not refer to ulterior benefits . . . the proximate ends are the only ends." [19]

The first point of relationship between the play impulse and the art impulse is that neither furthers directly the life processes of the organism. Spencer qualifies his statement that "the proximate ends are the only ends" by emphasizing that any exercise of a "faculty" *

---

* The present writers are employing the term "faculty" as Spencer used it; they do not recognize its validity when so used.

improves that "faculty." Therefore from this point of view an ulterior benefit also is to be derived from æsthetic and play activities. But since this ulterior benefit, improved functioning, comes also with forced functioning of the faculties, Spencer does not regard the practice effect a distinguishing feature of the æsthetic and the play activities.[20]

Spencer thus anticipates the Groos "practice theory" and indicates that it is an incomplete explanation of play.

Spencer mentions the fact that excess both of time and of energy is found when a given species' "faculties" have become so various and so efficient that the species is no longer exclusively occupied with the immediately urgent problems of existence. The resultant condition may be described best in Spencer's own words:

"The greater variety of faculty commonly joined with this greater efficiency of faculty, has a kindred result. When there have been developed many powers adjusted to many requirements, they cannot all act at once: now the circumstances call these into exercise and now those; and some of them occasionally remain unexercised for considerable periods. Thus it happens that in the more-evolved creatures, there often recurs an energy somewhat in excess of the immediate needs, and there comes also such rest, now of this faculty and now of that, as permits the bringing of it up to a state of high efficiency by the repair which follows waste."[21]

As a result of the fact that certain of the "faculties" are at times quiescent, their unused energy accumulates. Play consists of the functioning of those "faculties" not recently used, play is change of activity after an intervening period of disuse. It arises from the readiness of healthy muscles or organs to act. Spencer here anticipates a theory developed at great length by Patrick.[7] The following criticism therefore seems unjustifiable.

"But the most serious difficulty with Spencer's theory is that it does not explain the *form* taken either by the plays of children or of adults. His view is that men and animals in their surplus-energy moods . . . that is, in their play . . . would simply go on doing in a dramatizing way what they are accustomed seriously to do in their working moods. The horse would run, the tiger would jump, etc. . . . the man presumably would plow and reap and dig and write books and give lectures. But this is precisely what the man does not do. He goes fishing, etc."[22]

Spencer states that when the unemployed period is sufficiently long a given "faculty" may become so stored with energy that functioning becomes a definite organic need.   When natural discharge is precluded there comes a tendency to simulate the natural mode of discharge.   Under certain conditions almost any activity may be preferable to inactivity.   Spencer's words follow:

"Every one of the mental powers, then, being subject to this law, that its organ when dormant for an interval longer than ordinary becomes unusually ready to act . . . unusually ready to have its correlative feelings aroused, giving an unusual readiness to enter upon all the correlative activities; it happens that a simulation of those activities is easily fallen into, when circumstances offer it in place of the real activities." [23]

"Hence play of all kinds. . . . Hence this tendency to superfluous and useless exercise of faculties that have been quiescent.   Hence, too, the fact that these uncalled-for exertions are most displayed by those faculties which take the most prominent parts in the creature's life.   Observe how this holds from the simplest faculties upwards." [24]

Play, then, is very commonly simulation of the types of activity which an organ carries on when it is being forced to exercise directly the processes conducive to life.   Play activities are displayed most often by those parts of the body which are most significant in the creature's survival.*   Spencer writes:

"A rat, with incisors that grow continuously in adaptation to incessant wear they undergo, and with a correlative desire to use these incisors, will, if caged, occupy itself in gnawing anything it can get hold of.   A cat, with claws and appended muscles adjusted to daily action in catching prey, but now leading a life that is but in small degree predatory, has a craving to exercise these parts; and may be seen to satisfy the craving by stretching out her legs, protruding her claws, and pulling at some such surface as the covering of a chair or the bark of a tree.   And still more interesting in the giraffe, which when free is all day long using its tongue to pull down branches of trees, there arises, when in confinement, so great a need for some kindred exercise that it perpetually grasps with its tongue such parts of the top

* The criticism that Spencer fails to account for forms that play takes is therefore not wholly fair.   For examples of such criticism see: (a) McDougall, Wm., *Social Psychology*, p. 111; (b) Norsworthy and Whitley, *The Psychology of Chilahood*, p. 206 ff; (c) Patrick, G. T. W., *The Psychology of Relaxation*, pp. 32-33.

of its house as can be laid hold of . . . so wearing out the upper angles of doors, etc. This useless activity of unused organs, which in these cases hardly arises to what we call play, passed into play ordinarily so called where there is a more manifest union of feeling with the action." [25]

In the cases cited above the structure of a given animal determines the form that its play will take. In the lower animals it consists of mimic chase and mimic fighting. Examples of the latter follow:

"For dogs and other predatory creatures show us unmistakably that their play consists of mimic chase and mimic fighting. . . . They pursue one another, they try to overthrow one another, they bite one another, as much as they dare. And so with the kitten running after a cotton-ball, making it roll and catching it, crouching as though in ambush and then leaping on it, we see that the whole sport is a dramatization of the pursuit of prey . . . an ideal satisfaction for the destructive instincts in the absence of real satisfaction for them." [26]

With increased complexity of structural conformation there comes increased diversity in play behavior. In man play may take an almost unlimited number of forms. Nevertheless, certain play activities are almost certain to be engaged in by children, i.e., playing with dolls, playing soldier, etc. These activities are the dramatization of adult activities. Groos has elaborated at great length this general principle previously stated by Spencer. [1 9]

The instinctive basis of play is set forth by Spencer in the following paragraph:

"The sports of boys, chasing one another, wrestling, making prisoners, obviously gratify in a partial way the predatory instincts.* And if we consider even their games of skill, as well as the games of skill practiced by adults, we find that, significantly enough, the essential element running through them has the same origin. For no matter what the game, the satisfaction is in achieving victory . . . in getting the better of an antagonist. This love of conquest, so dominant in all creatures because it is so correlative of success in the struggle for existence, gets gratification from a victory at chess in the absence of ruder victories." [27]

---

* Interesting in this connection is the similar point of view set forth by McDougall in his *Social Psychology*, p. 110 ff.

In the latter part of the preceding quotation Spencer anticipates the principle of compensatory satisfaction. This conception has been greatly expanded since the day of Spencer.[28]

Those who have familiarized themselves with theories of compensatory behavior will recognize the modern tone of the following statement.[29]

"Nay, we may even see that playful conversation is characterized by the same element. In banter, in repartee, in 'chaff,' the almost-constant trait is some display of relative superiority . . . the detection of a weakness, a mistake, an absurdity, on the part of another. Through a wit-combat there runs the effort to obtain mental supremacy. That is to say, this activity of the intellectual faculties in which they are not used for purposes of guidance in the business of life, is carried on partly for the sake of the pleasure of the activity itself, and partly for the accompanying satisfaction of certain egoistic feelings which find for the moment no other sphere." [30]

The following summary of Spencer's discussion of play and art is given in order to illustrate clearly the scope of his discussion.

SUMMARY OF SPENCER'S DISCUSSION OF PLAY

1. Play and art are similar in that neither subserves in any direct way the processes conducive to life (pp. 627-28 *idem*).

2. Higher animals, not being occupied exclusively with their own maintenance, accumulate energy in unused "faculties." Inactivity may then become insufferable and escape therefrom is found in play, i.e., useless activity of unused organs (pp. 629-30 *idem*).

3. Useless activity is very commonly simulation of the types of activity which an organ carries on when it is being forced to subserve in a direct way the processes conducive to life (p. 639 *idem*.)

4. The play of dogs and of other predatory animals usually consists of mimic chase and mimic fighting (pp. 630-31 *idem*); in man a similar manifestation is dramatization.

5. The sports of boys gratify in a partial way the predatory instincts (p. 631 *idem*).

6. In games of skill the satisfaction consists in achieving victory . . . in getting the better of an antagonist (p. 631 *idem*).

7. In the absence of ruder victories, man's love of conquest secures

gratification of a victory at chess or from some other display of superiority (p. 631 *idem*). (Compensation.)

8. Games are the simulated activities resulting from the demand of the lower "faculties" for discharge of accumulated energy. The æsthetic sentiments are derived from a corresponding discharge of the accumulated energy in the higher "faculties" (p. 631 *idem*).

9. Æsthetic feelings result from harmonious, unimpeded action of the "faculties," the lower as well as the higher (p. 636 *idem*).

10. Play arises from the fact that certain states of consciousness are sought for their own sake, apart from ends (p. 647 *idem*).

11. The form that play shall take is a function of the level of development of the player. The following list displays various types of plays which correspond to various levels of development.

(a) Superfluous activity of the sensori-motor apparatus.

(b) Exercise of the higher coördinating powers in games and exercises.

(c) Mimic dances and accompanying chants of savages. There is here a predominance of substituted gratifications adapted to predatory life.

(d) Those more highly developed æsthetic products of ancient civilizations resulting in substitute gratification.

(e) Superfluous activity of the sympathies and altruistic sentiments giving rise to fine art, the highest form of play (pp. 647-48 *idem*).

12. As evolution continues play is destined to play an increasingly important part in human life (p. 648 *idem*).

The writers will avoid raising the question of whether the preceding ideas were original with Spencer. The charge has been made recently that Spencer obtained practically all of his educational philosophy from Priestley and others of his time. H. G. Good states that Spencer possessed a gift for expressing rather than for originating ideas.[31]

In reference to Spencer's book entitled *What Knowledge is of Most Worth,* Professor Good says: "Few, if any, other writers on education have attained a great reputation so cheaply; but perhaps fame rarely conforms to the facts." [32] It would be foreign to the purposes of the present writers to discuss this charge. They have based the foregoing discussion upon the fact that Spencer discussed play behavior with more than ordinary insight.

OTHER THEORIES OF PLAY

So much has been written about various aspects of play that space does not permit an adequate résumé of the various discussions. Brief summaries of a few of the significant writings will be presented.

Karl Groos ('96) elaborated at great length the theory that play is a means by which the young of a given species obtain practice in those forms of activity which in later life are necessary to sustenance. Groos' name is usually linked with the "practice theory of play." [1] [9]

The following statements have been made in criticism of this theory:

"Let us cease to blaspheme against the spirit of eternal youth by supposing (as Karl Groos does) that play means chiefly a preparation for the 'serious' work of life. Whatever has seriousness as its dominant note is a senile degeneration, a sad relapse from the healthy adventurous playfulness of childhood." [33]

"When we consider what the plays of children actually are, we discover, except in a limited number of imitative plays, but faint resemblance between them and the serious pursuits of adult man. They resemble rather the pursuits of primitive and prehistoric man, and many of them are like the sports of adults of the present day." [34]

"If the serious life of to-day consisted in escaping from enemies by foot, horse, or paddle, in living in close proximity to domestic animals, in pursuit of game with bow or gun, in subsisting on fish caught singly by hand, in personal combat with fist or sword, in throwing missiles, striking with a club or pursuing an enemy, in seeking safety in trees or caves, in living in tents or tree houses, in sleeping and cooking by a camp-fire, then we might venture to explain the play life of the child as 'an instinctive activity existing for purposes of practice or exercise with serious intent.'" [35]

"It would be a crude mistake on the part of nature to provide mankind with a period of immaturity in order to provide each child with practice in adult activities that were discarded by the race at the dawn of civilization. Injurious play, such as gambling and use of drugs, could not exist if nature was providing play as a preparation for certain future activities." [36]

"The idea that instincts are prophetic . . . looking forward to the occupations that the child must be ready to carry on when he reaches maturity . . . is the main fault of the instinct theory of play as stated by Groos." [37]

"The theory advanced by Professor Groos is that play is a *preparation for the business of life*. . . . No doubt, in some instances, especially if one considers primitive man, there is some such correspondence; but in most cases the preparatory effect of the various games is hard to trace. For instance, it might seem valuable to children of uncivilized races to indulge as they do in the running, catching games, because the adult savage depends largely on his agility and strength for his existence; but for what do these plays prepare a civilized child? . . . For catching a street car perhaps, or getting out of the way of an automobile. The preparation, if there is one, must be taken in a very general sense, for no close correlation can be found. Even if it does exist, as the theory suggests, it but indicates something further to be explained, for, 'Why does the child in his ignorance of adult needs react in just those ways which do thus train him?' The explanation needs itself to be explained." [38]

Comment regarding the above criticisms probably is unnecessary. It is to-day a well known fact that the child learns hand and eye coordination by a trial and error process and in a very real way his first lesson in driving a hammer is taken when he first attempts to bang his rattle against the side of his crib.[39]

Spencer has described the types of "play activities" engaged in by young animals and Breed has shown that the young chick's accuracy at pecking improves with practice.[40] It is true of course that maturation is a most significant factor in the development of many abilities. However, a certain amount of practice is essential.

Seashore has paraphrased the Groos "practice theory" of play with the necessary qualifications in the following words:

"Children seldom play with the intention of fitting themselves for life, nor are adults ordinarily conscious of serving this purpose in play. Children play, as do the rest of us, because it satisfies certain cravings and seems to be the eternally fit and natural thing to do. It is only in the larger, retrospective view that we realize how nature has wrought marvels of development through the operation of the play instincts." [41]

The Groos "practice theory" of play is therefore not invalid but simply incomplete.

"The Groos theory of play attempts to supply what the Spencer theory lacks, that is, to account for the actual form taken by the plays of children and young animals. Unfortunately, it gives little attention to the plays of adults." [42]

Professor Groos has supplemented his original theory by adding the concept of catharsis. Accordingly play is a kind of safety-valve for the expression of pent-up emotion.

" . . . fighting plays are among the natural or spontaneous activities of children and as long as they are freely indulged in, the child is free from hurtful emotions. If these activities are repressed, then no doubt would occur certain internal disturbances of a less healthful character. Where spontaneous responses are inhibited, readjustments are necessary and emotions are present. When the spontaneous response is resumed, the emotion subsides. In this way children's plays might seem to have a *catharsis* effect. In spontaneous unrestricted play, there would seem to be no such element present or necessary." [43]

The doctrine of catharsis is set forth clearly in the following:

"Catharsis . . . implies the idea of purging or a draining of that energy which has *anti-social possibilities*, and hence the cathartic value may be predicted of only certain play reactions. The value of football, boxing, and other physical contests in relieving the pugnacious tendencies of boys is readily apparent as examples. Without the numberless well organized set forms of play possessed by society which give a harmless outlet to the mischievous and unapplied energy of the young, the task of the teacher and parent would be appalling." [44]

G. Stanley Hall ('04) explained play as due to the fact that ontogeny repeats phylogeny. He pointed out that the individual rehearses the activities of his ancestors, repeating their life work in summative and adumbrative ways.[45]

Hall exhibited a normal human frailty in his estimate of Groos' first theory. His position follows:

The past holds the keys to all play activities. None survives unless based upon pretty purely hereditary momentum. The view of Groos that play is practice for future adult activities is very partial, superficial and perverse.[46]

Hall's contention that the individual cannot cut himself off entirely from his past is taken for granted at the present time. The trouble with Hall's theory is that it is based upon an invalid hypothesis (recapitulation).

"Theoretically, scientists do not believe that human nature has undergone such definite and well-marked changes due to the stages of culture through which it has passed. Practically, it is difficult on this theory to explain why boys like to go swimming and to live in caves at the same age, or why it is that children enjoy playing with toy boats and trains before they want a bow and arrow, or why the favorite toy of most girls under nine is a doll." [47]

McDougall ('08) considered play to be due to the ripening of the instinct of rivalry.[10] His point of view may be summarized thus:

If we ask—In what does this special adaptation (play) consist? The answer is—it consists in the tendency for the various instincts (on the skilled exercise of which adult efficiency depends) to ripen and to come into action in each individual of the species before they are needed for serious use. . . .
Play, then, is determined by the premature ripening of instincts. The ripening of any instinct in individuals of any species is liable to be shifted forwards or backwards in the age-scale during the course of racial evolution, so that the order of their ripening and of their appearances in the individual does not conform to the law of recapitulation.[48]

McDougall's two criticisms of the "Schiller-Spencer surplus energy theory" are as follows: (1) It does not account for the varied forms the play activities take. (2) It is not compatible with the fact that young animals, as well as children, often play until they are exhausted.

The writers feel that Spencer would have agreed with the first of these objections. McDougall's second criticism is met in the following statement by Patrick:

"As a rule people do not play when they are tired, that is, when that part of them is tired which they are using in play, but of course they get interested in their plays and sometimes go right on as a result of plot interest or from many other secondary causes. Consequently, a man might play chess when the parts of the brain involved in chess playing are already tired from his work, in order to defeat a rival and vindicate his reputation as a chess player, etc., etc." (From an unpublished letter in the possession of the writers.)

Karl Groos made a most discerning and significant observation when he pointed out the fact that surplus energy is not a *conditio sine qua non* of play.

"Notice the kitten when a piece of paper blows past. Will not any observer confirm the statement that just as an old cat must be tired to death or else already filled with satiety if it does not try to seize a mouse running near it, so will the kitten, too, spring after the moving object, even if it has been exercising for hours and its superfluous energies are entirely disposed of? Or observe the play of young dogs when two of them have raced about the garden until they are obliged to stop from sheer fatigue, and they lie on the ground panting, with tongues hanging out. Now one of them gets up, glances at his companion, and the irresistible power of his innate longings for the fray seizes him again. . . . And so it goes with end-less repetition, until we get the impression that the dog waits only long enough to collect *the needed strength, not* till *superfluous vigor urges him to activity.*" [49]

Miss Appleton ('10) wrote that play is that aspect of growth which involves the developmental exercise of maturing functions.[50] Growth, or the hunger for it, is the basic drive to play behavior. Play thus precedes the ability to function and gives rise to it. When a particular function has developed fully the play impulse in reference to that function subsides.

"Miss Appleton, in her comparative study of play already referred to, advances a *Biological theory* of play. She thinks that play is dependent on the structure of the body, and that the activity is of such character as will satisfy the needs of the growing body." [51]

It is obvious that the Appleton theory of play (like all others) is partial since it fails to take any account of the play activity of the adult.

Freud ('11) advanced the theory that man's basic desire is that of instinct gratification.[52] Lack of sex gratification gives rise to numerous substitute activities. These substitute activities occur under the domination of the "pleasure principle," i.e., the desire to obtain pleasure. This is most evident in the case of pleasurable day-dreaming which is frequently compensatory. It is because man is under the domination of the pleasure-principle that he is able to derive pleasure from situations intrinsically painful, e.g., a play in which tragedy is presented may be felt by him as highly enjoyable.

In a more recent publication[53] Freud has modified and qualified his earlier statements regarding play. He asserts that man is dominated by a "repetition-compulsion" as well as by the pleasure-principle. The pleasure-principle causes one to remember the pleasant experiences and to forget the unpleasant experiences. It even enables one to reconstruct his experiences in such fashion as to make them pleasurable. This gives rise to memory distortions and the so-called "happy days" of childhood. On the other hand, the "repetition-impulse" is a tendency that seems to go beyond the pleasure-principle. This compulsion appears to force the individual to repeat or to reënact earlier experiences without regard to their pleasant or unpleasant tone. In many instances the pleasure-principle enables one to derive some type of pleasure from the experience that it thus worked over, but this is not always true.

What concerns us here is the fact that Freud has modified his earlier position. He now asserts the probable operation of the two different principles in play behavior, i.e., the "pleasure-principle" and the "repetition-compulsion" principle. However, one is left in doubt as to whether the latter is able to operate independently of the former.

E. S. Robinson ('20) attempted to show by retrospective analysis that the child's make-believe play compensates for his lack of physical prowess and for the cramping influence of the environment in which he finds himself.[28] Robinson's concept of play as compensatory is to some extent similar to that of the Freudians. His phrase "lack of prowess" is suggestive of Miss Appleton's theory regarding play. Spencer too anticipated the principle of compensatory satisfaction. (See reference No. 27.)

G. T. W. Patrick ('16) stated that the play behavior of the adult is due to a demand of the higher cerebral centers for relaxation.[7]

" . . . there are some brain centers, or some brain tracts, or some forms of cerebral functioning, that are put under severe strain in our modern strenuous life and there must be some kind of activity which will relieve these centers, or these tracts, during a considerable portion of each waking day and involve other centers not so subject to exhaustion. Such activity we call play or sport. Perhaps the word 'relaxation' would be a more exact description of it." [54]

According to Patrick, play is due to a desire for a change of work. The theory is valid but also is partial. Furthermore, this basic conception was set forth previously by other writers.

Referring to the "recreation theory" Bowen and Mitchell have written the following:

"This idea of play is an old one. It was expressed 200 years ago by Lord Kames, English nobleman and philosopher, when he said, 'Play is necessary for man in order to refresh himself after labor.' A century ago Guts Muths, a German teacher who is sometimes called 'the father of physical training,' published a book entitled *Games for the Exercise and Recreation of Body and Mind*. Guts Muths, whose work was with children, emphasized the recreative value of play and also its value for development and training. . . . One of the strongest supporters in recent years was Professor Lazarus of the University of Berlin, who urged people to 'Flee from empty idleness to active recreation in play.' . . . Professor G. T. W. Patrick, of the University of Iowa, in his *Psychology of Relaxation*, sustains the recreation theory and goes farther to explain it than any previous writer." [55]

It was stated previously that any definition or "explanation" of play must be incomplete. This fact need not bother the psychologist or the educator. Slosson points to the futility of trying to state what electricity really is.

"You can make an-electrician mad . . . by interrupting his explanation of a dynamo by asking: 'But you cannot tell me what electricity really is.' The electrician does not care a rap what electricity 'really is' . . . if there really is any meaning to that phrase. All he wants to know is what he can do with it." [56]

The same statements might be made with equal validity regarding play. Play is behavior and is of importance to the educator *per se*.

The present writers will avoid offering any "explanation" of play. Indeed, the mere fact that children are organic beings is sufficient to account for the fact that they are active.

More than a century ago Guts Muths stated that complete quiescence is intolerable to the human being. Muths considered that this alone is sufficient to account for the phenomenon of play.

"Guts Muths (1796) considered the natural impulse to activity as the creator of play, and that ennui is always and only a favoring condition. The first object of play is the pleasure of activity, the second is the recovery of protection from ennui. . . . Ennui he considered as one of the most oppressive of evils—a sickness." [57]

Dewey recently has shown that all organic beings are naturally active and that it is therefore unnecessary to seek any further explanation for the fact that they are active than the fact that they are alive.

"As a matter of fact, however, the theory of surplus energy seems to be influenced by a survival of the once general conception that individuals are naturally averse to any kind of activity; that complete quiescence is the natural state of organic beings; and that some fear of pain or hope of pleasure is required in order to stir individuals to effort which in itself is painful. The fact of the case is that from intra-organic stimuli, the organism is in a constant state of action, activity indeed being the very essence of life. When the myth of natural quiescence is surrendered with its accompanying myth of the need of a special premium in order to arouse an inert agent, it ceases to be necessary to search for any special object in order to account for play. The only thing necessary is to state the conditions under which organic activity takes this or that form." [58]

Play may be regarded as consisting largely of the activities in which the individual engages "just because he wants to." The above statement has certain limitations. At certain times an individual may eat, sleep, etc., "just because he wants to." Of course such activities would not be regarded as play. But most of the remaining activities in the behavior stream (when such purely physiological reactions as eating, sleeping, etc., are eliminated) in which the child takes part *of his own volition* may be considered his play life. The writers have found this distinction a useful one in studying the child. They have therefore considered as play those behavior manifestations in general which the child exhibits "just because he wants to."

The present writers will make no attempt to explain the fact of play. They will content themselves with a discussion of the conditions under which various types of play occur. The goal is, of course, better to understand and control human behavior.

REFERENCES

1. Groos, Karl. *The Play of Animals.* New York. D. Appleton and Co. 1898. Pp. xxvi-341. (p. 2 f.)

2. Bowen, Wilbur P. and Mitchell, Elmer D. *The Theory and Practice of Organized Play.* New York. A. S. Barnes and Company. 1923. Vol. I, Pp. v:i-402. (p. 182.)

3. Schiller, Friedrich. *Essays, Æsthetical and Philosophical.* London. George Bell and Sons. 1875. 435 pp. (p. 112.)

4. Hobhouse, L. T. *Mental Evolution.* London. Macmillan and Company, Ltd. 1901. Pp. xiv-415. (p. 8.)

5. Schiller, Friedrich. *op. cit.* p. 113 f.

6. Schiller, Friedrich. *op. cit.* p. 71 ff. and 112 ff.

7. Patrick, G. T. W. *The Psychology of Relaxation.* Boston and New York. The Houghton Mifflin Company. 1916. Pp. viii-280. (p. 33.)

8. Lee, Joseph. Quoted by Curtis, Henry S., in *Education Through Play.* New York. The Macmillan Company. 1922. Pp. xix-359. (p. 3.)

9. Groos, Karl. *The Play of Animals.* New York. D. Appleton and Company. 1915. Pp. xxvi-341. (p. 5.)

10. McDougall, William. *Social Psychology.* Boston. John W. Luce & Co. 1918. 418 pp. (p. 111.)

11. Groos, Karl. *The Play of Animals. op. cit.* p. 23.

12. Patrick, G. T. W. *op. cit.* p. 32.

13. Curtis, Henry S. *op. cit.* p. 3.

14. Spencer, Herbert. *The Principles of Psychology.* In two Vol. New York. D. Appleton and Company. 1873. Vol. II. Pp. viii-648. (p. 635.)

15. Cabot, Richard C. *What Men Live By.* Boston. Houghton Mifflin Co. 1914. Pp. xxi-341. (p. 101.)

16. Lee, Joseph. *Play in Education.* New York. The Macmillan Company. 1923. Pp. xxiii-500. (p. viii.)

17. Gulick, Luther Halsey. *A Philosophy of Play.* New York. Charles Scribner's Sons. 1920. Pp. xvi-291. (p. 272.)

18. Ebbinghaus, Hermann. *Psychology; An Elementary Text.* Translated and edited by Max Meyer. Boston. D. C. Heath & Co. 1908. Pp. viii-215. (p. 198.)

19. Spencer, Herbert. *op. cit.* p. 627 f.

20. Spencer, Herbert, *op. cit.* p. 627.

21. Spencer, Herbert. *op. cit.* p. 629.

22. Patrick, G. T. W. *op. cit.* p. 32 f.

23. Spencer, Herbert. *op. cit.* p. 629.

24. Spencer, Herbert. *op. cit.* p. 630.

25. Spencer, Herbert. *op. cit.* p. 630.

26. Spencer, Herbert. *op. cit.* p. 630 f.

27. Spencer, Herbert. *op. cit.* p. 631.

28. Robinson, E. S. "The Compensatory Function of Make-Believe Play." *Psycho. Rev.* 1920, 27. Pp. 429-39.

29. Woodworth, Robert S. *Psychology; A Study of Mental Life.* New York. Henry Holt and Company. 1921. Pp. x-580. (p. 494.)

30. Spencer, Herbert. *op. cit.* p. 631.
31. Good, H. G. "The Sources of Spencer's Education." *Journal of Educational Research.* May, 1926. *13.* Pp. 325-336.
32. Good, H. G. *op. cit.* p. 335.
33. Cabot, Richard C. *op. cit.* p. 96.
34. Patrick, G. T. W. *op. cit.* p. 36.
35. Patrick, G. T. W. *op. cit.* p. 38.
36. Bowen, Wilbur P. and Mitchell, Elmer D. *op. cit.* p. 191.
37. Bowen, Wilbur P. and Mitchell, Elmer D. *op. cit.* p. 192.
38. Norsworthy, Naomi, and Whitley, Mary T. *The Psychology of Childhood* New York. The Macmillan Co. 1922. Pp. xix-375. (p. 207.)
39. Dorsey, George A. *Why We Behave Like Human Beings.* New York. Harper and Brothers. 1925. Pp. xv-512. (p. 345.)
40. (a) Breed, F. S. "The Development of Certain Instincts and Habits in Chicks." *Behavior Monographs.* 1911. *I.* pp. i-78.
    (b) Shepard, J. F., and Breed, F. S. "Maturation and Use in the Development of an Instinct." *Journal of Animal Behavior.* 1913. *III.* pp. 274-285.
41. Seashore, Carl. *Psychology in Daily Life.* New York. D. Appleton and Company. 1916. Pp. xvii-225. (p. 2.)
42. Patrick, G. T. W. *op. cit.* p. 33.
43. Patrick, G. T. W. *op. cit.* p. 42 f.
44. Carr, Harvey A. "The Survival Values of Play." *Investigations of the Department of Psychology and Education of the University of Colorado.* Vol. I, No. 2, Pp. 1-47. (p. 18.)
45. Hall, G. Stanley. *Youth.* New York. D. Appleton and Company. 1920. Pp. x-379. Chapter VI.
46. Hall, G. Stanley. *op. cit.* p. 74.
47. Norsworthy, Naomi, and Whitley, Mary T. *op. cit.* p. 208.
48. McDougall, William. *op. cit.* p. 113.
49. Groos, Karl. *The Play of Animals. op. cit.* p. 19.
50. Appleton, Lilla Estella. *A Comparative Study of the Play Activities of Adult Savages and Civilized Children; An Investigation of the Scientific Basis of Education.* Chicago. The University of Chicago Press. 1910. 94 pp.
51. Norsworthy, Naomi, and Whitley, Mary T. *op. cit.* p. 209.
52. Freud, Sigm. *Drei Abhandlungen zur Sexualtheorie.* Leipzig and Wien. F. Deuticke. 1905. 86 pp.
53. Freud, Sigm. *Beyond the Pleasure Principle.* The International Psycho-analytical Press. London. 1922. 90 pp. (pp. 11-17.)
54. Patrick, G. T. W. *op. cit.* p. 49.
55. Bowen, Wilbur P. and Mitchell, Elmer D. *op. cit.* p. 184.
56. Slosson, Edwin E. *Creative Chemistry.* New York. The Century Co. 1919. Pp. iii-311. (p. 71.)
57. Johnson, George E. *Education by Plays and Games.* New York. Ginn and Company. 1907. Pp. xiv-234. (p. 34.)
58. Dewey, John. In *A Cyclopedia of Education.* Edited by Paul Monroe. New York. The Macmillan Co. 1925. Vol. III and IV. Pp. xi-740. (p. 725.)

CHAPTER III

TECHNIQUES PREVIOUSLY EMPLOYED IN STUDYING PLAY BEHAVIOR

The play life of children is a phenomenon of many variables. The findings of a given investigation are therefore to a large extent a function of the technique employed. Chase noted this fact when the results obtained by the use of direct personal observation differed from those secured by questionnaire methods.[1] It therefore becomes necessary to evaluate various methods and to consider the results of investigations in the light of the techniques employed. This chapter presents a résumé of typical procedures employed by representative investigators. Data obtained by various techniques are also presented.

DEVICES USED IN IDENTIFICATION OF PLAY ACTIVITIES

The literature in the field reveals the following types of investigations:

    (a)   Questionnaire.
    (b)   Checking activities from a printed list.
    (c)   Personal observation.
    (d)   Pooling or averaging of opinions.
    (e)   The recreational survey.

(a) The Questionnaire Method

The questionnaire method predominated as a means of investigating play behavior during the last decade of the 20th century; this method is still commonly used. The impetus lent to this method was probably an outgrowth of the far-reaching results obtained by G. Stanley Hall and his students.

Monroe employed a very brief form of the questionnaire, asking children to write answers to the following questions:[2] "What games do you like to play in summer, and why?" Included in the study were 978 boys and 1072 girls ranging in age from seven to sixteen years. Monroe's data yielded 332 different play activities, 54 of which were mentioned only once. These 54 items were discarded and the remaining 278 games were grouped into nine categories under the following headings:

Type of Game.	Per Cent mentioning it.
Ball games	32
Chase games	31
Motion games	10
Occupation games	5
Parlor games	3
Love games	3
Animal games	1½
Guessing games	1½
Miscellaneous	14

The objection to the preceding classification is its subjectivity. It is extremely doubtful that two independent investigators would classify the list of activities in the same manner. The overlapping of the various categories is apparent.

It is of interest that Monroe fails to report the results obtained for the second question. *Why* do children like to play games during the summer?

Croswell used a more elaborate form of questionnaire[8] than did Monroe. However, his questions were of the same general type. Approximately 2,000 school children of Worcester, Massachusetts, were included in Croswell's study. The children were asked to give answers to "Questionnaire No. VIII, issued in the fall of 1896 by Clark University."

TOPICAL SYLLABI FOR CHILD STUDY

(Series for Academic Year 1896-7)

VIII.   Spontaneously Invented Toys and Amusements.

A. *For Children.* (Teachers are requested to ask their pupils to answer this part of the syllabus.)

Write your (a) name, (b) age, (c) sex, and (d) state whether you live in the city or country.

I. What toys or playthings do you use most (a) in winter, (b) in spring, (c) in summer, (d) in fall?

II. What games and plays do you play most (a) in winter, (b) in spring, (c) in summer, (d) in fall?

III. Which of these are (a) your favorite playthings? (b) your favorite plays? Do you use most of the toys and games you like best? If not, why not?

IV. Name other (a) games, and (b) playthings which you used when younger. Give age at which each was used most. Show your choice as above.

VIII. Describe any games you or your friends have invented. How long did you play them before giving them up? To what extent did other children imitate them?

IX. What do you play, or how do you amuse yourself (a) When alone? (b) When only two or three are together? (c) When more than three?

X. What do you do for amusement evenings?

XI. What games do you play on Sunday? What else do you do to amuse yourself?

"As a means of investigating the creative work of the child," says Croswell, "the following requests were made."

V. Describe any playthings, no matter how poor, which (a) you have ever made, (b) your friends have made.

VII. Describe anything you have repeatedly attempted to make, or wanted to do, but did not know how.

A questionnaire of the above nature assumes the child to be capable of introspective analysis and verbal report to an unwarranted degree. The preceding questionnaire is of interest at the present time merely because it is illustrative of a procedure that was at one time generally followed in obtaining data regarding the play behavior of children.

Croswell thought it desirable to classify the resultant data "according to their most prominent function in the development of the child." He accordingly placed in a single category those activities *"aiding most directly in the motor development."* In another main division he placed those activities *"productive of general idea not dis-*

tinctly motor." Sub-groupings were made under headings equally ambiguous; curves were plotted and labelled as follows: "Amusements tending toward physical development." "Interest in traditional amusements," etc.

(b) Checking Activities from a Printed List

While Croswell was investigating the play interests of the public school children of Worcester, Massachusetts, a similar study was being conducted in South Carolina by Zack McGhee.[4] Neither of these investigators was aware of the work of the other until after both studies had been completed. McGhee requested children to check their five favorite play activities from an extensive list. McGhee did not ask the children to explain *why* they were fond of particular activities, realizing that "children are not accustomed to analyze their likes and dislikes." ('00, p. 458 f.)

McGhee's study is more reliable than that of Croswell as the task set for the children was more nearly in accord with their abilities. The investigation was carried on at two times during the year, 4,566 children were examined in December and 4,152 in May. McGhee included several localities in his study.

McGhee classified the activities "according to the element of interest found in them." ('00, p. 459 f.) The following classifications resulted:

1. Groups of plays in which running is the predominant interest.
2. Groups of plays in which chance is predominant.
3. Groups of plays in which imitation is the predominant element.
4. Groups of plays in which rivalry plays the most important part, the object of the game being to best an opponent.
5. Groups of plays in which coöperation is predominant.

Categories such as those given above are obviously arbitrary and of questionable validity. For example, it is very difficult to identify those activities in which the element of rivalry predominates.

In spite of the fact that McGhee's classification is arbitrary his study is of considerable interest. McGhee found that two play activities were consistently and conspicuously popular among the boys. However, a correspondingly narrow range of popular activities was not demonstrated by the girls. Many activities were equally well-liked by the girls. The two most popular activities of the boys were baseball and football.* McGhee pointed out that a common element of these two games is their high degree of organization. Both of these games are played in accordance with rather carefully specified rules which are accepted by common consent. Among girls less than twelve years of age, unorganized plays, such as plays with dolls, jumping rope, etc., were decidedly popular. McGhee concluded that a conspicuous sex difference is apparent in the tendency of boys to prefer games requiring a high degree of organization. This tendency was not demonstrated by the girls studied.

One of the latest studies of play behavior is that of Terman.[5] Six hundred and forty-three gifted children were included in Terman's investigation. The children were asked to rate 90 play activities with respect to their interest in them, their knowledge of them, and the time devoted to them. Then followed an information test on plays and games.

Analysis of results yielded masculinity indices, maturity indices, and indices of sociability and activity as regards play interests.

No significant difference between gifted and control children was found in the masculinity indices. Maturity indices were one to two years higher for the gifted than for the control and were somewhat higher for boys than girls. Gifted children played alone slightly more than the control. They preferred playmates who were older more often than the control. The gifted children excelled greatly in all kinds of play information although they devoted a little less time to play than did the control group.

(c) Direct Personal Observation

Chase ('03) made a study of the street games of New York children.[1] Chase's study is of interest chiefly because of the technique employed. Chase assembled his data by the method of direct personal observation. Chase objected to the use of the questionnaire on the following grounds:

1. When the children are questioned relative to their play activities,

---

* Were McGhee's study to be repeated at the present time (1926) basket ball would doubtless be found to compete with football in popularity.

those games which have most recently been participated in are likely to receive undue emphasis.

2. The games most liked are not necessarily identical with those which are most frequently engaged in.

3. Children when questioned give very little information concerning gambling, craps, and other activities which are under the social ban. ('05, p. 503 f.)

In order that he might obtain more precise information than he thought possible by the use of the questionnaire method, Chase walked through the crowded tenement district of New York City from time to time during a period covering two years and noted the play life. The following items were recorded: (1) The different games that were being played. (2) The number of children playing each game. (3) The amount of interest. (4) The date.

Chase's list of the ten most popular play activities is unlike any lists which were compiled from the answers to questionnaires. Although Chase avoided the inherent weaknesses of the questionnaire his own procedure is of doubtful validity.

At Ipswich, Massachusetts, the then novel method of having observers stationed at various points in the city was employed.[6]   At a given time these observers made note of the play behavior of all children in sight, the attempt being to obtain by this method a cross-sectional view of the play life of Ipswich children.

At Cleveland, Ohio, this same procedure was tried on a much larger scale along with a variety of other procedures.[7]

Miss Ruth Andrus recently completed a study of the habits of the pre-school child by the use of the method of observation.[8]   Diaries of 52 children in four nursery schools in New York City were kept by 69 students, each student observing one child for 15 hours. Miss Andrus' study is illustrative of the enormous amount of time and labor involved when the observation method is employed in studying a small group of children.

With older children this method is not always feasible for the following reasons:

1. Errors in identifying plays and games are likely to be encountered.

2. Make-believe play and day-dreaming are seldom revealed by this method.

3. The child's play behavior is likely to be modified if he suspects himself to be under surveillance.

4. It is impossible to observe *all of the play behavior of any considerable number of children during all hours of the day and night.*

(d) Pooling or Averaging of Opinions

Naismith ('14) attempted to construct a chart showing the ages at which boys start playing various games, and the ages at which they cease to play them.[9] Naismith used the averages of estimates which he secured from questionnaires sent to "the leading directors of physical education in colleges, private preparatory schools, and high schools."

These directors presumably obtained their information by means of personal observation. A resultant chart presumed to show that some games are much more valuable than others on account of their longevity. The chart possesses some value. It would have been of much greater value had it resulted from an actual behavior study of children.

(e) Recreational Surveys

During the past dozen years there have been numerous recreational surveys. Many of these surveys have yielded lists of recreational facilities together with suggestions for the improvement and expansion of these facilities. Such surveys have been made in California ('14)[10] and New York ('19),[10] and in the following cities: Ipswich, Mass. ('19),[6] Cleveland, Ohio ('20),[7] Indianapolis ('14),[10] Madison, Wisconsin ('15),[10] Peoria, Illinois ('16),[10] and Gary, Indiana ('18).[10]

Most of these studies reveal little in regard to the extent to which children participate in the recreational facilities provided. The play behavior of the child is, of course, much more important to the psychologist than the play facilities provided for his use.

REFERENCES

1. Chase, J. H. "Street Games of New York City." *Ped. Sem.* 1905. *12,* 503-04.
2. Monroe, W. S. "Play Interests of Children." *American Education Review.* 1899, *4,* 358-65.
3. Croswell, T. R. "Amusements of Worcester School Children." *Ped. Sem.* 1899, *6,* 314-71.

4. McGhee, Zack. "Play Life of Some South Carolina Children." *Ped. Sem.* 1900, 7, 459-91.

5. (a) Terman, Lewis M. *Genetic Studies of Genius.* Palo Alto, Cal. Stanford University Press. 1925. Pp. xv-648. (pp. 437-39.)

(b) *The Twenty-Third Yearbook of the National Society for the Study of Education.* Bloomington, Illinois. The Public School Publishing Company. 1924. Chap. 9, pp. 155-169. (pp. 163-164.)

6. Ipswich Report. *Play and Recreation in a Town of* 6000. (A Recreation Survey of Ipswich, Massachusetts), Howard R. Knight. Russell Sage Foundation. Department of Recreation. New York City. 1919.

7. Cleveland Recreation Survey. The Survey Committee of the Cleveland Foundation. Vol. III. *Wholesome Citizens and Sparetime.* By John E. Gillin. 1920. 181 pp.

8. Andrus, Ruth. *A Tentative Inventory of the Habits of Children from Two to Four Years of Age.* New York; Teachers College, Columbia University, Contributions to Education. No. 160, 1924. 55 pp.

9. Naismith, James. "High School Athletics as an Expression of the Corporate Life of the School." (Chap. XVII of *The Modern High School.* Edited by Charles Hughes Johnston. New York. Charles Scribner's Sons. 1914. Pp. xiv-847.)

10. (a) *Indianapolis Recreation Survey.* Prepared for the General Civic Improvement Committee of the Indianapolis Chamber of Commerce. Compiled under the direction of the Playground and Recreation Association of America. 1914.

(b) Madison, *"The Four Lake City," Recreational Survey.* Prepared by a Special Committee of the Madison Board of Commerce. Madison, Wisconsin. Tracy and Kilgore, printers. 1915. Pp. ix-103.

(c) Peoria. *Report of the Recreation Conditions and Problems of Peoria, with Recommendations and Suggested System.* By James Edward Rogers. Peoria. 1916. Pp. 32.

(d) Gary. The Gary Public Schools. *Physical Training and Play,* by Lee F. Hanmer. General Education Board. New York. 1918. Pp. xix-35.

(e) California. California Recreational Inquiry Committee. *Report of the State Recreational Inquiry Committee.*

(f) New York. *New York Recreation Circular.* State of New York. Conservation Commission. Albany. 1919.

CHAPTER IV

THE METHOD EMPLOYED IN THE SERIES OF INVESTIGATIONS REPORTED HEREIN

The realization of the importance of identifying the activities in which children spontaneously engage at different ages has resulted in many investigations of play. Some of these investigations have been discussed in the preceding chapter. The subjective nature of play has limited the workers and the reports of the investigators are to no small degree controversial.

It was mentioned previously that the present writers would not attempt to define play. They have considered as play those behavior manifestations which individuals exhibit "just because they want to." The term play will be used to designate these multitudinous and diverse activities. The present chapter will include a description of a technique used for disclosing: (1) the play activities most commonly engaged in by representative persons from five to twenty-two years of age residing in certain communities; (2) the play activities best liked by these individuals; (3) the games and other play activities consuming the greatest amount of time; (4) the extent to which a given child participates with other children in his play activities, and (5) the effect upon play behavior of such variables as age, sex, race, season, intelligence, community, etc.

In the case of children old enough to read, the plan employed was to place before each individual a comprehensive list of 200 play activities, having him check each one in which he had engaged of his own volition during the week preceding the date of the investigation. In addition, each pupil was asked to indicate the three activities which had given him the most fun or which he liked best. He was asked also to indicate the one activity to which he thought he had given the most time. In the last of a series of six investigations the children were asked to identify and indicate those activities in which they had participated alone.

The development of this plan proceeded slowly. The general procedure was decided upon only after long deliberation. The plan of having the children check a printed list was adopted since it seemed the most feasible manner of obtaining significant data.

The questionnaire method was discarded because of the obvious limitations set forth by Thorndike; [1] the observation method was eliminated as it was thought to be too time consuming to permit securing sufficient data to make the results highly significant.

Some of the items of the list were obtained from the studies of Croswell and McGhee.[2] A few more were procured from the Cleveland Survey.[3] Several competent persons were asked to supplement the list. Since play is so subjective a phenomenon, it is impossible to compile a complete list. At the end of the list finally assembled spaces therefore were provided in which items omitted could be added.

A preliminary investigation was made at Hibbing, Minnesota, in Sept. 1923, for the purpose of determining whether the proposed technique would procure satisfactory results. The resultant data indicated that some of the children had checked all the activities in which they had participated at any time. Subsequent studies were made at Linwood, Eudora, and Tonganoxie, Kansas. During this preliminary work the following improvements were made in the technique:

First. The list of play activities was increased from 140 to 200 items. Certain of the activities at first included in the list were found to be indulged in only rarely. If two or three per cent only of the children were found to engage in an activity during the course of a week, the activity was removed from the list unless it was thought to be highly seasonal in character. The activities added were those most frequently indicated by the children in the blank spaces provided for that purpose.

Second. The alphabetical arrangement of the items of the list was abandoned. It was found that with alphabetical arrangement the first items of the list, i.e., "Anty-over," etc., were relatively unfamiliar to certain children and caused confusion and delay. As a means of enabling the children to comprehend the directions more readily the well-known activities were placed at the head of the list. These included such activities as "Football," "Basket ball," and "Baseball."

Third. The list of activities was found to be too long to be finished at a single sitting by third and fourth-grade pupils. Provision was made therefore for children in these grades to spend two days at the task.

Fourth. The directions to the teachers were changed repeatedly during the preliminary work and those finally used were as specific as those ordinarily employed for the giving of mental tests. Separate sets of directions were made out for teachers of the third and fourth grades. In these greater emphasis was placed on the fact that the play activities engaged in *during the past week only* were to be checked. The teachers of these grades were instructed to *read aloud* the list of activities to their pupils to insure comprehension.

Following is the list of activities chosen, an abbreviated form of the directions to the pupils, and certain supplementary data obtained from the pupils in the first four investigations.

PART A

What things have you been doing during the past week just because you wanted to?

Read through the following list of toys and games and, as you read through the list, draw a circle with your pencil around each number that stands in front of anything that you have been playing with *during the past week,* or anything that you have been doing *during the past week* just because you wanted to do it.

1 Football.
2 Basket ball.
3 Baseball with a hard ball.
4 Ball with an indoor or play-ground ball.
5 Just playing catch.

6 Volley ball.
7 Handball.
8 Golf.
9 Tennis.
10 Soccer.

11 Boxing.
12 Wrestling.
13 Fencing.
14 Checkers.
15 Chess.

16 Dominoes.
17 Marbles.
18 Roller skating.
19 Sliding on a playground slide.
20 Sliding on a toboggan slide.

21 Coasting on a coaster.
22 Coasting on a wagon.
23 Coasting on a sled.
24 Swinging.
25 Ice-skating.

26 Sleigh-riding.
27 Riding in an auto.
28 Driving an auto.
29 Riding a bicycle.
30 Horseback riding.

31 Rolling a hoop.
32 Rolling an auto tire.
33 Kiddie car.
34 Velocipede.
35 Watching athletic sports.

36 Excursions to woods, parks, country, etc.
37 Gathering fruit.
38 Gathering berries.
39 Gathering nuts.
40 Gathering flowers.

41 Collecting stamps, birds' eggs, and so on.
42 Just hiking or strolling.
43 Going to the movies.
44 Going to entertainments, concerts, and so on.
45 Going to parties or picnics.

46 Sight-seeing.
47 Attending lectures.
48 Visiting or entertaining company.
49 Chewing gum.
50 Smoking.

51 Having "dates."
52 Just loafing or lounging.
53 Social dancing.
54 Folk-dancing.
55 Card games, such as authors, bridge, whist.

56 Literary clubs.
57 Social clubs, or being with the gang.
58 Listening to the victrola.
59 Listening to the radio.
60 Playing the piano (for fun).

61 Playing other musical instruments for fun.
62 Looking at the Sunday "funny paper."
63 Reading jokes or funny sayings.
64 Reading the newspapers.
65 Reading short stories.

66 Reading books.
67 Telling or guessing riddles.
68 Telling stories.
69 Listening to stories.
70 Writihg letters.

71 Writing poems.
72 Telling fortunes or having fortunes told.
73 Hunting.
74 Fishing.
75 Boating or canoeing.

76 Camping out.
77 Building or watching bonfires.
78 Climbing porches, trees, fences, posts, etc.
79 Doing gymnasium work.
80 Doing stunts in the gymnasium.

81 Turning handsprings, cartwheels, etc.
82 Doing calisthenics.
83 Playing on the giant stride.
84 Playing teeter-totter.
85 Just running and romping.

86 Running races.
87 Hop, skip, and jump.
88 Jumping for distance.
89 Jumping for height.
90 Pole vaulting.

91 Leap Frog.
92 Hop-scotch.
93 Jumping or skipping rope.
94 Other hopping games played on sidewalk.
95 Follow your leader.

96 Fox and geese.
97 Hare and hounds.
98 Run sheep run.
99 Hide and seek.
100 Blind man's buff.

101 Hide the button.
102 Hide the thimble.
103 Anty-over.
104 Black man.
105 Other tag games.

106 Crack the whip.
107 Whistling.
108 Dodgeball.
109 Captain ball.
110 Dare base.

111 Prisoner's base.
112 Bean bags.
113 Duck on the rock.
114 Jacks.
115 Matching pennies.

116 Throwing dice or playing "Put and Take."
117 Stealing water melons, fruit, etc., for fun.
118 Playing pool.
119 Billiards.
120 Bowling.

121 Croquet.
122 Pitching horseshoes.
123 Quoits.
124 Mumbly peg.
125 Jackstraws.

3rd and 4th grades stop here 1st day *

126 Throwing rocks or stones.
127 Shinny on your own side.
128 Pillow fights.
129 Snowball fights.
130 Teasing somebody.

131 Teasing birds or animals.
132 Bow and arrows.
133 Shooting a gun.
134 Playing in the sand.
135 Wading in the water.

136 Building a dam.
137 Swimming.
138 Dressing up in older folks' clothing.
139 Playing circus.
140 Playing house.

141 Playing horse.
142 Playing store.
143 Playing school.
144 Playing church.
145 Playing Sunday school.

146 Playing doctor.
147 Playing nurse.
148 Playing bandit.
149 Playing soldier.
150 Playing cowboy.

151 Playing Indian.
152 Train conductor, engineer or brakeman.
153 Playing robber and police.
154 Playing movie actor or actress.
155 Playing other make-believe games.

156 Just imagining things.
157 Statuary.
158 Charades.
159 "Here I come"—"Where from?"
160 Tin-tin.

161 Post-office.
162 Spin the pan.
163 London Bridge.
164 Other singing games.
165 Just singing.

166 Drop the handkerchief.
167 Three deep.
168 Other ring games.
169 Old witch.
170 Pussy wants a corner.

* In order to avoid fatigue, the younger pupils used two periods on two successive days.

171 Making mud pies, mud dolls, etc.
172 Clay modeling.
173 Drawing with pencil, pen, chalk, or crayon.
174 Painting with water-colors.
175 Cutting paper things with scissors.

176 Making a scrap-book.
177 Taking snapshots.
178 Stringing beads.
179 Sewing, knitting, crocheting, etc., for fun.
180 Using a hammer, saw, nails, etc., for fun.

181 Digging caves or dens.
182 Building snow men, snow forts, snow houses.
183 Spinning tops.
184 Flying kites.
185 Walking on stilts.

186 Toy airplanes, toy balloons, toy parachutes.
187 Toy trains, ships, autos, wagons, etc.
188 Playing fire engine (or hook and ladder).
189 Looking at pictures.
190 Toy blocks.

191 Toy horn, toy drum, etc.
192 Dolls, doll carriages, doll clothes, etc.
193 Other toys.
194 Picture puzzles.
195 Wire puzzles, string puzzles.

196 Making or using a wireless or other electrical apparatus.
197 Playing with pet dogs.
198 Playing with pet kittens.
199 Playing with pet rabbits.
200 Playing with other pets.

PART B

Write on the blank lines below the names of any toys or games or other things which took up some of your time *during the past week,* and which you liked, *but which are not included in the printed list.*

201 ....   206 ....

202 ....   207 ....

203 ....   208 ....

204 ....   209 ....

205 ....   210 ....

Now go back and look at each circle that you have made. If you have made any circles in front of things that you did not actually do during the past week, draw a line through them.

PART C

Now look over all the numbers that you have put circles around and write on the blank lines below *the numbers* of the three things that gave you the most fun, or that you liked best. *If you are not sure, just guess.*

I liked number..........best of all. I liked number..........next best.

I liked number..........third best.

PART D

Now write on the blank line below *the number* of the one thing that took up most of your time. *If you are not sure, just guess.*

Number..........took up more of my time than anything else.

———

The following schools of Kansas City, Kansas, were included in the first three investigations *: the Douglass, Hawthorne, Lowell, Morse, and Riverview elementary schools; the Central Junior High School; the Northeast Junior High School; the Kansas City, Kansas, High School; and the Sumner High School. The selection of schools in Kansas City was made with a view to obtaining a fair sampling of the school population of the entire city. The Douglass Elementary School, the Northeast Junior High School, and the Sumner High School, all attended by colored children only, were selected in order that a sampling of negro children might be obtained. The Riverview and Morse elementary schools were selected because they were attended by white children with a social and economic status roughly comparable to that of the negro children. At Lawrence, Kansas, investigations were made in the Quincy and the Pinckney elementary schools, the Lawrence Junior High School, the Liberty Memorial High School, and the University of Kansas. The selection of schools in Lawrence was made merely with a view to obtaining a fair sampling of the city's school population. At Bonner Springs and at Moran, Kansas, the list was checked by all the pupils in the public schools.

In order that seasonal differences might be taken into account, the list was checked by the various school groups on three different dates: November 7, 1923; February 20, 1924; and April 30, 1924. The same printed list was used on each of the three dates.

In November, 1924, a similar investigation was made of the play activities of boys and girls in certain one-room rural schools of Kansas.

* The writers are especially indebted to Mr. R. L. Wise of the public schools of Kansas City, Kansas, for assistance in developing the sets of directions used for the administration of the Play Quiz.

The rural pupils checked the list in the fall of 1925 in order that the initial findings for country children might be verified.

Additional data were secured from more than 6,000 pupils of Kansas City, Missouri, in January of 1926. The reliability of the earlier findings for the city children was thus verified further.

Prior to making the last two investigations the Play Quiz was modified in such a manner as to permit the investigators to discover the extent to which a given child participates with other children in his play activities. The Quiz was modified further to permit the addition of several items not included in the original Quiz.

The total number of children studied is shown in Tables I and II. Separate tabulations were made for race groups and other sub-groups in such a manner as to permit both separate and collective computations.

After each investigation tables and graphs were made presenting the percentages of children of various ages in the various sub-groups who participated in each activity. After the first three investigations averages were obtained and graphs made.

TABLE I

NUMBER OF INDIVIDUALS OF GRADE III OR ABOVE INCLUDED IN SIX
INVESTIGATIONS OF PLAY BEHAVIOR.

| | City Children | | | | | | Country Children | | | | City Children |
| | Nov. 7 1923 | | Feb. 20 1924 | | Apr. 30 1924 | | Nov. 1924 | | Nov. 1925 | | Jan. 1926 |
Ages	B	G	B	G	B	G	B	G	B	G	Both Sexes
8½	98	100	90	97	80	99	89	85	35	39	84
9½	169	174	161	139	144	144	102	85	45	49	468
10½	182	215	169	199	160	176	102	103	67	53	935
11½	187	235	167	222	184	220	106	109	65	64	981
12½	249	326	201	289	176	266	101	83	79	69	748
13½	280	269	231	235	259	263	93	89	70	57	903
14½	274	301	252	282	238	278	67	68	50	35	946
15½	230	261	247	244	247	256	46	27	22	21	848
16½	210	251	181	223	193	235	..	..	..	..	573
17½	145	182	130	208	146	193	..	..	..	..	268
18½	115	120	170	174	130	167	..	..	..	..	82
19½	95	101	119	115	102	93	..	..	..	..	25
20½	50	73	73	124	59	76	..	..	..	..	5
21½	53	41	57	85	43	66	..	..	..	..	..
22*	79	44	105	114	68	88	..	..	..	..	..
University of Kansas Faculty					170	35					
Totals	2416	2693	2353	2780	2399	2655	706	649	433	387	6886

* Where age 22 occurs in this table and in the following tables data are presented for all persons studied whose chronological ages were 22 or above.

TABLE II

NUMBER OF CHILDREN BELOW GRADE III INCLUDED IN THREE
INVESTIGATIONS OF PLAY BEHAVIOR.

Ages	Nov. 1923		Feb. 1924		Apr. 1924		Totals	
	Boys	Girls	Boys	Girls	Boys	Girls	Boys	Girls
5½	65	68	38	49	20	25	123	142
6½	81	124	72	106	79	90	232	320
7½	102	98	94	104	89	123	285	325
8½	41	27	58	31	72	45	171	103
Totals	289	317	262	290	260	283	811	890

REFERENCES

1. Thorndike, E. L. *Educational Psychology*. Vol. I. New York. Teachers College. Columbia University. 1915. pp. xii-442. (pp. 32-37.)

2. (a) Croswell, T. R. "Amusements of the Worcester School Children." *Ped. Sem.* 1899, *6*, 314-71.

(b) McGhee, Zack. "A Study in the Play Life of Some South Carolina Children." *Ped. Sem.* 1900. *7*, 459-78.

3. Cleveland Recreational Survey. The Survey Committee of the Cleveland Foundation, Vol. III. *Wholesome Citizens and Sparetime*, by John E. Gillin. 1918. 181 pp.

CHAPTER V

GENERAL AGE GROWTH *

Undue emphasis upon periodicity in play behavior has resulted in the more important characteristic of play behavior, namely, its continuity, being obscured or underestimated. Of periodicity and rhythm in play, as in all development, there can be no doubt. But any thoughtful attempt to characterize a particular period must bring the conviction that the obvious characteristic traits of each period have their beginnings in preceding stages and merge gradually into succeeding ones.

Thorndike has stated that there is continuity of mental variations:

"Continuity of variations means two things,—the absence of regularly recurring gaps, such as those between 2 petals, 3 petals, 4 petals, and the like, and the absence of irregularly recurring gaps, such as those between mice and rats, between rats and squirrels, and the like." [1]

" . . . the discrete steps are exceedingly small like the steps of increase of physical mass by atoms. Intelligence, rate of movement, memory, quickness of association, accuracy of discrimination, leadership of men and so on are continuous in the sense that mass, amperage, heat, human stature and anemia are." [2]

"A misleading appearance of irregular discontinuity often arises from the insufficient number of cases measured. If only a few individuals are measured in a trait or if the scale is a fine one, there will of course be divisions on the scale or amounts of the trait unrepresented in any individuals." [3]

When human character traits are measured objectively continuity of variation is found to exist *invariably*. Classification of individuals according to types therefore usually is unwarranted and misleading. Such classification, however, is frequently employed. Team play and social participation are mentioned frequently as the characteristic activities of certain periods. Certain ages too are characterized as periods in which individualistic play predominates.

* A part of this chapter appeared in *The Journal of Applied Psychology*, April, 1927.

The difficulties inherent in classification of child development on the basis of age periods are revealed clearly by the diversity of opinion regarding the number and the duration of the periods of childhood. Few investigators agree either upon the number or the length of the periods. Chamberlain [4] has presented data showing the variety of age intervals resulting from attempts to differentiate certain periods in growth according to the degree of physical maturation therein found. The following attempts are examples of the conflicting opinions cited.

Lacassagne [5] recognizes the following periods of human life:

1.	Fœtal life	
2.	First childhood..............	Up to the 7th month.
3.	Second childhood...........	From 7th month to the 2nd year.
4.	Third childhood.............	From the 2nd year to the 7th year.
5.	Adolescence	From the 7th to the 15th year.
6.	Puberty	From the 15th to the 20th year.
7.	Adult age..................	From the 20th to the 30th year.
8.	Virility	From the 30th to the 40th year.
9.	"Age de retour"............	From the 40th to the 60th year.
10.	Old age....................	From the 60th year till death.

Tigerstedt [6] in his *Human Physiology* gives the common German division of life-periods as follows:

1. New-born child..........From birth to fall of navel-string. Age 4-5 days.
2. Suckling ....From 4-5 days to 7-9 months. (First dentition.)
3. Later childhood.........From 7-9 months to 7th year. (Second dentition.)
4. Boyhood ....From the 7th year to the 13th or 14th year.
5. Youth ....From the 13th or 14th year to age 19-21.
6. Mature age.............From the 19th or 21st year up to age 45 or 50.
7. Later manhood and old age. From age 45 or 50 on.

Macdonald [7] concludes that the human body has the following six periods of growth:

1. From birth to the 6th or 8th year.
2. From the 11th to the 14th year.
3. From the 16th to the 17th year.
4. From the 17th to the 30th year.
5. From age 30 to 50.
6. From age 50 on.

From the above examples, the difficulty of hard and fast classification of growth periods is at once apparent. However, the human organism possesses what seems to be a mania for cataloguing. The result has been manifold elaborate attempts to partition childhood into periods of development. These attempts have not been confined to physical maturation but have included almost every known human characteristic that manifests growth to any degree. Lesshaft [8] exemplifies a common tendency to develop "psychic" periods of growth:

1. The new-born child...............Chaos period.
2. To about the 2nd year.............Reflex rational period.
3. Up to school age.................Concrete imitation period.
4. Up to about 20 years.............Abstract imitation period.
5. Ripe age of man.................Critico-creative period.

Valentine,[9] from the point of view of developmental psychology, divides the life of the child as follows:

1. First few months of life. Instinctive period.
2. Up to the 6th or 7th year. Imitative period.
3. From about age 7 till puberty. Attentive period.

Guibert [10] recognizes four periods in childhood and youth as characterized by successive developments of aptitudes and mental functions:

1. New-born infant. Period of subjective and instinctive life.
2. Beginning before 6th month of life. Period of objective life.
3. Period of social life.
4. Period of professional and scientific life.

Sheldon [11] finds that the years of childhood from four to fourteen contain two distinctly marked periods:

1. Ages 4 to 10. Period of imitation.
2. Ages 10 to 14. Period of invention.

Certain writers have not been content with a differentiation of periods on the basis of certain fundamental universal human traits but have selected special interests and concocted epochs to correspond with changing manifestations of these interests. Miss Mary A. Barnes [12] finds the "historical sense" appearing as early as seven. This sense undergoes the following development:

1. From 7 or 8 to about 12 or 13. Period of striking biographies and events.

2. From 14 or 15 up to about entrance to college or after. Period of interest in "the statesman, thinkers, poets, as successors to the explorers and fighters of the earlier period."

3. College years. The age of monographic special study.

Again, Professor Earl Barnes and Miss Estelle M. Darrah [13] find the following periods of "law recognition."

1. From age 6 or 7 to age 10 or 12. Period of law-ignoring.
2. From age 10 or 12 to about age 16. Period of law-recognition. (Personal authority is replaced by obedience to rule and law.)

There has long existed a tendency for educational and sociological theorists to delimit the social development of the child and to ascribe to him periods in the development of social sense. The periods are defined often with little precision; the results of the various attempts are to no small degree controversial. The following is a popular example of this practice: [14]

1. Presocial stage...................This lasts most of the first year.
2. Imitative and socializing stage.....Culminates at about 3 years.
3. Individualizing stage.............Culminates at about 6 years.
4. Competitive socializing stage......Culminates at about 12 years.
5. Pubertal or transitional stage......Culminates at about 18 years.
6. Later adolescence...............Culminates at about 24 years.

The variation in periods which results when classification of growth stages is attempted may be occasioned by the very complexity of such vague traits as sociability, etc. The attempts to classify growth stages of play behavior on the basis of chronological age show that the disagreement in reference to age periods is not lessened when classification is made upon a single basis, namely, that of the play periods of childhood. There is no general agreement regarding either the number or the duration of the growth periods in connection with play manifestations. The following examples exemplify the existing confusion in this regard:

CLASSIFICATIONS OF GROWTH STAGES IN PLAY BEHAVIOR

Dr. Joseph K. Hart's classification: [15]

1. The segregative level..........Children to age 6, 7., or 8.
2. The group level..............Children to age 12, 13, 14, or 15.
3. The team level...............Upward to maturity.

Joseph Lee's classification: [16]

1. First three years..Creative impulse begins to manifest itself.
2. Ages 3 to 6......Age of impersonation.
3. Ages 6 to 11....."Big Injun" or age of self-assertion.
4. Ages 11 to 14...Age of loyalty.
5. Ages 14 to 21...Apprentice age.

George E. Johnson's classification: [17]

1. Ages 0 to 3.
2. Ages 4 to 6.
3. Ages 7 to 9.
4. Ages 10 to 12.
5. Ages 13 to 15.

Henry S. Curtis' classification: [18]

1. Ages 0 to 6...................................Imitative stage.
2. Ages 6 to puberty........................"Big Injun" stage.
3. Puberty on...............................Team games.

Luther Gulick's classification: [19]

1. Ages 0 to 3.............................Babyhood.
2. Ages 3 to 7.............................Early childhood.
3. Ages 7 to 12............................Childhood.
4. Ages 12 to 17...........................Early adolescence.
5. Ages 17 to 23...........................Later adolescence.

Bowen and Mitchell's classification: [20]

1. Ages 0 to 6...................Babyhood or early childhood.
2. Ages 6 to 12..................Later childhood.
3. Ages 12 to 15.................Early adolescence.
4. Ages 15 to 18.................Later adolescence.
5. Ages 18 to 40.................Maturity.

Croswell's classification: [21]

1. Ages 6 to 9..............Objects used symbolically.
2. Ages 9 to 13.............Vigorous exercise of the whole body.
3. Ages 14 and above........The creative spirit prevails.

Kirkpatrick's classification: [22]

1. First 5 years................Period of play.
2. Ages 5 to 10................Participation in team games.
3. Ages 12 and above..........Participation in games and sports.

It is obvious that few of the investigators agree upon *the number or the length* of the periods associated with the child's play life. One asks why such diversity of opinion exists. The writers feel that the complexity of play is one cause of this condition. Play is a behavior manifestation of so many variables that different aspects are conspicuous at different times and are observed by different writers as characteristic of the total phenomenon.

Most of the preceding classifications in reference to play were made prior to the introduction of quantitative measurement. Since the introduction of objective mental tests, not one test has been found which yields a very startling difference for groups in successive age levels. The tests all show continuity rather than periodicity in mental development. It is probable that these tests, which show no sudden evolution in the child's ability to think, furnish good illustrations of the child's intellectual growth. It seems obvious that most subjective descriptions of periods of development have been exaggerated somewhat; one reason being the fact that large differences within a given age group are always to be found. It is probable that periodicity exists only in the sense that one period of three or four years' duration differs from another period of similar length in conspicuous degree. The change from one period to another is always gradual, however, and never abrupt.

Continuity of growth is revealed by Tables III, and IV, which present for boys and girls respectively various play activities which are participated in by not less than 25 per cent of individuals of ages 8½ to 22½ inclusive. It is, of course, true that some of these activities are engaged in by much more than 25 per cent of individuals. These two tables show conclusively that there is a community of interest for persons of widely different ages.

TABLE III

PLAY ACTIVITIES ENGAGED IN BY MORE THAN 25% OF BOYS OF AGES
8½ TO 22 INCLUSIVE

    * Baseball with a hard ball.
    Just playing catch.
    Riding in an auto.
    Watching athletic sports.
    Going to the movies.

* November only.

Chewing gum.
Card games, such as authors, bridge, whist.
Listening to the victrola.
Listening to the radio.
Looking at the Sunday "funny" paper.

Reading jokes or funny sayings.
Reading the newspapers.
Reading short stories.
Reading books.
Writing letters

Whistling.
Teasing somebody.

TABLE IV

PLAY ACTIVITIES PARTICIPATED IN BY 25% OR MORE OF GIRLS OF ALL AGES
FROM 8½ TO 22½, INCLUSIVE

Listening to the victrola.
Playing the piano for fun.
Riding in an auto.
Writing letters.
Reading short stories.

Reading the newspapers.
Reading jokes or funny sayings.
Going to the movies.
Looking at the Sunday "funny" paper.
Going to parties or picnics.

Visiting or entertaining company.
Chewing gum.
Teasing somebody.
Listening to stories.
Gathering flowers.

Just singing.
Looking at pictures.

Table V presents for the boys studied the ranks of the play activities according to the frequency of participation therein at various age levels. Table VI shows similar data for the girls. A form of play is here included when it was found to be common to at least 20 per cent

of the persons of a given age.   Table V is to be read as follows: "Looking at the Sunday 'funny' paper," is the one activity of the entire list
of 200 that was engaged in most commonly by the boys from eight to
fifteen years of age.   "Reading books" was second in frequency for
the boys eight and ten years of age, third in frequency for the boys
nine and eleven years of age, fifth for those of ages fourteen and fifteen,
and seventh for age thirteen.   A blank space in the table indicates
that the particular activity was participated in by less than 20 per cent
of the pupils of the given age.

TABLE V-a

RANK IN FREQUENCY OF GAMES AND OTHER PLAY ACTIVITIES MOST COMMONLY
ENGAGED IN BY THE BOYS EIGHT TO FIFTEEN YEARS OF AGE.

Activity	Age							
	8	9	10	11	12	13	14	15
Looking at the Sunday "funny" paper.....	1	1	1	1	1	1	1	1
Reading books	2	3	2	3	4	7	5	5
Just playing catch *	3	2	2	3	3	3	3	3
Reading the newspapers	10	8	3	3	2	2	2	2
Chewing gum	7	7	3.	5	5	4	5	7
Drawing with pencil, pen, chalk, or crayon..	4	5	10	13	19	19	17	27
Whistling	5	6	4	8	13	14	11	14
Reading short stories	6	7	5	7	7	8	8	8
Just running and romping	8	4	6	20	19	21	..	..
Running races *	9	10	7	11	15	18	24	23
Cutting paper things with scissors	12	15	22	32	31	..	..	..
Gathering flowers *	11	13	12	18	22	23	26	..
Listening to stories	13	12	14	22	21	19	19	23
Football **	15	8	6	4	8	6	8	7
Riding in an automobile	16	11	5	7	6	5	5	4
Using a hammer, saw, nails, etc., for fun....	14	9	8	15	10	13	12	21
Going to the "movies"	26	17	8	6	5	6	4	4
Baseball with a hard ball *	18	14	8	7	6	6	6	6
Watching athletic sports	37	25	24	23	11	7	7	6
Listening to the victrola	17	12	9	12	17	16	13	14
Ball with an indoor or playground ball * ...	36	23	20	21	17	12	12	13
Reading jokes or funny sayings	26	18	13	10	10	9	9	9
Listening to the radio	25	23	16	21	12	4	9	10
Basket ball ***	..	38	29	27	15	10	8	11
Jumping for distance	18	15	11	14	13	16	15	18
Riding a bicycle	43	32	22	17	9	12	9	13
Playing with pet dogs	19	15	10	9	14	10	12	15
Jumping for height *	23	20	12	16	13	15	16	18
Wrestling	30	18	12	13	9	11	10	12
Teasing somebody	27	19	18	25	18	17	13	17
Throwing rocks or stones	22	16	13	19	16	15	14	19
Doing gymnasium work	..	..	..	..	27	21	14	20

* April data.   ** November data.   *** November and February data.

TABLE V-b

RANK IN FREQUENCY OF GAMES AND OTHER PLAY ACTIVITIES MOST COMMONLY
ENGAGED IN BY THE YOUNG MEN SIXTEEN YEARS OF AGE OR OLDER.

Activity	Age						University 22 or of Kansas	
	16	17	18	19	20	21	Older	Faculty
Reading the newspapers	1	1	1	1	1	1	1	1
Looking at the Sunday "funny" paper	2	2	2	2	2	4	3	9
Riding in an automobile	3	3	3	4	4	6	7	7
Going to the "movies"	4	4	4	3	2	3	4	11
Watching athletic sports	5	5	5	7	5	8	5	11
Just playing catch *	5	6	6	8	6	9	8	26
Chewing gum	6	8	8	10	7	14	16	22
Reading books	8	9	13	13	12	13	8	2
Baseball with a hard ball *	7	10	12	16	18	26	21	..
Reading short stories	9	9	10	11	10	15	12	13
Reading jokes or funny sayings	9	6	7	6	8	7	6	9
Driving an automobile	10	7	11	13	13	21	22	9
Listening to the radio	11	11	15	18	20	23	21	21
Football **	9	10	19	22	28	30	..	..
Basket ball ***	12	15	19	27	..	..	..	..
Listening to the victrola	13	13	9	9	9	5	9	11
Whistling	14	10	16	18	16	27	25	24
Riding a bicycle	14	25	..	..	..	..	..	..
Teasing somebody	15	12	17	20	14	21	21	19
Writing letters	17	17	10	5	3	2	2	4
Card games, such as authors, bridge, and whist	18	21	15	15	14	16	14	12
Having "dates"	16	14	14	12	11	10	11	21
Doing gymnasium work	18	22	15	14	14	22	21	..
Just "loafing" or lounging	22	27	22	15	13	12	12	15
Listening to stories	21	21	21	17	15	21	16	19
Ball with an indoor or playground ball *	14	15	16	17	17	22	19	..
Smoking	..	..	23	20	15	11	10	6
Visiting or entertaining company	..	27	26	20	22	27	17	5
Going to entertainments, concerts, etc.	20	20	24	25	24	20	18	3
Attending lectures	..	..	25	24	15	22	13	8
Excusions to woods, parks, country, etc. *	..	..	..	29	26	22	24	8
Just "hiking" or strolling	24	28	25	18	21	10	15	17

* April data.   ** November data.   *** November and February data

TABLE VI-a

RANK IN FREQUENCY OF GAMES AND OTHER PLAY ACTIVITIES MOST COMMONLY ENGAGED IN BY THE GIRLS EIGHT TO FIFTEEN YEARS OF AGE.

Activity	Age							
	8	9	10	11	12	13	14	15
Looking at the Sunday "funny" paper	1	1	1	1	1	1	1	1
Reading books	2	2	2	3	3	3	3	2
Jumping or skipping rope *	3	6	4	10	13	17	30	..
Reading short stories	6	3	3	4	5	5	6	3
Reading the newspapers	13	8	3	2	2	2	2	1
Drawing with pencil, pen, chalk, or crayon..	4	4	7	7	11	15	20	20
Just singing	7	5	5	6	7	10	10	12
Chewing gum	12	5	6	5	6	4	4	5
Playing the piano for fun	10	11	10	8	7	7	9	6
Riding in an automobile	13	11	9	10	8	8	5	3
Cutting paper things with scissors	5	6	8	12	14	25	29	..
Dolls, doll carriages, doll clothes, etc.	9	9	13	15	29	..	..	..
Listening to stories	9	15	16	14	18	21	22	21
Gathering flowers *	10	10	5	9	4	9	13	10
Playing house	9	16	25	28	..	..	..	..
Listening to the victrola	11	7	9	10	10	11	12	8
Looking at pictures	8	12	12	11	11	13	15	14
Going to the "movies"	20	23	18	12	9	6	8	5
Just running and romping	14	15	14	13	20	29	..	..
Playing school	14	15	14	20	26	..	..	..
Visiting or entertaining company	22	25	27	17	15	15	14	9
Swinging	15	19	23	23	27	..	..	..
Hide and seek	15	20	20	22	25	..	..	..
Running races	16	17	17	16	22	26	..	..
Telling or guessing riddles	17	18	21	16	19	20	23	25
Writing letters	15	13	15	13	12	12	11	7
Teasing somebody	25	23	19	17	14	14	13	13
Jacks *	18	14	19	17	28	32	..	..
Reading jokes or funny sayings	21	16	11	9	8	6	7	4

* April data.

TABLE VI-b

RANK IN FREQUENCY OF GAMES AND OTHER PLAY ACTIVITIES MOST COMMONLY
ENGAGED IN BY THE YOUNG WOMEN SIXTEEN YEARS OF AGE OR OLDER.

Activity	16	17	18	19	20	21	22 or Older	University of Kansas Faculty
Reading the newspapers	1	1	1	2	2	2	1	1
Riding in an automobile	3	2	2	3	4	5	5	6
Reading short stories	4	5	7	10	10	6	6	4
Writing letters	7	5	3	1	1	1	2	5
Going to the "movies"	5	4	5	5	6	7	5	10
Looking at the Sunday "funny" paper	2	2	4	7	9	15	16	10
Reading books	5	8	13	15	21	14	13	5
Playing the piano for fun	6	7	11	7	9	15	10	12
Visiting or entertaining company	7	6	6	4	3	5	3	2
Reading jokes or funny sayings	6	3	8	9	11	12	9	10
Listening to the Victrola	9	9	9	6	8	8	8	11
Just singing	10	13	17	15	12	11	12	12
Chewing gum	8	10	12	18	21	20	20	..
Having "dates"	13	11	7	4	3	4	11	..
Social dancing	16	16	10	8	5	3	7	..
Watching athletic sports	11	12	12	13	16	14	15	18
Gathering flowers *	14	17	13	12	15	8	10	7
Going to parties or picnics	15	13	14	13	14	13	16	14
Teasing somebody	11	13	15	14	17	17	14	..
Attending lectures	..	..	..	19	19	18	13	8
Going to entertainments, concerts, etc.	15	15	14	11	7	12	4	3
Just "hiking" or strolling	20	21	14	10	11	9	6	7
Social clubs or being with the gang	19	24	19	13	18	13	9	..
Card games, such as authors, bridge, and whist	21	23	19	16	16	10	17	12

* April data.

From tables V and VI, it is at once obvious that there is considerable permanence of play interest from age to age. These tables give striking evidence of the difficulty attendant upon classification of play activities in certain age groups. The gradual transition in play behavior from year to year is again revealed in the favorite activities of children of various ages. (See Tables VII and VIII.) There is considerable permanence in favorite activities and the best liked activities tend to be those most frequently participated in. The play trends which characterize a given age group seem to be the result of gradual changes occurring during the growth period. These changes are not sudden and sporadic, but are gradual and contingent. Nor can any age or group of ages between 8½ and 22½ inclusive be designated social or individualistic on the basis of the play behavior therein revealed.

TABLE VII-a

RANK IN FREQUENCY OF GAMES AND OTHER PLAY ACTIVITIES LIKED BEST BY THE BOYS EIGHT TO FIFTEEN YEARS OF AGE.

Activity	Age							
	8	9	10	11	12	13	14	15
Football *	1	1	1	1	2	1	2	2
Baseball with a hard ball **	2	2	2	2	3	3	3	3
Basket ball ***	4	3	4	3	1	2	1	1
Boxing	3	4	3	6	7	9	8	8
Marbles	4	5	6	9	10	..	..	..
Just playing catch **	5	5	3	4	5	7	9	9
Playing cowboy	5	7	5	10	..	..	..	..
Wrestling	6	8	4	8	8	10	..	..
Roller skating	5	4	5	3	6	5	10	..
Horseback riding	6	9	10	8	10	10	11	..
Looking at the Sunday "funny" paper	5	6	9	9	10	..	..	..
Riding a bicycle	6	7	4	4	4	4	6	9
Riding in an automobile	7	8	9	10	8	7	7	12
Going to the "movies"	8	7	7	5	6	5	5	7
Reading books	8	8	9	11	10	8	8	8
Ball with an indoor or playground ball **	..	4	8	8	6	7	10	9
Running races **	8	8	8	..	..	..	..	..
Coasting on a wagon	8	8	..	..	..	..	..	..
Driving an automobile	..	..	..	10	11	6	4	4
Tennis **	..	..	..	..	11	9	7	5
Watching athletic sports	..	..	..	..	10	8	10	6
Hunting *	..	..	..	..	11	9	6	6
Jumping for height **	..	10	11	7	9	11	10	9
Pole vaulting **	10	10	11	7	11	7	8	11
Having "dates"	..	..	..	..	..	10	10	11
Listening to the radio	..	..	..	..	..	..	10	10

* November data.   ** April data.   *** November and February data.

TABLE VII-b

RANK IN FREQUENCY OF GAMES AND OTHER PLAY ACTIVITIES LIKED BEST BY THE
YOUNG MEN SIXTEEN YEARS OF AGE OR OLDER *

Activity	16	17	18	19	20	21	22 or Older	University of Kansas Faculty
Basket ball **	1	1	1	1	3	2	10	..
Football ***	2	2	2	2	2	9	11	..
Baseball with a hard ball	3	4	8	3	9	9	7	..
Driving an automobile	4	3	3	8	6	5	8	4
Going to the "movies"	6	6	8	6	4	6	6	..
Tennis ****	5	8	6	7	7	3	7	10
Having "dates"	6	5	5	5	1	1	2	11
Hunting ***	7	11	7	10	12	..	..	..
Watching athletic sports	8	7	4	5	1	4	1	10
Reading books	9	12	9	8	9	7	4	1
Social dancing	11	14	11	10	10	8	5	..
Listening to the radio	10	10	5	6	3	2	5	..
Riding in an automobile	12	13	9	11	10	9	11	10
Reading short stories	9	9	9	9	9	9	9	9
Reading the newspapers	..	..	10	8	6	5	3	3
Smoking	..	..	10	9	11	8	8	7
Card games, such as authors, bridge, and whist	..	..	12	10	11	9	7	8
Going to entertainments, concerts, etc.	..	..	..	..	..	..	..	2

* The following activities were popular, but it is difficult to rank them on the basis of their popularity: ball with an indoor or playground ball, just playing catch, golf, gathering flowers (April data), attending lectures, visiting or entertaining company, social clubs or being with the gang, listening to the victrola, playing for fun musical instruments other than the piano, and swimming.

** November and February data.

*** November data.

**** April data.

TABLE VIII-a

RANK IN FREQUENCY OF GAMES AND OTHER PLAY ACTIVITIES LIKED BEST BY THE
GIRLS EIGHT TO FIFTEEN YEARS OF AGE *

Activity	Age							
	8	9	10	11	12	13	14	15
Roller skating	1	1	4	5	5	6	..	..
Dolls, doll carriages, doll clothes, etc.	2	2	3	7	..	..	..	..
Riding in an automobile	3	2	4	6	4	4	5	5
Reading books	5	2	4	2	2	1	2	1
Going to the "movies"	4	4	2	1	1	2	1	1
Playing the piano for fun	6	4	1	3	3	3	4	4
Playing school	6	6	5	..	..	..	..	..
Jacks **	7	6	5	10	..	..	..	..
Basket ball ***	..	..	..	8	7	4	7	7
Playing house	8	5	..	..	..	..	..	..
Looking at the Sunday "funny" paper	6	3	2	4	5	5	9	11
Listening to the Victrola	8	7	5	9	8	7	10	12
Going to parties or picnics	..	..	5	8	5	4	5	7
Watching athletic sports	..	..	..	..	..	6	6	6
Doing gymnasium work	..	..	..	..	..	6	7	8
Sewing, knitting, crocheting, etc., for fun	..	8	6	9	6	5	8	9
Having "dates"	..	..	..	..	..	7	6	6
Reading short stories	..	..	..	..	..	7	9	9
Social dancing	..	..	..	..	8	5	3	2
Dressing up in older folks' clothing	11	6	..	..	..	..	..	..

* The following activities were popular, but it is difficult to rank them on the basis of their popularity: riding a bicycle; social clubs or being with the gang; driving an automobile; going to entertainments, concerts, etc.; and just "hiking" or strolling.
** April data. *** November and February data.

TABLE VIII-b

RANK IN FREQUENCY OF GAMES AND OTHER PLAY ACTIVITIES LIKED BEST BY THE
YOUNG WOMEN SIXTEEN YEARS OF AGE OR OLDER.*

Activity	Age						22 or Older
	16	17	18	19	20	21	
Social dancing	3	2	1	1	1	1	1
Reading books	1	1	4	5	7	2	3
Going to the "movies"	2	3	3	6	6	10	8
Playing the piano for fun	4	6	6	3	2	8	4
Having "dates"	5	4	2	2	3	3	6
Riding in an automobile	6	5	5	4	8	6	5
Watching athletic sports	7	7	6	8	7	5	12
Going to parties or picnics	8	9	8	7	9	9	9
Driving an automobile	9	8	7	9	10	8	11
Reading short stories	10	7	9	9	8	6	8
Visiting or entertaining company	11	8	10	6	10	7	3
Going to entertainments, concerts, etc.	12	10	8	6	4	4	1
Card games, such as authors, bridge, and whist	..	12	11	8	7	5	9
Just "hiking" or strolling	13	11	9	8	5	7	3
Social clubs or being with the gang	13	12	9	8	9	8	8
Writing letters	..	13	10	10	13	10	7
Gathering flowers **	..	..	12	10	12	12	7
Reading the newspaper	..	..	12	11	11	11	9
Just singing	..	11	11	12	11	12	11

* The following activities were popular, but it is difficult to rank them on the basis of their popularity: listening to the victrola; doing gymnasium work; basket ball; tennis; and sewing, knitting, crocheting, etc., for fun. ** April data.

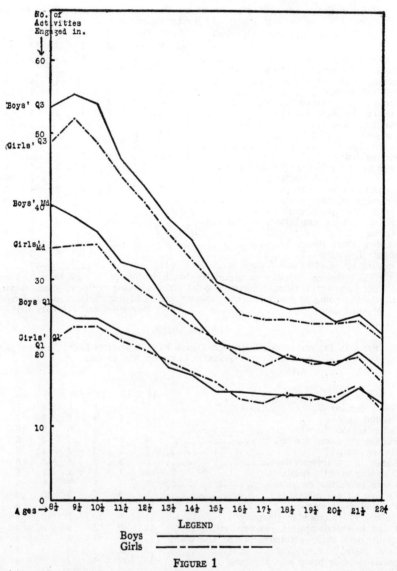

FIGURE 1

The number of different play activities engaged in by boys and girls of various ages. Average of findings from three separate investigations. Dispersion of the two middle quartiles also shown. See Table IX, p. 59.

NUMBER OF PLAY ACTIVITIES PARTICIPATED IN
BY INDIVIDUALS OF VARIOUS AGE LEVELS

Figure 1 and Table IX show the median, the lower, and the upper quartiles of the number of activities engaged in by the children of various ages.   It will be noted that the younger subjects studied not only engaged in a larger number of activities but also manifested greater variability than the older ones.   The middle fifty per cent range is larger for ages $8\frac{1}{2}$ to $14\frac{1}{2}$ than for any of the later periods.   This condition holds for both sexes and for each of the three seasons.   The median number of activities participated in by boys of age eight is forty.   By age sixteen this number has diminished to twenty with slight decrease subsequently.   Data obtained from the members of the faculty of the University of Kansas suggest a continued, though gradual, narrowing of play interest with increase of age.   This finding may be due to the fact that adults tend to become more conventional in their use of their leisure, whereas children find greater opportunity for versatility of interest.   This finding, however, may be due to the limitations of the Quiz, the list having been made for children.

Figure 1 shows that the transition from age to age in reference to the number of different activities participated in is very gradual.   It brings out clearly the fact that there are no age levels at which the

TABLE IX

THE NUMBER OF DIFFERENT PLAY ACTIVITIES INDULGED IN BY PERSONS OF DIFFERENT AGES. DATA FOR ALL THREE SEASONS TAKEN COLLECTIVELY. DISPERSION OF THE TWO MIDDLE QUARTILES.

Ages	No. of boys	Q1	Md	Q3	No. of girls	Q1	Md	Q3
8	286	26.50	40.11	53.81	323	21.55	34.44	48.75
9	466	24.71	38.45	55.36	459	23.72	34.75	52.06
10	500	24.73	36.57	54.00	593	23.72	34.89	48.63
11	530	22.77	32.29	46.50	684	21.61	30.65	44.25
12	618	21.69	31.40	42.82	873	20.51	28.32	40.59
13	766	18.07	26.48	38.39	752	18.93	26.30	36.46
14	759	17.04	25.13	35.26	849	17.46	23.85	32.81
15	723	14.76	21.59	29.80	746	16.17	22.04	29.40
16	588	14.72	20.40	28.30	699	13.99	19.77	25.39
17	438	14.43	20.79	27.27	598	13.27	18.33	24.88
18	413	14.19	19.39	26.15	463	14.81	19.90	24.62
19	313	14.25	19.04	26.48	308	13.87	18.61	24.00
20	178	13.31	18.40	24.36	285	14.27	18.59	24.15
21	155	15.34	20.29	25.75	196	16.00	19.57	24.50
22 and up.	267	13.16	17.71	22.67	240	12.77	16.53	22.09

NOTE: Figures 1 to 6 inclusive, and Tables IX to XI inclusive, appeared in *The Pedagogical Seminary*, June, 1926.

diversity of play interest suddenly decreases or increases by spurts.

Figure 2 gives the percentages of girls and the percentages of boys of various ages who indicated that they had been jumping or skipping rope during the course of a single week. The arrows in this figure indicate the age level at which exactly 25 per cent of the girls engaged in the diversion.

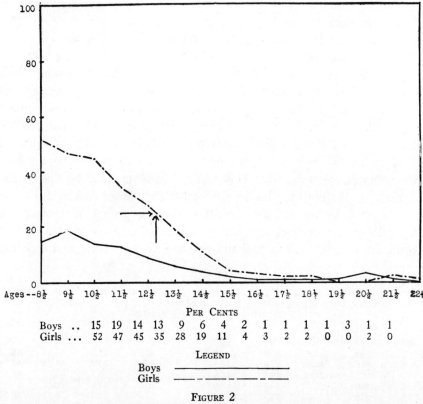

Ages--	8½	9½	10½	11½	12½	13½	14½	15½	16½	17½	18½	19½	20½	21½	22+

PER CENTS

	8½	9½	10½	11½	12½	13½	14½	15½	16½	17½	18½	19½	20½	21½	22+
Boys ..	15	19	14	13	9	6	4	2	1	1	1	1	3	1	1
Girls ...	52	47	45	35	28	19	11	4	3	2	2	0	0	2	0

LEGEND

Boys —————————————
Girls —— —— —— —— ——

FIGURE 2

Percentages of boys and girls who indicated that they had jumped or skipped rope during the course of a week. Average of findings from three separate investigations.

Figure 2 reveals a situation which is typical of that found for most of the 200 play activities. Periodicity in play certainly is not portrayed by such graphs. The following statements offer distinct contrast to the present findings in this regard.

"Because of its connection with the recapitulation theory, it is significant to note that the interest in the universal game of hide-and-seek culminates at ten, then suddenly drops." [23]

"It is even said that the prevalent gum-chewing habit culminates at this time (adolescence) and affords work for the developing muscles." [24]

"The interest in music which suddenly develops at this time (age 15) occasionally amounts to a passion. . . ." [25]

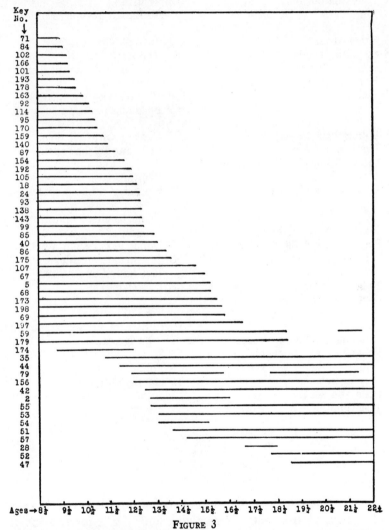

FIGURE 3

Ages at which more than 25% of girls were found to engage in various activities. Average of findings from three separate investigations. See Table X, p. 62.

TABLE X

(KEY TO FIGURE 3)

71 Writing poems.
84 Playing teeter-totter.
102 Hide the thimble.
106 Drop the handkerchief.
101 Hide the button.

193 Other toys.
178 Stringing beads.
163 London Bridge.
92 Hop-scotch.
114 Jacks.

95 Follow your leader.
170 Pussy wants a corner.
159 "Here I come" "Where from?"
140 Playing house.
87 Hop, skip, and jump.

154 Playing movie actor or actress.
192 Playing with dolls, doll carriages, doll clothes, etc.
105 Other tag games.
18 Roller skating.
24 Swinging.

93 Jumping or skipping rope.
138 Dressing up in older folks' clothing.
143 Playing school.
99 Hide and seek.
85 Just running and romping.

40 Gathering flowers.
86 Running races.
175 Cutting paper things with scissors.
107 Whistling.
67 Telling or guessing riddles.

5 Just playing catch.
68 Telling stories.
173 Drawing with pencil, pen, chalk, or crayon.
198 Playing with pet kittens.
69 Listening to stories.

197 Playing with pet dogs.
59 Listening to the radio.
179 Sewing, knitting, etc., for fun.
174 Painting with water-colors.
35 Watching athletic sports.

44 Going to entertainments, concerts, and so on.
79 Doing gymnasium work.
156 Just imagining things.
42 Just hiking or strolling.
2 Basket ball.

55 Card games, such as authors, bridge, whist.
53 Social dancing.
54 Folk-dancing.
51 Having dates.
57 Social clubs, or being with the gang.

28 Driving an auto.
52 Just loafing or lounging.
47 Attending lectures.

The above activities are listed in the order in which they drop below the 25% level in frequency of participation. Data for girls only.

TRANSITORINESS AS SHOWN BY THE AGE LEVELS AT WHICH
MORE THAN 25% OF GIRLS OF VARIOUS AGE LEVELS WERE
FOUND TO ENGAGE IN THE VARIOUS ACTIVITIES

Figure 3 shows the ages at which more than 25 per cent of the children participated in a given activity. Culmination of the line indicates that fewer than 25 per cent of the children participated in the activity portrayed. The key numbers are given in the vertical column on the left. The age levels are indicated on the horizontal line at the bottom of the page. The activity represented by the number may be identified by reference to Table X.

The reader must not assume that when a given play activity drops below the 25 per cent level it disappears suddenly. The waning is in most instances very gradual.

Figure 3 shows that marked participation in the various play activities becomes less frequent as chronological age advances. The gradual decrease in participation must be apparent at once to the reader.

Similar data are presented for the boys in Figure 4 and in Table XI. The results corroborate the findings for the girls, showing that play activities wax and wane gradually.

In Figure 5, the solid line was made by connecting the right-hand extremities of the horizontal lines of Figure 3. The other lines of Figure 5 were made from similar seasonal charts for the girls. It will be noted that in Figure 5 the seasonal lines show that there is no single age level at which a sudden decrease in diversity of play occurs. Figure 6 reveals a corresponding situation for the boys.

It is, of course, true that these data do not tell the whole story regarding play behavior. For example, a small boy may think himself to be playing football when his game is not at all the same as would be a game of football played by high school or college boys. The same is true of many other activities. The real age differences with respect to a given activity may be qualitative. In the latter case, they are to be ascertained by the method of a detailed psychological analysis of *how* persons of various age levels participate in recreational activities. The subjective nature of such analyses make them difficult and of questionable validity. Too, the enormous individual differences that exist among the members of a group of the same chronological age make doubtful the advisability of a program to discover such tendencies.

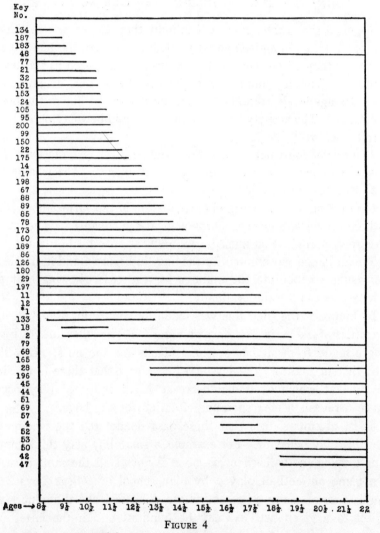

FIGURE 4

Ages at which more than 25% of boys were found to engage in various activities. Average of findings from three separate investigations. See Table XI, p. 65.
  * November only.

It is to be remembered that the findings herein presented do not prove that classification of play activities on the basis of chronological age is not a useful device. It is difficult to make a comparison of the

TABLE XI

(Key to Figure 4)

134 Playing in the sand.
187 Toy trains, ships, autos, wagons, etc.
183 Spinning tops.
 48 Visiting or entertaining company.
 77 Building or watching bonfires.

 21 Coasting on a coaster.
 32 Rolling an auto tire.
151 Playing Indian.
153 Playing robber and police.
 24 Swinging.

105 Other tag games.
 95 Follow your leader.
200 Playing with other pets.
 99 Hide and seek.
150 Playing cowboy.

 22 Coasting on a wagon.
175 Cutting paper things with scissors.
 14 Checkers.
 17 Marbles.
198 Playing with pet kittens.

 67 Telling or guessing riddles.
 88 Jumping for distance.
 89 Jumping for height.
 85 Just running and romping.
 78 Climbing porches, trees, fences, posts, etc.

173 Drawing with pencil, pen, chalk, or crayon.
 60 Playing the piano (for fun).
189 Looking at pictures.
 86 Running races.
126 Throwing rocks or stones.

180 Using a hammer, saw, nails, etc., for fun.
 29 Riding a bicycle.
197 Playing with pet dogs.
 11 Boxing.
 12 Wrestling.

* 1 Football.
133 Shooting a gun.
 18 Roller skating.
  2 Basket ball.
 79 Doing gymnasium work.

 68 Telling stories.
165 Just singing.
 28 Driving an auto.
196 Making or using a wireless or other electrical apparatus.
 45 Going to parties or picnics.

 44 Going to entertainments, concerts, and so on.
 51 Having "dates."
 69 Listening to stories.
 57 Social clubs, or being with the gang.
  4 Ball with an indoor or playground ball.

 52 Just loafing or lounging.
 53 Social dancing.
 50 Smoking.
 42 Just hiking or strolling.
 47 Attending lectures.

* November only.

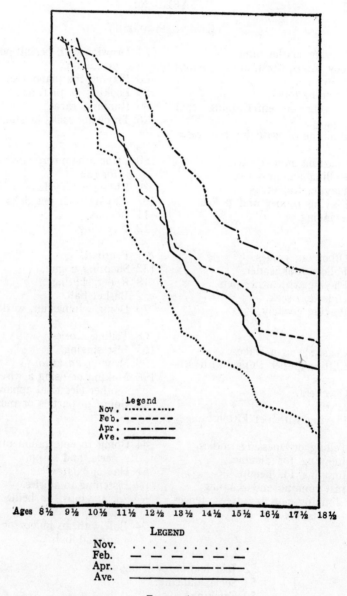

FIGURE 5

Ages at which various play curves drop below the 25 per cent level. Data for girls only.

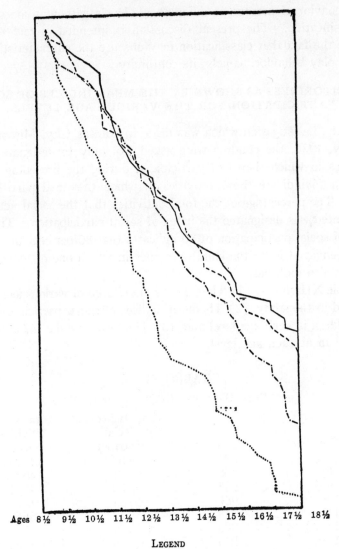

Ages 8½ 9½ 10½ 11½ 12½ 13½ 14½ 15½ 16½ 17½ 18½

LEGEND

Nov.   . . . .
Feb.   — — — — — —
Apr.   — · — · — · — ·
Ave.   —————————

FIGURE 6

Ages at which various play curves drop below the 25 per cent level. Data for boys only.

play behavior of persons of different age levels without some system of classification. The present discussion is intended merely to emphasize the fact that classification may obscure the characteristic feature of play behavior, namely, its continuity.

TRANSITORINESS AS SHOWN BY THE MEAN INDICES OF SOCIAL PARTICIPATION FOR THE VARIOUS AGE LEVELS

In the investigation which was made in Kansas City, Missouri, in January, 1926, the children were asked, not only to designate those activities in which they had participated during the preceding week, but also to indicate those activities in which they had participated *alone*. The percentage of the total activities that the social activities represented was designated the index of social participation. Thus an index of social participation of 80 indicates that 80 per cent of the activities engaged in by the child were ones in which one or more other children also took part.

Table XII shows: (1) The number of children of various age levels included in the study, (2) The mean indices of social participation for the children in each age level and, (3) The mean number of activities engaged in at each age level.

TABLE XII
Play Data for 6,886 Children

C.A.	Frequencies	Mean Indices of Social Participation	Mean No. of Activities Engaged in
7½	84	62.01	44.26
8½	468	63.25	40.56
9½	935	61.70	42.37
10½	981	60.58	37.67
11½	748	58.12	36.86
12½	903	55.69	34.01
13½	946	55.65	31.52
14½	848	52.92	28.58
15½	573	52.28	27.45
16½	288	50.56	25.91
17½	82	52.04	24.93
18½	25	52.32	25.50
19½	5	57.50	25.50
Total	6886		

Figure 7 shows the mean index of social participation of each age-level group. Very large individual differences exist at every age level in this regard but the differences between the mean indices of social participation at the various ages are extremely small. There is a tendency for children to become slightly less social in their play with increase in chronological age. However, on the basis of these data, it would be

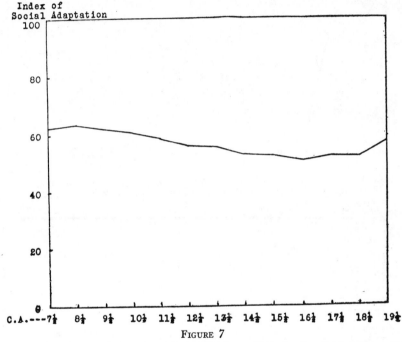

FIGURE 7

Relationship between index of social participation and C. A. See Table XII, p. 68. See also Chap. XIII, p. 203 ff.

impossible to designate the play of any age level as primarily social or individualistic in nature. Conspicuous differences in these regards are not revealed by the technique employed.

AGE LEVELS AT WHICH THE PLAY CURVES MOST COMMONLY REACH THEIR PEAKS

Inspection of the 200 different play curves similar to those shown in Figure 2, page 60, of this chapter, reveals that in most instances, the modes of the curves are to be found at ages 8½, 9½, and 10½. This

No. of Play
Activity Curves

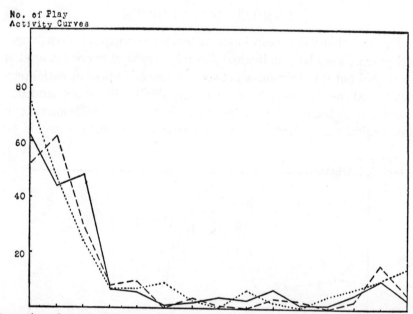

Ages 8½   9½   10½   11½   12½   13½   14½   15½   16½   17½   18½   19½   20½   21½   22-

FIGURE 8-A. The number of play activity curves which reached their peaks at various
age levels. Data for boys only, by seasons. See Table XIII, p. 71.

No. of Play
Activity curves.

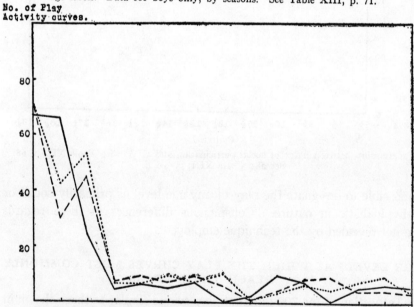

Ages--8½   9½   10½   11½   12½   13½   14½   15½   16½   17½   18½   19½   20½   21½   22-

FIGURE 8-B. The number of play activity curves which reached their peaks at various
age levels. Data for girls only, by seasons. See Table XIII, p. 71.

Nov. ————————   Feb. — — — — — — —.   Apr. . . . .

situation holds both for boys and for girls and similar results were found for each of the three seasons of the year.

It is not to be understood that the mode of a given play curve is always a great deal higher than any other point of the curve. In most cases the peak of a given curve is only slightly higher than the next highest point. Nevertheless, when it is remembered that as many as twelve hundred curves were inspected (200 for each sex and 400 for each of three seasons), and when it is borne in mind that the situation remains unchanged when the data are partitioned by sexes and by seasons, the validity of this phenomenon is verified.

TABLE XIII

THE AGE LEVELS AT WHICH THE PLAY CURVES REACH THEIR PEAKS

Ages	Nov. 1923 Boys	Nov. 1923 Girls	Feb. 1924 Boys	Feb. 1924 Girls	Apr. 1924 Boys	Apr. 1924 Girls
8½	62	67	52	69	74	71
9½	44	66	62	30	47	42
10½	48	24	30	45	24	53
11½	7	4	8	7	7	6
12½	6	6	10	9	7	6
13½	1	5	1	7	9	9
14½	2	7	4	9	3	7
15½	4	0	1	6	0	10
16½	3	2	0	1	6	1
17½	7	9	4	3	2	3
18½	1	7	3	8	0	6
19½	1	0	0	9	4	4
20½	5	5	3	4	6	7
21½	10	6	17	5	10	9
22 or above	3	5	5	3	13	3

The above table is to be read as follows:—Of the 200 boys' play curves that were made using data assembled in Nov. 1923, sixty-two were at maximum height at age 8½; forty-four were at maximum height at age 9½, etc., etc.

The columns do not add to exactly 200 because in some instances the curves were bi-modal. Double credit was given in such instances, two age levels each being considered a maximum height.

GROUP VARIABILITY AT VARIOUS AGE LEVELS

Greater variability was manifested by the *groups* of younger children than by the *groups* of older ones. The largest range of activities was found for the children in chronological age groups 8½, 9½, and 10½. This condition was found in each of the first three investigations. It is significant that the particular play activities which were found to vary most from group to group were precisely those which were most popular with the younger children. This was found to be true in almost every instance.

TYPES OF PLAY ACTIVITIES PARTICIPATED IN BY YOUNGER CHILDREN AS COMPARED TO OLDER ONES

The fact has been emphasized already that attempts at classification are hazardous. Nevertheless, the play behavior of young children *is* different from that of persons more mature. The present discussion perhaps will be better systematized if an attempt is made to list the *types* of activities participated in by persons of varying degrees of maturity. It is to be remembered that the types listed are not clearcut categories and that the purpose is to describe rather than to disclose clear-cut types.

In general it was found that the play activities engaged in by the youngest individuals (8½-10½) are of the following types: *

(1) Activities involving pleasurable bodily movements usually of a rhythmic sort.
(2) Activities involving hiding and finding.
(3) Activities involving the imitation of adults.
(4) Activities involving a relatively high degree of skill.
(5) Activities which involve efforts at construction.
(6) Activities which depend for their enjoyment primarily upon sense organ stimulation.
(7) Tag games.
(8) Singing games and ring games (for girls chiefly).

At the upper age levels the play activities which were usually discarded could be classified thus:

(2) Activities involving hiding and finding.
(3) Activities involving the imitation of adults.
(7) Tag games.
(8) Singing and ring games.

OLDER PERSONS MORE CONSERVATIVE IN THEIR PLAY BEHAVIOR THAN ARE YOUNGER PERSONS

It has been shown previously that: (1) The older subjects studied engaged in a smaller number of activities than the younger ones. (2) The middle fifty per cent range in number of activities participated in

* (Examples of these various types are to be found in Chap. VII, pp. 83 to 107, in which a detailed discussion of sex differences is presented.)

frequently diminished as age advanced. (3) Very few of the play curves reached their peaks beyond age 10½. (4) The older persons engaged in fewer distinct types of activities. All these findings posit greater conservatism in the play behavior characteristic of adults.

The general conservatism of the older individuals in play behavior was indicated further by the fact that they varied less during the course of the year than the younger children, i. e., they engaged in fewer seasonal activities. It is true that high school and college boys have such seasonal activities as baseball, basket ball, football, etc., but the younger boys have, in addition to these, such other seasonal or transitory activities as:

Gathering nuts.
Coasting on a sled.
Snowball fights.
Building snow men, snow forts, snow houses, etc.
Flying kites.
Playing marbles.
Play Jacks.
Shinny.
Walking on stilts.
Rolling a hoop.
Swinging.
Sliding on a playground slide.
Hide and seek.
Roller skating.
Wading in the water.
Spinning tops, etc., etc.

Not all of the activities of the preceding list are confined to any one season of the year. Some of them seem to come and go as transitory crazes such as Mah Jong, cross-word puzzles, etc. However, in the case of young children, such transitory activities are much more numerous than they are in the case of adults. In most instances they continue only for a few days or a few weeks among the young children whereas the longevity of such activities is greater for adults.

The greater variability of the younger children was demonstrated again in the range of best liked activities, the range being conspicuously greater for the younger children than for the older ones. (See Tables VII and VIII, p. 55 ff.) Greater variation was demonstrated also in the range of activities consuming the most time. Versatility of interest is a conspicuous feature of the play of young children.

Woodworth offers the following interesting speculation in reference to the cause of the tendency for young children to engage in a larger and more varied assortment of plays and games than older ones.

"As the child grows older, the 'economy of effort' motive becomes stronger, and the random activity motive weaker, so that the adult is less playful and less responsive to slight stimuli. He has to have some definite goal to get up his energy, whereas the child is active by preference and just for the sake of activity."

SUMMARY

Previous investigations of play with subsequent emphasis upon periodicity have tended to obscure the most important characteristic of play behavior, namely, its continuity. Any thoughtful attempt to characterize a particular period must bring the conviction that the obvious characteristic traits of each period have their beginnings in preceding stages and merge gradually into succeeding ones.

From extensive investigations of the play activities of unselected children, the present writers found that there is considerable permanence of the play interests of groups of children of various ages. The changes are not sudden and sporadic. The play trends which characterize a given age group seem to be the result of gradual changes occurring during the growth period. It was found that no age between $8\frac{1}{2}$-$22\frac{1}{2}$ inclusive, could be designated social or individualistic on the basis of the play behavior therein revealed.

The younger subjects studied engaged in a larger number of activities than the older ones. The median number of activities participated in by the boys of age $8\frac{1}{2}$ was 40; at $16\frac{1}{2}$, the median was 20. A slight decrease occurred subsequently. The transition from age to age was very gradual. The investigations show clearly that there are no age levels at which diversity of play interest suddenly decreases or increases by spurts.

Through the use of a technique employing the index of social participation, an attempt was made to discover whether the play of certain ages is predominately more social than at others. Very large individual differences existed at every age level but the differences between the mean indices of social participation at the various ages were extremely small. There was a tendency for children to become slightly less social in their play with increase in chronological age. However, on the basis of the data secured, it would be impossible to designate the play of any age level as primarily social or individualistic in nature. Conspicuous differences in these regards were not revealed by the technique employed.

Individuals become more and more conservative in their play as chronological age advances. This was brought out through the following data: (1) The older subjects engaged in a smaller number of activities than the younger ones. (2) The middle fifty per cent range was progressively diminished as age advanced. (3) Very few of the play curves reached their peaks beyond age 10½. (4) The older children engaged in fewer distinct types of activities.

REFERENCES

1. Thorndike, E. L. *Educational Psychology.* (Briefer Course.) New York. Teachers College, Columbia University. 1915. Pp. xii-442. (p. 402.)

2. Thorndike, E. L. *op. cit.* p. 403.

3. Thorndike, E. L. *op. cit.* p. 404.

4. Chamberlain, Alexander Francis. *The Child; A Study of the Evolution of Man.* New York. The Walter Scott Publishing Co. 1911. Pp. xii-498. (Pp. 51-107.)

5. Chamberlain, A. F. *idem.* p. 70.

6. *Idem.* p. 71.

7. *Idem.* p. 72.

8. *Idem.* p. 80.

9. *Idem.* p. 80.

10. *Idem.* p. 81 f.

11. *Idem.* p. 83.

12. *Idem.* p. 87 f.

13. *Idem.* p. 88.

14. Kirkpatrick, E. A. *The Individual in the Making.* Boston. Houghton Mifflin Co. 1911. Pp. ix-339. (p. 59 f.)

15. Quoted in *The Normal Course in Play.* Prepared by the Playground and Recreation Association of America. New York. A. S. Barnes and Co. 1925. Pp. x-261. (p. 71.)

16. Quoted in *The Normal Course in Play.* *op. cit.* p. 71.

17. Johnson, George Ellsworth. *Education by Plays and Games.* New York. Ginn & Co. 1907. Pp. xiv-234. (p. 65 ff.)

18. Curtis, Henry S. *Education Through Play.* New York. The Macmillan Co. 1921. Pp. xix-359. (p. 10 f.)

19. Quoted by G. Stanley Hall in *Youth.* New York. D. Appleton and Co. 1920. Pp. x-379. (p. 83.)

20. Bowen, Wilbur P. and Mitchell, Elmer D. *The Theory and Practice of Organized Play.* New York. A. S. Barnes and Co. 1923. Vol. I. Pp. viii-402. (p. 249 f.)

21. Croswell, T. R. Amusements of Worcester School Children. *Ped. Sem.* 1899, *6*. Pp. 314-71. (p. 331.)

22. Kirkpatrick, E. A. *Fundamentals of Child Study.* New York. The Macmillan Co. 1903. Pp. xxi-384. (p. 152.)

23. Pringle, Ralph W. *Adolescence and High-School Problems.* Chicago. D. C. Heath & Company. 1922. Pp. x-386. (p. 13.)

24. Pringle, Ralph W. *op. cit.* p. 69.

25. Pringle, Ralph W. *op. cit.* p. 70.

CHAPTER VI

THE PLAY PREFERENCES OF CHILDREN BELOW GRADE III

The fact has already been mentioned that in the case of children below the third grade the Play Quiz was not used for obtaining data in reference to play behavior. It would have been possible, of course, for the primary teachers to read the list of play activities to their pupils and have them indicate whether or not they had engaged in each activity read. This procedure has advantages but it was discarded since difficulties in understanding might have ensued. It was felt, too, that the memory of the young child might not be reliable.

To reveal the play behavior of children below Grade III, the following plan was developed and used. Each pupil was asked to mention the five things which he liked best to do at home. After securing these five choices, an equal number of favorite school activities was secured. The two lists were secured since preliminary investigations revealed that the activities best liked at home were not always those enjoyed most at school. The two lists obtained from each child were treated together for it was felt that composite treatment would afford the best overview of the child's total play life. It was decided that it would be inadvisable to distinguish the order of the various preferences. The writers felt that the method used in obtaining the data would not justify such refinement of technique.

Data were secured from children in the following Kansas towns: Kansas City, Lawrence, Bonner Springs, and Moran. In order that seasonal differences might be taken into account investigations were made on each of three different dates: Nov. 7, 1923, Feb. 20, 1924, and Apr. 30, 1924. The data were subsequently grouped simply by ages and sexes and graphs made therefrom. Separate charts also were made for each of the three seasons of the year.

Table II (p. 43), shows by seasons the number of boys and girls below Grade III, included in the three studies. Tables XIV and XV present lists of those activities which were mentioned with sufficient frequency to justify the computation of percentages. In spite of a certain inaccuracy due to the technique employed, which perhaps secured the things uppermost in mind rather than the actual preferences, the results are indicative probably of genuine preferences. Distinct differences are revealed between the sexes in their play favorites at these age levels. The same technique was used for boys and for girls. The early divergence in interests is a fact of significance both to the psychologist and to the curriculum-maker.*

TABLE XIV

RANK IN FREQUENCY OF GAMES AND OTHER PLAY ACTIVITIES LIKED BEST BY BOYS BELOW THE THIRD GRADE IN CERTAIN KANSAS COMMUNITIES.

Activity	Age			
	5	6	7	8
Ball or baseball	1	1	1	1
Blocks	2	13	..	..
Playing with a wagon	3	4	11	7
Playing house	4	3	11	17
Playing horse	5	2	9	8
Hide and seek	6	4	2	2
Playing tag	7	11	3	3
Drawing	7	11	15	15
Playing school	8	5	8	4
Playing in the sand pile	8	21	12	18
London Bridge	9	..	..	..
Marbles	9	6	5	4
Football	11	6	3	4
Cowboy and Indian	10	7	8	5
Playing train	10	9	13	..
Skipping	10	11	14	19
Farmer in the dell	11	8	17	12
Sliding on the playground slide	15	9	4	10
Writing on the blackboard, writing with colored crayons, etc...	15	10	11	13
Running races	15	10	10	11
Swinging	14	10	10	10
Playing robber and police	..	17	7	14
Basket ball	..	..	17	8
Playing on the teeter-totter	..	15	13	8
Reading	..	15	11	10

* These and other sex differences will be discussed in Chapter VII.

TABLE XV

RANK IN FREQUENCY OF GAMES AND OTHER PLAY ACTIVITIES LIKED BEST BY GIRLS
BELOW THE THIRD GRADE IN CERTAIN KANSAS COMMUNITIES.

Activity	Age			
	5	6	7	8
Playing house	1	1	1	1
Dolls	2	3	4	5
Playing school	4	2	2	2
Hide and seek	10	4	2	3
Playing tag	8	7	3	4
Ball or baseball	3	5	8	7
Drawing	4	11	12	10
Mulberry bush	5	8	16	20
Blocks	6	..	..	..
Skipping	7	11	11	11
Making things	7	..	18	16
Ring around the roses	9	5	7	7
Playing in the sand pile	9	18	..	33
Jumping rope	7	4	2	2
Drop the handkerchief	17	9	7	15
Farmer in the dell	..	9	7	15
Swinging	13	11	6	6
Reading	16	10	7	9
Sliding on the playground slide	17	10	7	8
Playing on the teeter-totter	17	14	10	10
Writing on the blackboard, writing with colored crayons, etc...	13	12	9	17
Working, doing chores, etc.	16	13	13	9
Jacks	..	..	12	9

Individual differences in play preference were enormous. The amount of individual difference is not shown in the tables. That 800 different activities were mentioned by the children is indicative of the extent of individual variation. During the reports of the children, it was noted that the children reported with great frequency that they liked to help some one in the performance of certain tasks. Again and again the primary child testified that he liked to "help mamma," do this or that, or to "help grandma or grandpa or uncle," with this or that homely enterprise. Such assistance as could be rendered by a five-year-old child would in most instances be of a superfluous nature. It is probable that assistance was sometimes tolerated at the sacrifice of time and efficient performance.

The difficulty of analyzing and classifying responses falling under the head of "helping some one" must be apparent at once to the reader. It was impossible for the teacher to tell exactly what part the child took in the experience reported by him. Therefore this activity or series of activities was not included in Tables XIV and XV. It is important for the student to realize that this tendency was reported frequently by the children, that its popularity is evidence of a fundamental human drive, the desire for new experience.

Table XVI presents some of the specific items which the primary children mentioned to their teachers as among their five best-liked home-activities. Most of the activities listed in Table XVI would ordinarily be regarded as onerous tasks. Thus, eighteen of these small children stated that "washing dishes" was one of the best-liked home activities. It is highly probable that most of the children were too young to be trusted with this task and that the actual assistance rendered was negligible. That supervision was involved and activity restricted is indicated by the assertion of one youngster that she liked to "wash and wipe the dishes *alone*," and by the statement of a small boy that he liked "to put coal in the furnace *if allowed*." Such qualifications, although not specifically mentioned, probably apply to many of the preferences displayed in Table XVI. It is evident, therefore, that many of the preferences result not from *actual participation* in certain activities but from a *desire to participate* in varied and novel activities. These data give evidence of the impulse to obtain new experience, of the deep-rooted desire for physical and mental activity on the part of the growing child.

Dewey has pointed to children's desire to "help":

"Children want to 'help'; they are anxious to engage in the pursuits of adults which effect external changes: setting the table, washing dishes, helping care for animals, etc. In their plays they like to construct their own toys and appliances. With increasing maturity, activity which does not give back results of tangible and visible achievement loses its interest. . . . Observable results are necessary to enable persons to get a sense and a measure of their own powers." [1]

TABLE XVI

SOME OF THE THINGS WHICH PRIMARY CHILDREN LIKE TO DO WHEN
AT HOME

Girls	Boys
Wash the dishes.	Cut and chop wood.
Wipe the dishes.	Help father at the store.
Wash and wipe the dishes *alone*.	Take the wagon to the post-office.
Set the table.	Pick apples.
Clean house.	Go to the store.
Cook.	Run errands.
Sweep.	Bring in the coal, wood, etc.
Make candy.	Make the fire.
Sew center pieces.	Haul fodder.
Feed the chickens.	Feed bran to the hog.
Gather eggs.	Put coal in the furnace (if allowed).
Clean the yard.	Help papa paint the house.
Put the dishes away.	Get the mail.
Sweep the porch.	Milk the cow.
Make beds.	Rake the yard.
Help with the washing.	Plant flowers.
Help scrub.	Help plow.
Work at the store (father's).	Pound coal.
Put the dishes away.	Help father at the butcher shop.
Take care of the baby.	Make the dog house.

It is evident that the tasks mentioned by Dewey are not too onerous
to appeal to the child who is too young to have had real experience
with them.   Collectively the above lists evidence the fact that the
growing child craves new experiences for the sake of the experience.
Groos has pointed to the fact that such activity facilitates the development of the child's inherited abilities.[2]   Seashore, too, has commented
on this phenomenon:

"Growth through play is evident in the development of the social nature
of the child, and is especially marked in the development of his consciousness of kinship with a group. . . . Child play reproduces on its level the
struggles and achievements of developed social life . . . the child ـ . . gradually approaches the stern, adult realities, taught and trained, hardened
and softened, warmed and cooled, roused and rationalized, through those
very engagements, in play, which without break or loss of their original

character gradually blend into the duties, responsibilities, opportunities and achievements of adult life." [3]

And again: "Children seldom play with the intention of fitting themselves for life, nor are adults ordinarily conscious of serving this purpose in play. Children play, as do the rest of us, because it satisfies certain cravings and seems to be the eternally fit and natural thing to do. It is only in the larger, retrospective view that we realize how nature has wrought marvels of development through the operation of the play instincts." [4]

In the last analysis the child's desire to help is the means which nature has provided for his self-help. The parent and the teacher who are cognizant of this fact will give the child permission to "help" whenever it seems desirable to do so. It is important that the parent or teacher attempt to turn the impulse to help to good account. Certain psychologists hold that *any* response that an organism is capable of making *may* be attached (at least theoretically) to any situation to which it be sensitive. Multitudinous forms of redirection which satisfy the desire for new experience are therefore possible. The parent and teacher should recognize that it is dangerous and unwise to repress or suppress such a powerful original drive to activity. They should recognize the strength of the drive and seek diligently to direct it in such a way as to facilitate maximum growth.

REFERENCES

1. Dewey, John: *Democracy and Education*. New York. The Macmillan Co. 1921. Pp. xii-434. (p. 239.)
2. Groos, Karl: *The Play of Man*. New York. D. Appleton and Co. 1908. Pp. ix-412. (p. 2.)
3. Seashore, Carl: *Psychology in Daily Life*. New York and London. D. Appleton and Co. 1916. Pp. xvii-225. (p. 7.)
4. Seashore, Carl: *op. cit.* p. 2.

CHAPTER VII

SEX DIFFERENCES

Popular thinking assumes conspicuous differences between the sexes in most traits. The average person has no hesitancy in describing dogmatically these differences. Striking differences have been emphasized in intelligence. Terman and Hollingworth have demonstrated conclusively that sex differences have been exaggerated in regard to this function.[1] [2] The outstanding differences pointed to by earlier investigators have not been found when objective measures have been employed. The conspicuous and vital fact regarding the sexes in reference to intelligence is their likeness.

Salient data are available regarding intelligence. Little experimentation has been carried on in reference to other traits. Large sex differences are generally assumed.

When human traits or activities are objectively measured it is found that continuity of variation exists. Therefore classification usually affords a very incomplete description of the data.

Sex differences in play behavior have been overemphasized by previous investigators. Play behavior is a function of so many variables that it is unsatisfactory to characterize most activities as belonging primarily to one sex or the other. In some instances the present writers found that a given play activity is engaged in more frequently, by younger boys than by girls of the same ages, but that the opposite of this situation exists at the upper age levels, older girls engaging more frequently in the same activity than older boys. This was found for "Just hiking or strolling," and for "Social clubs or being with the gang."

The following quotation reveals that others are cognizant of the difficulties attendant upon cataloguing play activities according to sex.

"The idea that certain games and occupations are for boys and others for girls is a purely artificial one that has developed as a reflection of the conditions existing in adult life. It does not occur to a boy that dolls are not just as fascinating and legitimate a plaything for him as for his sister, until some one puts the idea into his head." [3]

The amount of sex difference may be studied best by examination of the graphs made for each of the 200 activities. Each graph shows the percentages of boys and of girls of various ages who engaged in each activity. Lack of space has prevented the inclusion of all of these graphs or the data from which they were made. However, an overview of sex differences in play behavior may be obtained by examining the lists of activities here given in which sex differences are conspicuous.

Table XVII presents those activities which are more commonly engaged in by boys than by girls. The activities are arranged in order of merit, those activities showing the largest amount of sex difference being listed toward the top of the page. Table XVIII presents a similar list showing the activities in which girls participate more frequently than boys. Table XIX displays a list of activities in which the sexes participate with approximately equal frequency.

TABLE XVII

PLAY ACTIVITIES MORE COMMONLY PARTICIPATED IN BY BOYS THAN BY GIRLS AT PRACTICALLY EVERY AGE

Football.
Using a hammer, saw, nails, etc., for fun.
Wrestling.
Marbles.
Riding a bicycle.

Climbing porches, trees, fences, posts, etc.
Throwing rocks and stones.
Playing cowboy.
Boxing.
Whistling.
Shooting a gun.

Playing Indian.

Playing robber and police
Basket ball.
Baseball with a hard ball.

Driving an auto.
Watching athletic sports.
Smoking.
Jumping for distance.

Jumping for height.
Mumbly peg.
Flying kites.
Making or using a wireless, or other electrical apparatus.
Snowball fights.
Pole vaulting.

Just playing catch.
Coasting on a wagon.
Rolling an auto tire.
Fishing.
*Playing pool.

Pitching horseshoes.

Playing with bow and arrows.
Swimming.
Digging caves or dens.
Spinning tops.
Playing with toy trains, ships, autos, wagons, etc.
Playing fire engine (or hook and ladder).
Running races.
Matching pennies.
Coasting on a coaster.

Playing bandit.
Playing soldier.
Playing with pet dogs.
Playing with an indoor or playground ball.

Horseback riding.
Rolling a hoop.
Walking on stilts.
Hunting.
Building or watching bonfires.
Building a dam.

* In the case of some activities the sex difference is slighter than would perhaps have been expected because of the fact that few members of either sex engaged in the particular activity.

TABLE XVIII

PLAY ACTIVITIES MORE FREQUENTLY PARTICIPATED IN BY GIRLS THAN BY BOYS AT PRACTICALLY EVERY AGE

Playing with dolls.
Visiting or entertaining company.
Playing house.
Just singing.
Sewing, knitting, crocheting, etc., for fun.

Playing the piano (for fun).
Writing letters.
Jumping or skipping rope.
Dressing up in older folks' clothing.
Playing school.

Social dancing.
Jacks.
Playing movie actor or movie actress.
London bridge.
Stringing beads.

Going to parties or picnics.
Folk-dancing.
Just imagining things.
Looking at pictures.
Gathering flowers.

Going to entertainments, concerts, and so on.
Playing with pet kittens.
Playing Sunday school.
Drop the handkerchief.
Cutting paper things with scissors.

Teasing somebody.
Just hiking or strolling.
Hop, skip, and jump.
Playing nurse.
Listening to the victrola.

Sleigh-riding.
Reading short stories.
Telling or guessing riddles.
Telling fortunes or having fortunes told.
Hop-scotch.

Hide-and-seek.
Playing store.
Playing other make-believe games.
Statuary.

"Here I come." "Where from?"
Tin-tin.
Other singing games.
Old witch.
Pussy wants a corner.

Making mud pies, mud dolls, etc.
Painting with water-colors.
Making a scrapbook.
Taking snapshots.
Roller skating.

TABLE XIX

PLAY ACTIVITIES WHICH ARE PARTICIPATED IN ABOUT AS COMMONLY BY
ONE SEX AS BY THE OTHER

Dominoes.
Sleigh-riding.
Riding in an auto.
Excursions to the woods, parks,
country, etc.
Attending lectures.

Doing calisthenics.
Just running and romping.
Follow your leader.
Run, sheep, run.
Anty-over.

Chewing gum.
Having "dates."
Card games, such as authors, bridge,
whist.
Looking at the Sunday "funny"
paper.
Reading jokes or funny sayings.

Blackman.
Crack the whip.
Dodgeball.
Croquet.
Jackstraws.

Reading the newspapers.
Reading books.
Listening to stories.
Writing poems.
Doing gymnasium work.

Pillow fights.
Playing in the sand.
Post-office.
Three deep.
Other ring games.

Clay modeling.
Drawing with pencil, pen, chalk, or
crayon.
Other toys.
Picture puzzles.
Playing with pet rabbits.
Playing with other pets.

TYPES OF ACTIVITIES COMMONLY PARTICIPATED IN BY BOTH SEXES OF AGES 8½ TO 12½ INCLUSIVE

For boys and girls of ages 8½ to 12½ inclusive there is considerable unanimity of interest in play activities. In order that the reader
may observe the *chief* characteristic of the sexes in reference to play,
namely, the likeness, the writers have compiled in Table **XX** a list of
the types of activities in which both boys and girls of ages 8½ to 12½
participate. All of the activities of the list are participated in by some
children of each sex; some of the activities, however, are much more
frequently participated in by one sex.

The writers found that girls took part much more frequently than boys in some of the activities. These are designated (§). Those in which boys participated much more frequently than girls are marked (‡). The activities in which the boys indulged only to a slightly greater extent than girls are marked (†). Those activities in which girls participated only slightly more frequently than the boys are designated (*).

TABLE XX

Types of Play Activities Commonly Participated in by Children of Ages 8½ to 12½ Inclusive

(1) Activities involving pleasurable bodily movements, usually of a rhythmic sort.

Girls	Boys
Riding in an auto.	Riding in an auto.
* Swinging.	Swinging.
* Roller skating.	Roller skating.
† Sliding on a playground slide.	Sliding on a playground slide.
* Playing teeter-totter.	Playing teeter-totter.
§ Jumping or skipping rope.	‡ Rolling an auto tire.
	‡ Coasting on a wagon.
	‡ Coasting on a coaster.

(2) Activities which involve the hiding and finding of objects or the concealment of one's own person.

Girls	Boys
§ Drop the handkerchief.	Drop the handkerchief.
* Blind man's buff.	Blind man's buff.
* Hide the button.	Hide the button.
* Hide the thimble.	Hide the thimble.
* Hide and seek.	Hide and seek.

(3) Activities which involve the imitation of older persons.

Girls	Boys
§ Playing school.	Playing school.
§ Playing house.	† Playing horse.
* Playing store.	‡ Playing cowboy.
§ Playing movie actor or actress.	‡ Playing soldier.
§ Playing with dolls, doll carriages, doll clothes, etc.	‡ Playing robber and police.

(4) Activities which involve a rather high degree of motor skill.

Girls	Boys
Follow your leader.	Follow your leader.
* Hop, skip, and jump.	Hop, skip, and jump.
§ Jacks.	‡ Spinning tops.
§ Sewing, knitting, crocheting, etc., for fun.	‡ Marbles.
	‡ Mumbly peg.
	‡ Track and athletic events.

(5) Activities which consist of efforts at construction.

Girls	Boys
* Drawing with pencil, pen, chalk or crayon.	Drawing with pencil, pen, chalk or crayon.
* Cutting paper things with scissors.	Cutting paper things with scissors.
§ Sewing, knitting, crocheting, etc., for fun.	Using a hammer, saw, nails, etc., for fun.
Fixing or repairing something.	‡ Fixing or repairing something.
Helping somebody with his work.	Helping somebody with his work.

(6) Activities which seem to depend almost wholly upon sensory stimulation, as for example:

Girls	Boys
Chewing gum.	Chewing gum.
* Listening to the victrola.	Listening to the victrola.
† Building or watching bonfires.	Building or watching bonfires.
§ Gathering flowers.	Gathering flowers.
Whistling.	‡ Whistling.
§ Just singing.	Just singing.

(7) Tag games.

Girls	Boys
Other tag games.	Other tag games.
* Drop the handkerchief.	Drop the handkerchief.
* Three deep.	Three deep.

(8) Singing games.

Girls	Boys
§ London Bridge.	London Bridge.
Other singing games.	Other singing games.

(9) Activities which involve reading.

Girls	Boys
* Reading jokes or funny sayings.	Reading jokes or funny sayings.
* Reading the newspapers.	Reading the newspapers.
* Reading short stories.	Reading short stories.
* Reading books.	Reading books.
Reading or looking at magazines.	Reading or looking at magazines.

(10) Miscellaneous activities.

Girls	Boys
Going to the movies.	† Going to the movies.
§ Writing letters.	Writing letters.
Looking at the Sunday "funny" paper.	Looking at the Sunday "funny" paper.
Watching athletic sports.	‡ Watching athletic sports.

It is apparent from Table XX that the play life of pre-adolescent girls and boys has many elements in common. Both sexes engage in activities which involve pleasurable bodily movement, the hiding and finding of objects, imitation of older persons, bodily activity and motor skill, skill in construction, sensory gratification, reading, and singing. The difficulty of hard and fast classification of play data has been pointed out previously. Nevertheless, in order that the present discussion may be better systematized, an attempt will be made to present types of activities in which sex differences were found. The writers have compiled the lists with a full realization of the *overlapping* of the categories. The inclusion of several activities under different headings is a result of the awareness of the overlapping. Hard and fast classifications can not be drawn. The following rather convenient divisions facilitate description of the data.

TYPES OF ACTIVITIES IN WHICH CONSPICUOUS SEX DIFFERENCES ARE FOUND
Ages 5½ to 8½ inclusive.*

Active, vigorous plays and games.

One difference appeared consistently throughout the investigations that were conducted. This was the conspicuous tendency for boys to

---

* The children of age 8½ here discussed were children who had not reached the third grade in school.

engage more frequently than girls in extremely active plays and games and for the girls to participate more frequently than boys in games sedentary in character. This difference appeared at a very early age. Inspection of the tables presented on pages 78 and 79 reveals that the activity best liked by boys below Grade III is "Ball or baseball." The girls' most frequently mentioned preference is "Playing house." Other activities preferred by boys are:

Hide and seek.   Playing horse.
Tag.   Playing football.
              Playing cowboy and Indian.

Boys of ages 5½ and 6½ indicated also a preference for "Playing with blocks," "Playing house, "Playing London Bridge," etc., but the popularity of these activities declined rapidly as chronological age advanced.

Activities other than "Playing house," which appeared frequently among the preferences of the girls are:

Playing with dolls.   Swinging.
Playing school.   Jumping rope.
              Playing tag.

Other of the best-liked activities of the primary boys and girls may be identified by inspection of the Tables XIV and XV, presented on pages 78 and 79. It will be noted from these tables that "Playing football," and "Playing with dolls," are about the only activities confined almost exclusively to one sex or the other. Most of the activities of the lists were participated in both by boys and by girls. Sex differences were not revealed to the extent previous writers have indicated.

TYPES OF ACTIVITIES IN WHICH CONSPICUOUS SEX DIFFERENCES ARE FOUND

Ages 8½ to 12½

It was pointed out previously that the primary boys studied frequently engaged in extremely active plays and games. This tendency was found also for boys of ages 8½ to 12½ inclusive. The activities more frequently participated in by boys than by girls of these ages include:

Football.	Climbing porches, trees, fences, posts, etc.
Boxing.	
Wrestling.	Throwing rocks or stones.
	Snowball fights.
Using a hammer, saw, nails, etc., for fun.	Playing cowboys.
	Playing robber and police.
	Track events.

There is a difference also in the *way* in which the sexes play certain games. For example, both girls and boys engage in basket ball, indoor baseball, etc., but girls seem to exert less energy in these play activities. In general, the writers noted that the girls tended to avoid active participation in certain games which afforded extremely vigorous diversion for the boys.

ACTIVITIES WHICH INVOLVE MUSCULAR DEXTERITY, SKILL AND STRENGTH

A difference between the sexes was found in the persistent tendency of the boys to turn to activities which posit muscular dexterity, skill and strength. Many of the activities listed on pages 85 and 86 are of this type. Additional activities of slightly different type which can be characterized as requiring a marked degree of motor skill and coordination were engaged in more frequently by the boys than by the girls. Among these are the following:

Spinning tops.	Mumbly peg.
Marbles.	Walking on stilts.

Some activities in which the girls participated more frequently than the boys required muscular skill and coördination. Among these are:

Jacks.	Jumping or skipping rope.
Sewing, knitting, crocheting, etc., for fun.	

In general, it may be said that activities which require a marked degree of motor skill were much less numerous in the lists of activities frequently participated in by girls than in those of the boys.

ACTIVITIES INVOLVING THE ELEMENT OF COMPETITION

Noticeable also was the relatively great frequency with which the boys turned to activities involving the element of competition. This tendency was not revealed to so marked a degree by the girls studied. The following activities involving the element of competition were engaged in frequently by the boys.

Football.	Wrestling.
Boxing.	Snowball fights.
	Track events.

ORGANIZED PLAYS AND GAMES

Another important difference revealed clearly in the lists of activities most frequently engaged in is the greater degree of organization necessary for participation in many of the boys' games. The boys' games tend to conform to recognized and accepted codes of rules. They involve coöperation to a greater extent and likewise submission to an arbiter. Girls, on the other hand, were found to play few games in which a high degree of organization is required. Their pastimes were more often individual in nature. The boys' games which best exemplify a high degree of organization are:

Football.	Baseball with a hard ball.
Basket ball	Track events.

It has been said frequently that girls enjoy witnessing athletic sports, boys preferring to participate in them. The present studies showed the boys to be more fond than the girls of watching athletic sports.

SEDENTARY ACTIVITIES AND ACTIVITIES INVOLVING RE-STRICTED RANGE OF ACTION

Young girls seem to find it necessary to obtain their play life through activities within the home or very near the home. Such a restriction does not exist to the same extent for boys. Therefore, the boys studied took part much more frequently than the girls in certain activities requiring a relatively wide geographical radius, i.e.:

Horseback riding.	Hunting.
Gathering nuts.	Fishing.
	Flying kites.

PLAY ACTIVITIES INVOLVING INDIRECT RESPONSES, THE USE OF LANGUAGE, ETC.

It is noteworthy that girls' activities involve the use of language to a slightly greater extent than do those of boys. This is seen clearly in such activities as:

Visiting and entertaining company.	Reading the newspapers.
Writing letters.	Reading short stories.
Reading jokes or funny sayings.	Reading books.
	Teasing somebody.

In the investigations herein reported sex difference as regards the percentage of individuals participating therein was marked only for the first two of the above activities. In the case of the others, the difference was small but consistently in favor of the girls.

It is common knowledge that girls and women are relatively voluble as compared with men. Jesperson states that, as compared with boys, girls are found to learn to talk at a younger age and to stutter and stammer less often. Too, they suffer less frequently from other speech defects.[4]

Earlier maturing may account for the fact that girls participate more frequently than boys in activities involving the use of language but it may be due merely to a tendency toward greater loquaciousness on the part of the girls. It may be that girls turn more frequently than boys to play activities involving the use of language because of the indirect gratification of certain desires so obtained.

Previous citation has been given to the fact that girls read more than boys. The differences between the sexes in this regard were not large. However, the sex differences in reference to the *popularity* of book-reading, and the relative *amounts of time* devoted to book-reading were significant.

Table XXI shows how "Reading books," ranked in favor among the 200 activities of the Play Quiz, according to the children's own statements. Table XXI is to be read as follows:—"Reading books" is the one activity of the entire list of 200 that was most frequently selected as one of their three favorite activities by the males of age 21½ included in the investigation of February, 1924. This activity was second in popularity among white boys of ages 12½, 13½, and 17½, included in the investigation of January, 1926.

It will be noted from Table XXI that "Reading books," was most frequently selected as one of their three favorite activities by *two* groups only of males, one of these groups being the members of the faculty of the University of Kansas, the other, students of age 21½. The greater popularity of book-reading among girls is indicated by the fact that *ten* groups of girls gave book-reading rank one in popularity. Examination of Table XXI reveals further evidence of the girls' greater fondness for book-reading, i.e., the groups of girls report fondness for book-reading much more frequently than the groups of boys.

Table XXII shows how "Reading books" ranked among the list of 200 games, sports, and other play activities in reference to the relative amount of time consumed by the activity. Table XXII is to be read as follows: According to the children's own judgments "Reading books," consumed more time than any other one activity for boys of ages 9½, 20½, and 22½, included in the investigation of November, 1923. However, this activity consumed more time than *any other activity* for the girls of ages 9½ to 18½ inclusive.

It will be noted from Table XXII that "Reading books," was judged to consume more time than any other activity by 23 groups of boys and by 49 groups of girls. It is at once apparent that the girls studied spent a greater proportion of their leisure time in reading books than did the boys.

Table XXIII displays by sex the *percentages* of individuals of various age levels who indicated that "Reading books," was *one of their three favorite leisure-time activities.* The amount of sex difference is at once apparent. Separate tables and graphs were made for the seasonal data and for each of the sub-groups studied, but since the amount of sex difference was found to be approximately the same for each sub-group, the data have been treated collectively in Table XXIII.

Table XXIII shows clearly that book-reading is more often a favorite activity among girls than among boys. Between ages 10½ and 16½ inclusive, book-reading is mentioned as one of three favorites by almost twice as large a percentage of girls as of boys.

Table XXIV displays by sex the percentages of individuals who indicated that "Reading books," was the one activity that had consumed more of their leisure time than any other of the list of 200 leisure-time activities. The data obtained from the six separate investigations are given composite treatment in Table XXIV. It will be noted that at most age levels a larger percentage of girls than of boys judged book-reading to have consumed more of their leisure time than any other activity.

It is interesting to speculate regarding the educational implications of the above findings. The sex differences are clearly marked. Recent writers have emphasized the fact that the problem of the modern school is to teach children to *want to read* rather than merely to impart reading ability. Professor Morrison has said that in the appraisal of the learning product the vital question is, "What does the pupil do when he is on his own?" As a means of appraising the learning product, Professor Morrison furnishes the pupil with ready access to a liberal amount of material written in French, German, or Latin, as the case may be, and then sees what the pupil does without supervision or requirement. If the pupil reads, this fact is taken as evidence that the real learning product has been obtained. If the pupil does not read, it is inferred that, regardless of test results, the real learning product (adaptation) has not been obtained.[5]

If education be regarded as a process of habit-formation it is evident that girls acquire the reading adaptation at earlier ages than boys.

One logically asks what effect the above sex difference in reading adaptation has upon school work. Much attention has recently been given to the fact that girls obtain better marks in school work, fail less often, and experience a smaller percentage of elimination from school than boys. Several attempts have been made to explain these facts but no single explanation seems to be wholly satisfactory. School marks are doubtless a function of many and diverse elements and it seems probable that no single statement will suffice to explain why girls progress through school more rapidly than boys.

In a Master's thesis recently completed by Mae M. Gale at the University of Kansas, the Terman Group Intelligence Test and the Stanford Achievement Examination were administered to 268 boys and 326 girls in the Junior High School of Lawrence, Kansas.[6] It was found that the girls surpassed the boys by a larger margin in *reading* than in any other subject.

If the finding in reference to the girls' superior reading ability represents a general situation it seems likely that this sex superiority may be due in part to the fact that the girls spend a greater proportion of

TABLE XXI

How Activity No. 66, "Reading Books, Just for Fun," Ranked Among a List of 200 Games, Sports, and Other Play Activities in Reference to Popularity.

Ages	Nov. 1923	Feb. 1924	Apr. 1924	Nov. 1924 (Rural)	Nov. 1925 (Rural)	Jan. 1926 (White)	Jan. 1926 (Negro)
				Boys			
8½	‡	13	‡	5	8	4	‡
9½	9	5	‡	11	‡	14	‡
10½	‡	8	11	‡	‡	11	‡
11½	15	8	‡	11	8	3	13
12½	11	11	6	12	9	2	‡
13½	7	2	6	‡	‡	2	‡
14½	9	6	6	‡	10	4	12
15½	10	6	5	‡	‡	5	10
16½	8	6	11	*	*	3	*
17½	5	7	10	*	*	2	*
18½	7	7	‡	*	*	*	*
19½	8	8	5	*	*	*	*
20½	13	12	12	*	*	*	*
21½	20	1	‡	*	*	*	*
22 or above	2	3	8	*	*	*	*
K. U. Faculty Men	*	*	1				
				Girls			
8½	8	3	16	4	‡	8	4
9½	11	5	9	7	1	10	‡
10½	3	5	7	7	5	5	6
11½	2	2	2	‡	4	4	8
12½	2	2	1	9	2	2	4
13½	2	2	1	4	3	2	3
14½	1	2	2	5	1	1	4
15½	2	1	2	‡	‡	2	3
16½	2	1	3	*	*	2	*
17½	2	1	1	*	*	*	*
18½	12	2	6	*	*	*	*
19½	7	4	5	*	*	*	*
20½	5	7	17	*	*	*	*
21½	1	2	7	*	*	*	*
22 or above	12	3	11	*	*	*	*
K. U. Faculty Women	*	*	2				

* No data assembled.
‡ Mentioned by less than 5% of individuals.

their leisure time at reading books than do the boys. If the above hypothesis is accepted it follows that the data herein presented point the way to an evaluation of extra-curricular activities.

The writers will not attempt to account for the fact that the girls are more fond than the boys of book-reading. It is probable that numerous factors produce this situation. The writers have sought

TABLE XXII

How Activity No. 66, "Reading Books, Just for Fun," Ranked Among a List of 200 Games, Sports, and Other Play Activities in Reference to Time Consumed.

Ages	Nov. 1923	Feb. 1924	Apr. 1924	Nov. 1924 (Rural)	Nov. 1925 (Rural)	Jan. 1926 (White)	Jan. 1926 (Rural)
			Boys				
8½	‡	‡	‡	4	‡	‡	‡
9½	1	1	‡	‡	3	3	‡
10½	9	1	9	3	‡	5	‡
11½	2	1	7	‡	1	1	‡
12½	2	2	3	5	2	1	4
13½	3	2	3	‡	4	1	6
14½	3	2	3	‡	2	1	6
15½	2	2	4	‡	‡	1	‡
16½	5	2	3	*	*	1	*
17½	2	2	1	*	*	1	*
18½	3	1	1	*	*	*	*
19½	2	1	1	*	*	*	*
20½	1	1	1	*	*	*	*
21½	3	1	7	*	*	*	*
22 and up	1	1	2	*	*	*	*
K. U. Faculty Men	*	*	1	*	*	*	*
			Girls				
8½	2	5	‡	3	2	3	2
9½	1	2	1	2	1	8	‡
10½	1	1	2	2	2	2	5
11½	1	1	1	2	6	2	3
12½	1	1	1	3	1	1	1
13½	1	1	1	1	2	1	1
14½	1	1	1	1	3	1	1
15½	1	1	1	1	‡	1	2
16½	1	1	1	*	*	1	*
17½	1	1	1	*	*	1	*
18½	1	1	1	*	*	*	*
19½	2	1	1	*	*	*	*
20½	‡	1	8	*	*	*	*
21½	1	1	1	*	*	*	*
22 and up	3	1	4	*	*	*	*
K. U. Faculty Women	*	*	1	*	*	*	*

* No data assembled.
‡ Mentioned by less than 3% of individuals.

merely to point to the above rather marked sex difference in reference to fondness for book-reading and to emphasize the fact that "to give boys and girls a love of books means far more than to teach them to read."

TABLE XXIII

PERCENTAGES OF INDIVIDUALS OF VARIOUS AGE LEVELS WHO STATED THAT "READING BOOKS, JUST FOR FUN," WAS ONE OF THEIR THREE FAVORITE LEISURE TIME ACTIVITIES. COMPOSITE RESULTS OF ALL INVESTIGATIONS WHICH WERE MADE

Ages	No. of Males	%	No. of Females	%
8½	531	6.7	568	11.1
9½	796	6.1	781	8.7
10½	874	4.9	969	10.5
11½	898	6.3	1064	13.7
12½	1010	7.6	1243	15.8
13½	1113	11.0	1104	20.0
14½	1024	10.2	1135	21.4
15½	932	12.1	943	21.4
16½	684	11.8	709	29.0
17½	421	14.7	583	25.9
18½	415	8.7	461	17.6
19½	316	10.4	309	13.9
20½	182	6.5	273	12.1
21½	153	11.7	192	20.8
22 or above	262	15.5	246	15.4
K. U. Faculty	135	29.7	35	25.7

TABLE XXIV

PERCENTAGES OF INDIVIDUALS OF VARIOUS AGE LEVELS WHO INDICATED THAT "READING BOOKS, JUST FOR FUN," HAD CONSUMED MORE OF THEIR LEISURE TIME THAN ANY OTHER ACTIVITY OF A LIST OF 200 GAMES, SPORTS, AND OTHER PLAY ACTIVITIES. COMPOSITE RESULTS OF ALL INVESTIGATIONS WHICH WERE MADE.

Ages	No. of Males	%	No. of Females	%
8½	531	1.9	568	5.3
9½	796	4.7	781	5.4
10½	874	8.1	969	7.7
11½	898	7.6	1064	8.7
12½	1010	7.1	1243	12.7
13½	1113	7.7	1104	19.7
14½	1024	6.8	1135	17.2
15½	932	9.7	943	16.4
16½	684	10.4	709	23.6
17½	421	14.3	583	24.4
18½	415	7.5	461	14.5
19½	316	10.8	309	10.0
20½	182	15.9	273	8.8
21½	153	12.4	192	14.6
22 or above	262	17.9	246	12.2
K. U. Faculty	135	21.0	35	17.1

HIDING GAMES

Girls were found to engage more frequently than boys in each of the following hiding games. The difference is not especially marked for any one activity but was consistent in every case.

Drop the handkerchief.   Hide the button.
Blind man's buff.   Hide the thimble.
                   Hide and seek.

It is possible that the girls engage more commonly than boys in each of the preceding activities simply because they are sedentary in character. It is difficult to disentangle sedentariness from such a factor as indirection.

CONSERVATIVE PLAYS AND GAMES

It is of interest that the girls showed less seasonal change in their play than did the boys. This was true both for the activities participated in, those mentioned as favorites, and those which consumed the largest amount of time. It was noticeable particularly in the case of the activities best liked and those which consumed the greatest amount

TABLE XXV-a

RANK IN FREQUENCY OF GAMES AND OTHER PLAY ACTIVITIES TO WHICH THE BOYS EIGHT TO FIFTEEN YEARS OF AGE THOUGHT THEY HAD GIVEN THE MOST TIME.*

Activity	Age							
	8	9	10	11	12	13	14	15
Baseball with a hard ball **	1	1	1	2	2	3	2	3
Football ***	2	2	2	1	1	1	3	2
Basket ball ****	..	5	4	5	2	2	1	1
Reading books	..	3	5	4	4	4	4	4
Riding a bicycle	5	5	3	3	5	5	5	6
Marbles	3	4	6	7	4	..	..	..
Boxing	4	5	5	6	..	..	..	..
Playing cowboy	2	5	5	..	..	..	..	..
Roller skating	5	6	6	7	5	7	..	..
Going to the "movies"	6	5	5	6	6	6	6	7
Horseback riding	6	6	6	7	6	..	..	..
Driving an automobile	..	..	..	..	..	7	6	5
Listening to the radio	..	..	..	..	..	..	8	8
Having "dates"	..	..	..	..	..	..	9	8
Just "loafing" or lounging	..	..	..	..	..	..	9	8
Tennis **	..	..	..	..	..	7	9	8
Just playing catch	6	6	6	7	6	..	..	..
Watching athletic sports	..	..	..	..	..	7	8	7
Hunting ***	..	..	..	..	..	4	4	5

* The following activities consumed much time, but it is difficult to rank them on the basis of the time consumed: jumping for distance, pole vaulting, jumping for height, coasting on a wagon, riding in an automobile, doing "stunts" in the gymnasium, playing with pet dogs, spinning tops, making or using a wireless or other electrical apparatus, and fishing.
** April data.
*** November data.
**** November and February data.

TABLE XXV-b

RANK IN FREQUENCY OF GAMES AND OTHER PLAY ACTIVITIES TO WHICH THE YOUNG MEN SIXTEEN YEARS OF AGE OR OLDER THOUGHT THEY HAD GIVEN THE MOST TIME.*

Activity	16	17	18	Age 19	20	21	22 or Older	University of Kansas Faculty
Football **	2	1	1	1	3	4	5	..
Basket ball ***	1	2	2	3	8	..	..	..
Reading books	4	3	3	2	1	1	1	1
Baseball with a hard ball ****	3	4	5	..	..	..	..	..
Driving an automobile	4	5	4	5	7	5	8	4
Just "loafing" or lounging	5	7	6	5	2	2	3	..
Reading the newspapers	8	7	7	4	4	2	2	2
Having "dates"	7	7	7	4	5	5	5	..
Going to the "movies"	9	8	9	5	3	7	11	..
Listening to the radio	8	8	..	..	..	..	..	..
Attending lectures	..	..	..	5	2	3	4	..
Just "hiking" or strolling	..	..	..	..	..	5	7	..
Reading short stories	..	..	7	8	9	8	7	5
Writing letters	..	..	..	..	10	10	12	..
Social clubs or being with the gang	..	..	..	..	5	5	6	..
Social dancing	10	10	10	10	10	5	..	..
Doing gymnasium work	..	9	8	11	..	..	..	..
Hunting **	4	4	6	..	..	..	..	..
Tennis ****	4	4	4	5	5	3	..	..
Watching athletic sports	4	4	5	7	..	..	..	..

* The following activities consumed much time, but it is difficult to rank them on the basis of the time consumed: going to entertainments, concerts, etc.; visiting or entertaining company; card games, such as authors, bridge, and whist; playing for fun musical instruments other than the piano; running races (April data); smoking, swimming; riding in an automobile; going to parties or picnics; and playing golf.
** November data.
*** November and February data.
**** April data.

of time. See Tables VII, VIII, XXV, and XXVI. Table VIII shows that the favorite activities of girls (ages 8½ to 12½) were "Playing with dolls," and "Going to the movies." The activity consuming the largest amount of time was "Reading books." None of the activities revealed large seasonal variation.

The boys' favorite activities were "Football," "Baseball," and "Basket ball." These were the activities which also consumed the greatest amount of the boys' time. These activities are of course seasonal. The present writers found "Basket ball," to be less seasonal than "Football," or "Baseball."

The girls' conservatism was shown when the individual age groups were studied. The greater variability of the male in play was apparent at all ages.

Conservatism on the part of the girls may be due to the fact that girls mature more rapidly than boys. However, it may be due merely to the fact that range in play behavior is greatly restricted for girls. It is common·knowledge that girls are required to conform more rigorously to conventional demands than boys and this principle probably holds for play behavior, unusual play activities on the part of the girls being quickly suppressed.

TABLE XXVI-a

RANK IN FREQUENCY OF GAMES AND OTHER PLAY ACTIVITIES TO WHICH THE GIRLS EIGHT TO FIFTEEN YEARS OF AGE THOUGHT THEY HAD GIVEN THE MOST TIME.*

Activity	Age							
	8	9	10	11	12	13	14	15
Reading books	3	1	1	1	1	1	1	1
Dolls, doll carriages, doll clothes, etc.	1	4	2	3	..	..	..	..
Jacks **	2	4	3	4	..	..	..	..
Playing the piano for fun	2	3	2	2	2	2	2	2
Roller skating	3	2	3	3	6	6	..	..
Riding in an automobile	4	5	3	3	6	6	4	5
Sewing, knitting, crocheting, etc., for fun	..	4	3	3	5	4	3	5
Playing school	..	3	3	4	6	..	..	..
Playing house	4	4	4	..	..	..	..	..
Writing letters	3	5	4	..	..	..	..	..
Jumping or skipping rope **	5	5	4	3	..	..	..	..
Gathering flowers **	5	5	4	5	6	..	..	..
Going to the "movies"	..	..	3	3	3	3	3	3
Going to parties or picnics	..	5	5	4	6	6	3	6
Basket ball ***	..	..	..	4	6	6	3	4
Visiting or entertaining company	..	..	4	4	6	5	3	4
Social dancing	..	..	..	..	..	5	3	6
Having "dates"	..	..	..	..	..	..	4	6
Reading short stories	..	..	..	..	..	..	4	4
Reading the newspapers	..	..	..	..	4	4	3	6
Doing gymnasium work	..	..	..	..	..	6	6	5
Listening to the radio	5	5	5	4	5	6	..	..
Ball with an indoor or playground ball **	..	..	4	4	4	6	..	..

* The following activities consumed much time, but it is difficult to rank them on the basis of the time consumed: watching athletic sports, just singing, social clubs or being with the gang, listening to the victrola, just "hiking" or strolling, and running races.
** April data.
*** November and February data.

TABLE XXVI-b

RANK IN FREQUENCY OF GAMES AND OTHER PLAY ACTIVITIES TO WHICH THE YOUNG WOMEN SIXTEEN YEARS OF AGE OR OLDER THOUGHT THEY HAD GIVEN THE MOST TIME.*

Activity	16	17	18	Age 19	20	21	22 or Older	University of Kansas Faculty
Reading books	1	1	1	1	1	1	1	1
Playing the piano for fun	2	3	6	5	7	7	6	..
Having "dates"	4	4	2	2	3	4	6	..
Visiting or entertaining company	3	7	3	3	2	5	2	4
Going to the "movies"	4	2	..	..	..	..	..	..
Social clubs or being with the gang	5	6	5	2	4	2	5	..
Reading short stories	5	5	4	7	7	7	8	7
Reading the newspapers	5	5	8	9	7	6	7	5
Social dancing	7	8	5	6	5	3	6	..
Writing letters	..	8	5	6	7	6	4	3
Going to entertainments, concerts, etc.	7	8	5	6	3	5	5	3
Attending lectures	..	..	7	4	6	6	3	2
Just "loafing" or lounging	..	8	7	6	5	6	7	4
Riding in an automobile	6	8	8	8	7	7	..	..
Going to picnics or parties	7	8	8	9	8	8	..	..
Sewing, knitting, crocheting, etc., for fun	5	8	7	7	7	8	9	5
Gathering flowers **	..	..	..	9	7	7	8	4
Just "hiking" or strolling	..	..	..	..	7	6	8	4

* The following activities consumed much time, but it is difficult to rank them on the basis of the time consumed: just imagining things; card games, such as authors, bridge, and whist; just singing; drawing with pencil, pen, chalk, or crayon; driving an automobile; reading jokes or funny sayings; doing gymnasium work; watching athletic sports; tennis; and listening to the victrola.
** April data.

There is another hypothesis which may explain the greater conservatism of the girls. It may be that girls are more able to endure situations in their play behavior which would prove monotonous to boys. Thorndike quotes Heymans and Wiersma to the effect that only 38 per cent of men reach or exceed the median of women in patience.[7] Cabot, too, has observed that girls seem to possess more patience in their play activity than boys. Cabot makes the following statement:

"Boys seldom stay long in a swing without contriving 'stunts' to put variety and adventure into the drowsy motion; but I have seen girls swing indefinitely without variation or check."[8]

Cannon, too, has observed that male cats are less patient than females. He found that young male cats are more restive and excited when fastened to a holder than females.

"In my earliest observations on the movements of the stomach I had difficulty because in some animals the waves of contraction were perfectly evident, while in others there was no sign of activity. Several weeks passed before I noticed that this difference was associated with difference in sex. In order to be observed with Röntgen rays the animals were restrained in a holder. Although the holder was comfortable, the male cats, particularly the young males, were restive and excited on being fastened to it, and under these circumstances gastric peristaltic waves were absent; the female cats, especially if elderly, usually submitted with calmness to the restraint, and in them the waves had their normal occurrence." [9]

NUMBER OF DIFFERENT PLAY ACTIVITIES ENGAGED IN BY BOYS AND GIRLS

Table IX, page 59, shows the median number and the middle fifty per cent range of the activities engaged in by the sexes.

It will be noted that the median and quartile lines of the girls fall slightly beneath those of the boys in every age interval. Similar results were found when the data were partitioned by seasons. It seems that girls engage in a slightly smaller number of activities than do boys at all ages *when each age group is considered as a distinct unit.*

AGES OF GREATEST SEX DIFFERENCES IN PLAY BEHAVIOR

For certain of the 200 play activities sex differences are conspicuous at every age level. Inspection of the graphs for all activities reveals the fact that the boys' and girls' curves deviate most at ages 8½ to 10½ inclusive.

The fact that sex difference is greatest among children at the younger age levels may be due to the tendency of little children to simulate the activities of elders of their own sex. Small girls tend to play house, to play with dolls, etc., while small boys take part in activities of the following sorts: "Playing cowboy," "Bandit," "Indian," "Robber and police," etc. With increase of maturity imitative games are less frequent and sex differences consequently less pronounced.

It is noticeable further that as chronological age increases the sexes tend to engage more frequently in the same activities. It is likely that increase in maturity brings greater opportunity for social intercourse between the sexes, and consequent opportunity for participation in common activities.

ELIMINATION OF CERTAIN ACTIVITIES AS CHRONOLOGICAL AGE ADVANCES

A large number of the activities of the Play Quiz was not engaged in by adults. Less than 60 per cent of the 200 activities were engaged in by as many as 1 per cent of adults. Table XXVII presents the percentages of the 200 activities that were engaged in by less than 1 per cent of individuals of various ages. Data are presented for the sexes. Eighty-five of the boys' activities (42.5 per cent) and 112 of the girls' activities (56.0 per cent) were engaged in by less than 1 per cent of those individuals 22 or above in chronological age.

It is interesting that girls tend to abandon more activities in early years than do boys. This may be due to a fact previously emphasized. Girls mature more rapidly than boys and maturity correlates with narrowing of play interests.

It is significant that between the ages 14½ to 18½ inclusive, the girls as a *group* engaged in a slightly larger number of activities than the boys. This seems inconsistent in the light of the previous statement in respect to the earlier maturation of the girls. The probable explanation for this apparent inconsistency is to be found in the *types* of activities participated in by boys of ages 14½ to 18½. At these ages boys engaged in numerous games involving team work. Boys are therefore drawn to common activities and are afforded less

TABLE XXVII

PERCENTAGES OF THE 200 ACTIVITIES OF THE PLAY QUIZ THAT WERE ENGAGED IN BY LESS THAN 1% OF INDIVIDUALS OF VARIOUS AGES.

Ages	Boys No. of Act.	Boys % of Act.	Girls No. of Act.	Girls % of Act.
8½	..	..	..	..
9½	..	..	..	..
10½	..	..	..	..
11½	..	..	..	..
12½	..	..	3	1.5
13½	1	.5	10	5.
14½	15	7.5	15	7.5
15½	24	12.	27	13.5
16½	50	25.	43	21.5
17½	60	30.	50	25.
18½	70	35.	68	34.
19½	80	40.	85	42.5
20½	83	41.5	89	44.5
21½	84	42.	93	46.5
22½ and up	85	42.5	112	56.

opportunity to engage in individual ones. The girls of corresponding chronological ages engaged less frequently in games which require coöperative effort. They are, therefore, more free to turn to individualistic activities.

SUMMARY

Popular thinking assumes conspicuous sex differences in play. The present series of investigations revealed that both sexes participate in *most* play activities and engage in many with *equal* frequency. Therefore, it is difficult and unsatisfactory to classify various plays and games as characteristic ones of one sex or the other.

Sex differences result from many variables. The present studies revealed that young boys engage more frequently than young girls in certain activities, while the opposite situation exists in subsequent periods. Extensive and reliable information must be at hand before generalizations are justified.

Conspicuous differences, although not the rule, are to be found between the sexes in play behavior. The boys studied engaged more frequently than the girls in the following types of activities:

> Active, vigorous plays and games.
> Plays and games involving muscular dexterity and skill.
> Games involving competition.
> Organized plays and games.

The girls, however, engaged more frequently than boys in the following:

> Sedentary activities and activities involving restricted range of action.

The girls were more conservative in their play life; they displayed less variability than did the boys.

The largest sex differences were found at ages 8½ to 10½ inclusive. As chronological age increased the sexes tended to engage more frequently in the same activities. Consequently sex differences were not so pronounced at the higher age levels.

REFERENCES

1. Terman, Lewis M. *The Measurement of Intelligence.* Boston. Houghton Mifflin Co. 1916. Pp. xvii-362. (p. 63 ff.)

2. Hollingworth, Leta S. "Variability as Related to Sex Differences in Achievement." *American Journal of Sociology.* Jan. 1914. *19,* Pp. 510-530.

3. Dewey, John and Dewey, Evelyn. *Schools of To-morrow.* New York. E. P. Dutton & Company. 1915. 316 pp. (p. 115.)

4. Jesperson, Otto. *Language; Its Nature, Development and Origin.* New York. Henry Holt and Co. 1923. 448 pp. (p. 146).

5. Morrison, H. C. *The Practice of Teaching in the Secondary School.* Chicago. The University of Chicago Press. 1926. Pp. viii-661.

6. Gale, Mae L. *A Study in Pupil Achievement.* Unpublished Master's Thesis on file at Watson Library. The University of Kansas, Lawrence, Kansas. 1926.

7. Thorndike, E. L. *Educational Psychology.* (Briefer Course.) New York. Teachers College. Columbia University. 1915. Pp. xii-442. (p. 349.)

8. Cabot, Richard C. *What Men Live By.* Boston. Houghton Mifflin Co. 1914. Pp. xxi-341. (p. 131.)

9. Cannon, Walter B. *Bodily Changes in Pain, Hunger, Fear, and Rage.* New York. D. Appleton and Company. 1920. Pp. xiii-311. (p. 14.)

CHAPTER VIII

A COMPARISON OF THE PLAY ACTIVITIES OF TOWN AND COUNTRY CHILDREN *

CURRENT OPINION

Much theoretical material has been published from time to time regarding the play behavior of country and town children. In this literature one can find many contradictory statements. The following quotation is illustrative of the speculative writing frequently found:

"Country children, contrary to popular belief, do not play as great a variety of games as children in towns or cities where there are playgrounds. They are handicapped particularly in respect to facilities for gymnastic activities, so that the city child who is within reach of a well-conducted playground is better off, even with all the disadvantages of city life, than the country child for whom no provision has been made." [1]

O'Shea offers no evidence in support of the above assertion other than the following paragraph which seems to indicate that his opinion is the outcome of what may be termed an invoice of the observable facilities for play:

"The country school building is often located on a small plot of ground which does not afford sufficient space for the games and plays which children like and in which they should indulge. The farmers protest if the pupils make use of the fields adjoining the school grounds for any of their games. In some rural districts the teacher is under constant criticism because her pupils overrun the property adjoining the school, when they do not have room to play their games on the school grounds. Some important surveys of country life recently have been completed and they show that, except in rare instances, no one has devoted time or thought to providing facilities for plays and games for children in the country." [2]

Charters too has asserted that country children are lacking in opportunity to play.

* The graphs presented in this chapter appeared in *The Pedagogical Seminary*, September, 1926.

"Country children even more than city children need to have an opportunity to play. The city children frequently do not have the space, but the
country children do not live close enough together to congregate in groups
sufficiently large to play and very often the variety of games that they can
play is very narrow." [3]

Charters' statement also is based probably upon observation. Such
a qualitative statement as "the variety of games is very narrow" leaves
much to be desired in the way of specific description of the activities
country children actually engage in.

It is clear that objective data are needed. The series of investigations herein described reveal that play is a function of numerous
variables. A survey of play behavior should therefore include much
more than an invoice of observable material facilities that might at
first thought appear to be the necessary prerequisites of play.

The rural children studied were pupils in one-teacher rural schools.
No data were tabulated except those received from rural schools having enrollments of less than 25 pupils, the intention being to investigate
the play behavior of children living in *genuinely* rural environments.
Table I (p. 42 of Chap. 4) shows the number of rural pupils included
in the study. Tables XXVIII to XXXI show some of the findings. It
will be noticed at once that the games and other play activities of the
rural children differ in certain respects from those of the children
living in towns and villages.

SIGNIFICANT DIFFERENCES IN REFERENCE TO SPECIFIC ACTIVITIES

Figure 9 shows the extent to which the town and the country
children attended moving-picture shows during the course of a single
week. The results displayed have been verified in two ways: (a) By
repetition of the first investigation, (b) By partitioning the data
derived from a single investigation.

It is apparent in Figure 9 that the rural children attended the
moving-picture show much less frequently than the town children.
It was found likewise that rural children attended church and Sunday
school much less frequently than town children.

Figure 10 shows the relative frequency with which town and country boys went hunting during the week. The findings for "Shooting a
gun," are almost identical with those for "Going hunting."

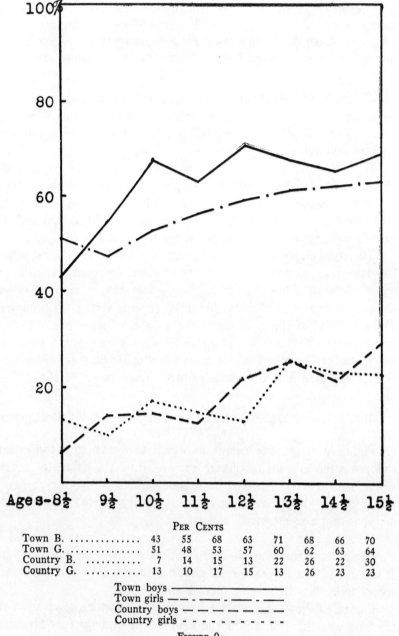

	PER CENTS							
Town B.	43	55	68	63	71	68	66	70
Town G.	51	48	53	57	60	62	63	64
Country B.	7	14	15	13	22	26	22	30
Country G.	13	10	17	15	13	26	23	23

Town boys ——————————
Town girls —— · —— · —— · —— ·
Country boys —— —— —— —— ——
Country girls - - - - - - - - - -

FIGURE 9

Percentages of town and country children who went to the movies.

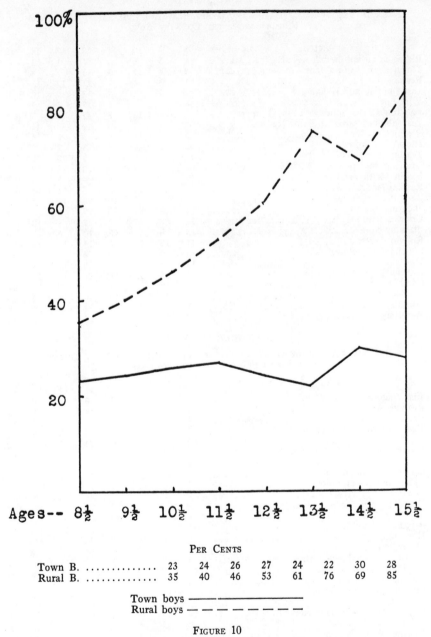

Ages--	8½	9½	10½	11½	12½	13½	14½	15½

PER CENTS

	8½	9½	10½	11½	12½	13½	14½	15½
Town B.	23	24	26	27	24	22	30	28
Rural B.	35	40	46	53	61	76	69	85

Town boys —————
Rural boys — — — — — — —

FIGURE 10

Percentages of town and country boys who went hunting during the course of a week.

TABLE XXVIII

RANK IN FREQUENCY OF GAMES AND OTHER PLAY ACTIVITIES MOST COMMONLY ENGAGED IN BY THE COUNTRY BOYS.

Activity	8	9	10	11	12	13	14	15
Riding in an automobile	4	3	6	4	1	1	1	1
Throwing rocks or stones	8	4	2	2	5	7	8	2
Reading books	1	3	4	7	11	12	13	9
Just running and romping	2	1	1	3	3	9	10	9
Whistling	3	2	2	1	5	3	7	6
Looking at the Sunday "funny" paper	6	4	13	8	2	6	5	5
Just playing catch	5	5	12	10	12	12	11	10
Reading the newspapers	25	21	11	6	3	7	3	3
Horseback riding	12	6	14	4	8	2	6	5
Teasing somebody	11	9	7	9	6	10	2	5
Drawing with pencil, pen, chalk, or crayon	7	8	5	6	10	12	18	17
Playing with pet dogs	10	5	3	5	4	5	9	7
Reading short stories	10	12	11	13	8	11	12	7
Listening to stories	9	10	23	18	20	18	14	18
Shooting a gun	..	28	31	20	19	8	10	4
Using a hammer, saw, nails, etc., for fun	12	7	7	7	7	4	10	11
Chewing gum	12	8	17	15	10	6	7	8
Running races	11	12	12	14	15	14	19	16
Looking at pictures	13	9	8	8	14	15	17	12
Just singing	13	13	10	12	9	13	13	13
Cutting paper things with scissors	9	17	15	19	23	21	25	22
Climbing porches, trees, fences, posts, etc.	12	10	6	11	8	10	13	19
Reading jokes or funny sayings	20	22	15	13	10	14	9	10
Hunting	27	18	24	17	12	3	5	6
Wrestling	22	16	16	18	13	15	15	11

TABLE XXIX

RANK IN FREQUENCY OF GAMES AND OTHER PLAY ACTIVITIES MOST COMMONLY ENGAGED IN BY THE COUNTRY GIRLS.

Activity	8	9	10	11	12	13	14	15
Just singing	2	2	6	3	3	2	4	1
Reading short stories	2	3	5	3	4	3	4	5
Reading books	1	3	4	8	8	10	12	8
Just running and romping	3	1	1	4	10	10	9	12
Black man	3	15	17	20	21	17	14	12
Looking at the Sunday "funny" paper	2	2	3	2	5	6	5	11
Listening to stories	4	5	15	15	12	15	11	11
Playing the piano for fun	12	20	11	13	10	13	14	14
Riding in an automobile	8	7	2	1	1	1	2	1
Looking at pictures	7	8	7	5	6	6	7	6
Drawing with pencil, pen, chalk, or crayon	3	6	3	7	2	6	10	3
Swinging	6	7	17	13	20	20	21	12
Playing school	5	14	15	20	21	17	15	12
Hop, skip, and jump	6	6	13	22	25	33	31	12
Playing teeter-totter	10	7	19	21	34	..	..	..
Cutting paper things with scissors	6	9	6	8	9	16	14	12
Teasing somebody	17	8	6	7	6	3	8	4
Playing with pet dogs	10	4	5	13	5	7	12	10
Playing with pet kittens	11	11	6	9	14	15	18	7
Whistling	13	6	9	11	7	8	7	8
Visiting or entertaining company	14	19	14	14	10	5	8	3
Chewing gum	10	5	9	10	7	6	6	4
Reading the newspapers	20	6	6	2	1	1	1	2
Reading jokes or funny sayings	2	3	12	6	9	4	6	2
Telling or guessing riddles	23	18	17	16	17	15	13	9
Dolls, doll carriages, doll clothes, etc.	12	10	8	24	..	..	..	..
Listening to the Victrola	17	12	21	17	16	19	20	6

TABLE XXX

RANK IN FREQUENCY OF GAMES AND OTHER PLAY ACTIVITIES LIKED BEST BY THE COUNTRY BOYS.

Activity	Age							
	8	9	10	11	12	13	14	15
Baseball with a hard ball	1	1	1	2	3	4	2	4
Hunting	8	3	5	4	2	1	1	1
Horseback riding	1	2	3	1	1	3	3	5
Football	2	1	2	3	6	6	7	2
Basket ball	6	6	7	8	8	7	4	4
Just playing catch	..	4	4	8	8	7	8	..
Driving an automobile	..	9	8	5	9	2	2	3
Shooting a gun	..	9	9	7	7	4	5	..
Riding in an automobile	5	4	6	7	8	..	..	..
Riding a bicycle	..	..	9	6	5	8	6	..
Ball with an indoor or playground ball	5	8	9	9	..	..	7	..
Reading books	4	8	..	8	10	..	..	..
Wrestling	8	8	8	7	..	10	7	..
Playing with pet dogs	7	7	10	..	..	..	..	..
Running races	8	8	..	10	..	..	..	..
Looking at the Sunday "funny" paper	3	..	7	7	..	9	..	..
Black man	..	8	9	..	..	..	..	..

TABLE XXXI

RANK IN FREQUENCY OF GAMES AND OTHER PLAY ACTIVITIES LIKED BEST BY THE COUNTRY GIRLS.

Activity	Age							
	8	9	10	11	12	13	14	15
Horseback riding	3	1	1	1	3	1	1	4
Riding in an automobile	4	4	3	2	1	2	3	1
Swinging	2	2	..	..	..	8	..	..
Reading books	4	7	7	..	7	4	4	..
Looking at the Sunday "funny" paper	1	..	2	3	9	4	7	..
Dolls, doll carriages, doll clothes, etc.	6	3	4	6	..	..	..	..
Driving an automobile	..	..	..	..	4	5	3	2
Basket ball	..	..	6	6	6	8	7	3
Playing the piano for fun	7	5	5	4	2	4	2	..
Social dancing	..	..	..	..	..	..	6	2
Playing house	5	7	8	7	..	..	..	..
Playing teeter-totter	6	..	..	..	..	..	..	..
Just playing catch	6	7	7	7	..	..	..	..
Playing with pet kittens	7	..	..	..	..	..	..	..
Playing with pet dogs	6	..	..	..	..	..	..	..
Anty over	..	6	..	..	..	..	..	..
Black man	7	7	..	..	..	..	..	..
Going to the "movies"	..	..	..	7	..	3	..	..
Going to parties or picnics	..	..	..	..	8	4	..	..
Visiting or entertaining company	..	..	..	7	8	9	7	3
Ball with an indoor or playground ball	..	..	..	7	5	10	1	1
Teasing somebody	..	..	..	..	5	7	7	..
Having "dates"	..	..	..	..	..	..	..	5
Gathering flowers	..	..	..	..	5	..	..	..
Just singing	..	..	8	..	..	6	..	..
Going to entertainments, concerts, etc.	..	..	..	..	..	..	5	5
Sewing, knitting, crocheting, etc., for fun	..	..	..	..	..	..	8	5

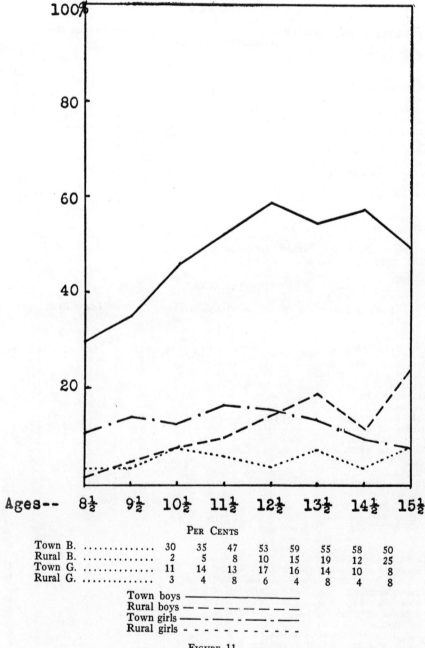

	Per Cents							
Town B.	30	35	47	53	59	55	58	50
Rural B.	2	5	8	10	15	19	12	25
Town G.	11	14	13	17	16	14	10	8
Rural G.	3	4	8	6	4	8	4	8

Town boys ————————
Rural boys — — — — — — — —
Town girls —— · —— · —— · ——
Rural girls - - - - - - - - - - -

FIGURE 11

Percentages of town and country children who rode bicycles during the course of one week.

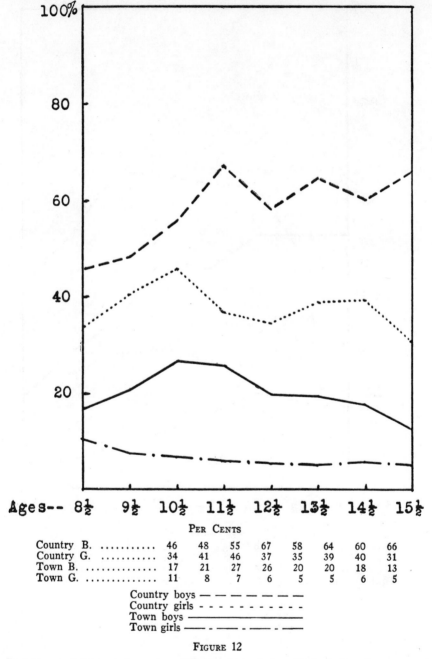

Ages--	8½	9½	10½	11½	12½	13½	14½	15½

PER CENTS

Country B.	46	48	55	67	58	64	60	66
Country G.	34	41	46	37	35	39	40	31
Town B.	17	21	27	26	20	20	18	13
Town G.	11	8	7	6	5	5	6	5

Country boys — — — — — — —
Country girls - - - - - - - - - - -
Town boys ———————————
Town girls —— - —— - —— - —— - ——

FIGURE 12

Percentages of town and country children who rode horseback during the course of one week.

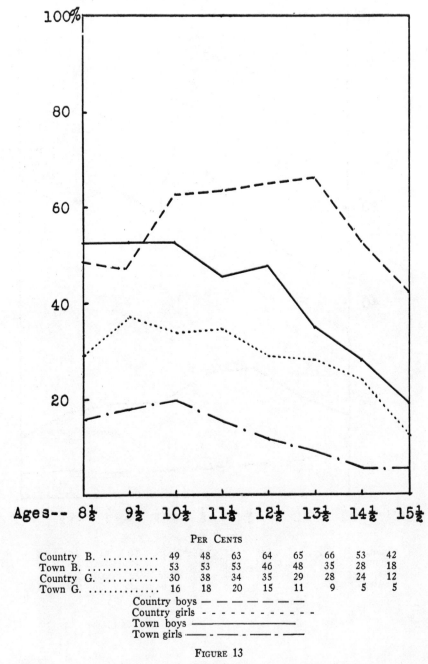

FIGURE 13

Percentages of town and country children who climbed porches, trees, fences, etc. during the course of one week.

Figure 11 shows that "Bicycle riding," was much more frequently engaged in by town boys than by country boys. The country boys, on the other hand, engaged more often in "Horseback riding." Figure 11 sets forth the findings for "Bicycle riding," and Figure 12 gives the findings for "Horseback riding." It may be seen from Figure 12, that although the boys rode horseback more often than the girls living in the same environment, country girls engaged in this activity more frequently than city boys.

It may be inferred that the preceding data prove rather conclusively that play behavior is a function of environment. The data presented seem to show that participation in *certain* activities is a matter of the accessibility of the facilities requisite for participation therein. There are, however, numerous differences in the recreational activities of town and country children that are not to be accounted for on this basis.

Figure 13 shows that the country children climbed "Porches, trees, fences, posts, etc.," more commonly than the town children. It cannot be maintained that porches, trees, etc., are inaccessible to the town children included in the present series of studies.

Boys participated more frequently than girls of the same environment in this activity. But it is significant and interesting that country girls took part in this form of play behavior almost twice as frequently as the town boys of corresponding chronological ages.

Figure 14 shows that the country childen played "Blackman," much more frequently than the town children. This difference is especially marked at ages 14½ to 15½. Figures 14, 15 and 16 illustrate typical activities in which country children participated more often than town or city children. Few of the town children of ages 14½ to 15½ played "Blackman," "Anty-over," "Teeter-totter," etc., yet a considerable number of country children engaged in these activities. Only four or five per cent of the town boys of ages 14½ to 15½ participated in playing "Anty-over," while over 25 per cent of country children of these ages were found to have engaged therein. The data for girls of the two groups reveal similar differences in this regard.

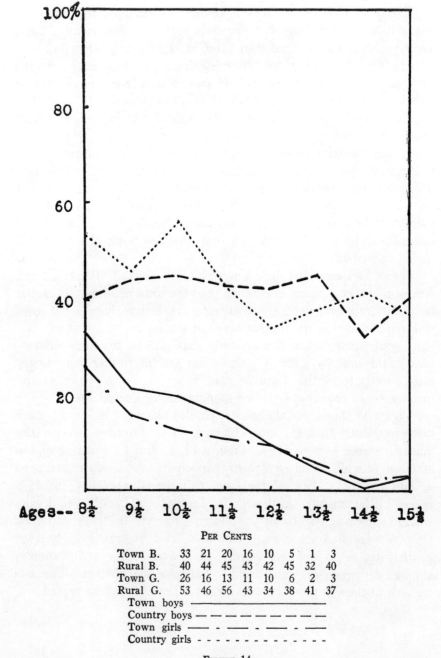

PER CENTS

Town B.	33	21	20	16	10	5	1	3
Rural B.	40	44	45	43	42	45	32	40
Town G.	26	16	13	11	10	6	2	3
Rural G.	53	46	56	43	34	38	41	37

Town boys ——————————
Country boys — — — — — — — — —
Town girls —— · —— · —— · ——
Country girls - - - - - - - - - - - - -

FIGURE 14

Percentages of town and of country children who were found to play blackman as
frequently as once per week.

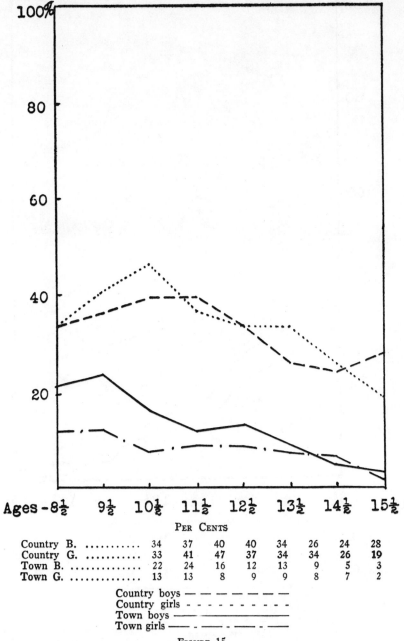

Ages –	$8\frac{1}{2}$	$9\frac{1}{2}$	$10\frac{1}{2}$	$11\frac{1}{2}$	$12\frac{1}{2}$	$13\frac{1}{2}$	$14\frac{1}{2}$	$15\frac{1}{2}$

PER CENTS

Country B.	34	37	40	40	34	26	24	28
Country G.	33	41	47	37	34	34	26	19
Town B.	22	24	16	12	13	9	5	3
Town G.	13	13	8	9	9	8	7	2

Country boys — — — — — —
Country girls - - - - - - - -
Town boys ————————
Town girls —— - —— - —— - ——

FIGURE 15

Percentages of town and country children who played anty-over during the course of one week.

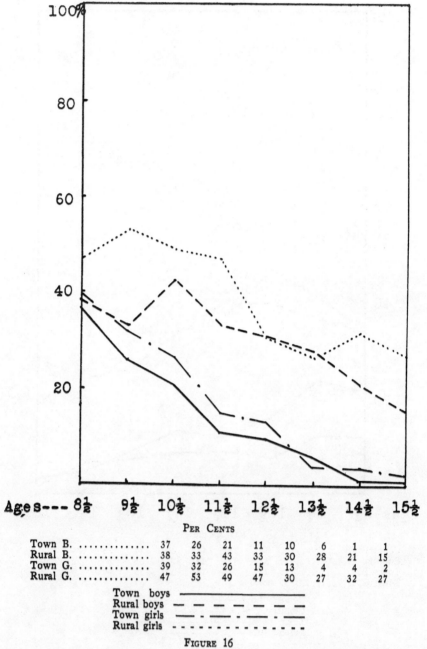

Ages---	8½	9½	10½	11½	12½	13½	14½	15½

Per Cents

	8½	9½	10½	11½	12½	13½	14½	15½
Town B.	37	26	21	11	10	6	1	1
Rural B.	38	33	43	33	30	28	21	15
Town G.	39	32	26	15	13	4	4	2
Rural G.	47	53	49	47	30	27	32	27

Town boys ——————
Rural boys — — — — — —
Town girls —— · —— · —— · —
Rural girls - - - - - - - - - - - -

FIGURE 16

Percentages of town and country children who played teeter-totter.

MEDIAN NUMBER OF PLAY ACTIVITIES ENGAGED IN

Figure 17 shows the median number of play activities engaged in by town boys as compared with country boys. Figure 18 presents similar data for town and country girls. Country boys of ages $8\frac{1}{2}$ to $10\frac{1}{2}$ inclusive, engaged in fewer activities than the town boys of the same ages. Country boys older than $10\frac{1}{2}$ were found to engage in a larger number of activities than the town and city boys of corresponding ages. The curves for the girls are similar; the difference, however, is less marked at the younger ages.

Each of the three investigations of town children yielded curves similar to those presented in Figs. 17 and 18 for city children. A subsequent investigation of rural children yielded data which corroborate those presented in Figures 9 and 10.

Figures 17 and 18 show that the country children of ages $11\frac{1}{2}$ and above engage in a *larger* number of activities than town children of corresponding chronological ages. These findings are opposed to the opinions expressed by O'Shea and Charters in this regard.

The fact that rural children beyond the age of $11\frac{1}{2}$ participated in a larger number of play activities than city children of corresponding ages may be accounted for in the following manner:

Younger rural children are less able than town children (or older rural children) to go far from their homes. Hence, the younger rural children probably have less opportunity to participate in group plays and games. Older rural children, however, were found to participate in a greater variety of recreational activities than the town children of the same chronological ages. This condition may be explained on the basis that individual and group specialization in play are possible to a greater extent for city children. There is obviously greater opportunity for individual preferences in play activities to be gratified in the city than in the country. Specialization and individualization undoubtedly result in narrowing the range of activities in which a particular group takes part. It is likely further that country children have less opportunity to congregate in relatively homogeneous age groups. Thus, it may be that the play activities of the rural group are chosen in accord with the wishes and needs of the average person in the group. Certainly if rural children are to

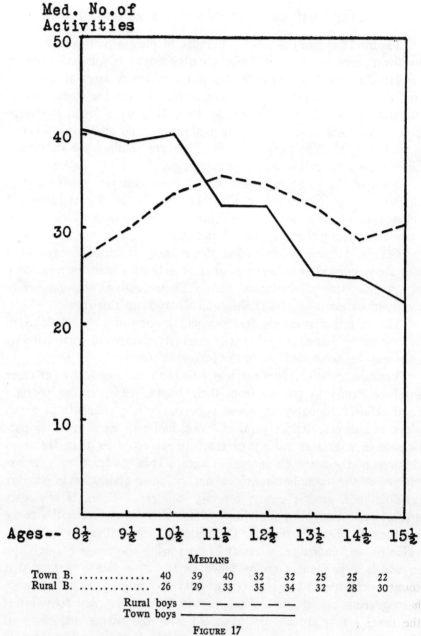

Med. No.of
Activities

FIGURE 17

Median number of play activities engaged in by town versus rural boys.

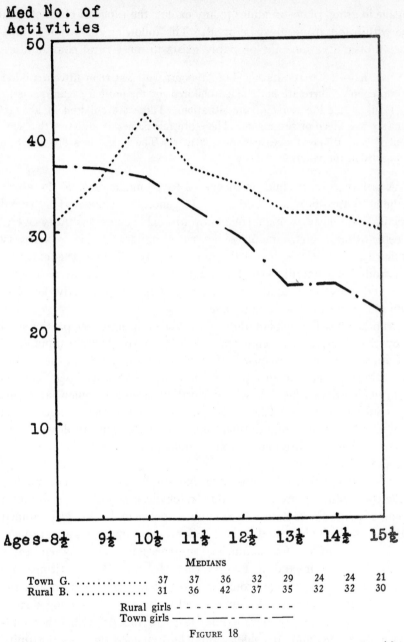

Med No. of
Activities

Ages—8½   9½   10½   11½   12½   13½   14½   15½

MEDIANS

Town G. 37   37   36   32   29   24   24   21
Rural B. 31   36   42   37   35   32   32   30

Rural girls - - - - - - - - - - -
Town girls ——— - ——— - ——— - ———

FIGURE 18

Median number of different play activities engaged in by town versus country girls.

engage in group plays or games to any extent, the range of chronological age within the group must be great. The following quotation is illustrative of a situation that probably exists in most rural communities:

"We have 2,300 rural schools in Missouri with less than fifteen children to the school. There are not enough children for the ordinary team games.

"This is not the worst of the situation. There are children of all ages from six to sixteen or seventeen. There are few games or athletics that children of such different ages can do together. The older ones are fewer in number than the younger children." [4]

A group of rural children of ages 8 to 14 might engage, therefore, in the activities in which children of 11 generally engage. This would explain the relatively high frequency of such games as "Anty-over," "Teeter-totter," etc., among older rural children. Since maturity ordinarily posits narrowing of the range of play behavior, this explanation would account likewise for the fact that rural children of ages 11½ and above participate in a larger number of play activities than town children of corresponding ages.

Another possible explanation of the types of activities participated in by the older country children, and the relatively large number of activities participated in, may be found in the differences in the mental age ratings of the two groups of children. Numerous investigations have yielded data which show that rural children are somewhat below city children in mental age. The relatively lower mental age of the rural child may cause him to turn to play activities that are less mature in nature than his chronological age would posit but which correspond to his mental age.

It is equally plausible to assume that the lower mental age ratings of the rural children are not a causal factor but a result of the situation revealed by the above data. In administering mental tests it is assumed that the individuals tested have similar environmental backgrounds, equal opportunities for acquiring information, etc. When these assumptions are invalid it follows that the mental age ratings are invalid also. It is evident from the above data that the rural and the city children do not have the same social contacts. The younger rural children have relatively few opportunities to mingle with other children of like ages and the older rural children have little opportunity to congregate in relatively homogeneous age groups. It is difficult to equate ability to learn and opportunity to learn. One can only speculate, therefore, in reference *to how much less stimulating* a given environment may be. Certain it is that the environments of the town and the country children are quite different and this environmental difference *may have* an influence upon the mental age ratings of the two groups of children.

The writers are offering these hypotheses not dogmatically but simply as interesting speculations.

THE SINGING AND WHISTLING OF TOWN AND COUNTRY CHILDREN

Figure 19 shows the percentages of town boys and town girls who indicated that they had engaged in activity No. 165, "Just singing" during the course of the week preceding a given investigation. It will be noted that Figure 19 presents the findings for three separate investigations and that the results of all investigations are strikingly similar. Singing is apparently an activity little affected by the seasons. There is, however, a conspicuous sex difference as regards the extent to which town children engaged in this activity. The girls engaged in singing more frequently than the boys at each season of the year. It is to be noted further that there was a consistent decrease in the incidence of singing with increased chronological age. The decrease, however, is more rapid for the boys than for the girls.

Figure 20 shows the percentages of town boys and town girls who indicated that they had engaged in activity No. 107, "Whistling." It is noticeable again that the seasonal results are similar. Whistling does not seem to be a seasonal activity. The boys engaged in whistling more commonly than the girls during each season of the year.

Figure 21 shows the percentages of town and country children who engaged in whistling. Figure 21 shows that the boys of each environment whistle more frequently than the girls of the same environment and that the country children whistle more commonly than the town children. Between ages 12½ to 15½ inclusive more than twice as many rural girls as town girls engage in this activity. Older *rural girls* whistle *more* frequently than *town boys* of the same ages!

In Figure 21 the curves for the town children were made after aver-

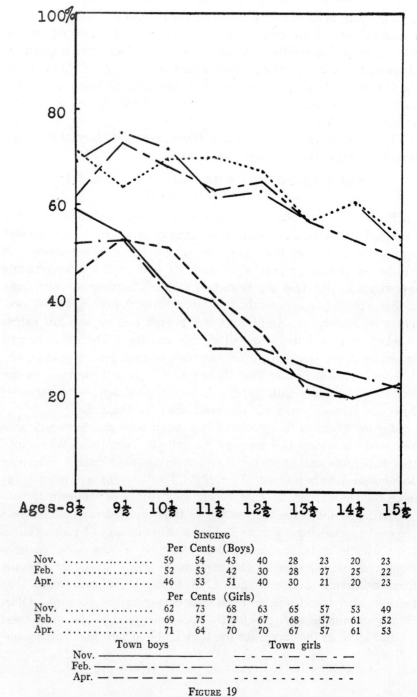

	Per	Cents	(Boys)					
Nov.	59	54	43	40	28	23	20	23
Feb.	52	53	42	30	28	27	25	22
Apr.	46	53	51	40	30	21	20	23

	Per	Cents	(Girls)					
Nov.	62	73	68	63	65	57	53	49
Feb.	69	75	72	67	68	57	61	52
Apr.	71	64	70	70	67	57	61	53

Town boys   Town girls

Nov. ——————————   — — — — — — — — —
Feb. —— · —— · —— · —— ·   — — · — — · — — ·
Apr. — — — — — — — —   · · · · · · · · · · · · · · ·

FIGURE 19

Percentages of town children who indicated that they had engaged in singing
during the course of a week.

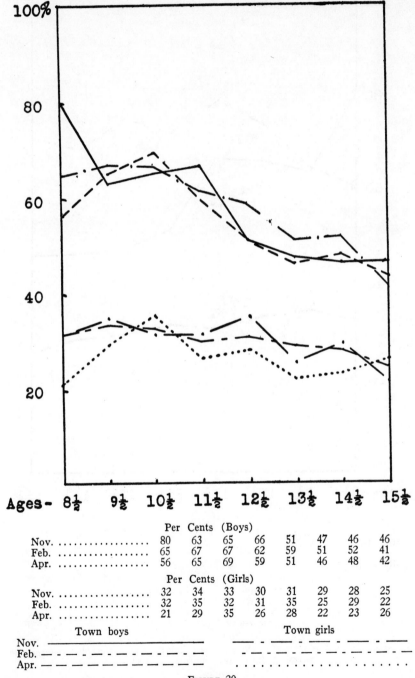

Ages-	8½	9½	10½	11½	12½	13½	14½	15½

	Per Cents (Boys)							
Nov.	80	63	65	66	51	47	46	46
Feb.	65	67	67	62	59	51	52	41
Apr.	56	65	69	59	51	46	48	42
	Per Cents (Girls)							
Nov.	32	34	33	30	31	29	28	25
Feb.	32	35	32	31	35	25	29	22
Apr.	21	29	35	26	28	22	23	26

Town boys	Town girls
Nov. ——————————	— · — · — · — · —
Feb. — · — · — · — · —	· — · — · — · — · —
Apr. — — — — — — — —	··················

FIGURE 20

Percentages of town children who engaged in whistling during the course of a week.

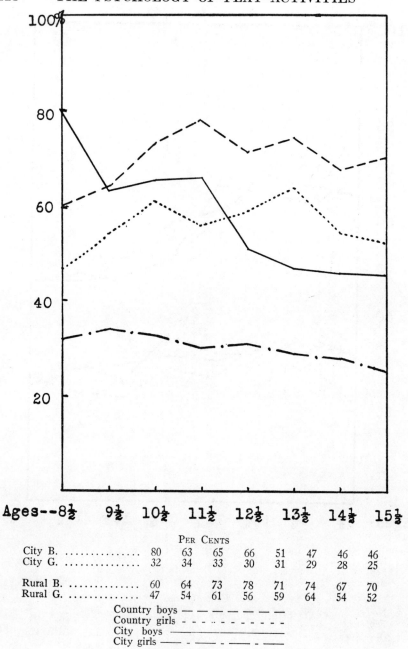

Ages—	8½	9½	10½	11½	12½	13½	14½	15½
PER CENTS								
City B.	80	63	65	66	51	47	46	46
City G.	32	34	33	30	31	29	28	25
Rural B.	60	64	73	78	71	74	67	70
Rural G.	47	54	61	56	59	64	54	52

Country boys — — — — — — —
Country girls - - - ·· - - - - - -
City boys ——————
City girls —— - —— - —— - ——

FIGURE 21

Percentages of town and country children who indicated that they had engaged in whistling during the course of a week.

aging the results obtained from the three separate town investigations and the curves for the country children were made after averaging the results obtained from the two separate rural investigations. The repetition of the investigations prevented obtaining unreliable data due to unusual conditions which might attend a single investigation. The fact that similar curves were obtained when the data were partitioned tends to validate the findings.

Figure 22 shows that the girls of a given environment sing more often than the boys of the same environment and that country children sing more than town children. Between ages 13½ to 15½ inclusive more than twice as many rural boys as town boys engaged in singing. At these age levels *country boys* sang as often as *town girls*.

The preceding figures are indicative of the extent to which town life tends to suppress two very natural modes of self-expression. They probably reveal differences in the amount of social pressure brought to bear upon children reared in town as compared to children reared in the country. For obvious reasons, singing and whistling are discouraged among town children. Where many persons are working together not even humming is permissible.

Judd has recently discussed the extent to which the individual is a product of social forces and has voiced his protest against attempts to formulate the plans of the school on a psychology of the individual.

"In arguing for the recognition of the psychology of social institutions, it is by no means denied that there is a psychology of individual mental life. What is said is that individual psychology should be studied as a part of the more inclusive science of the psychology of mankind. It is not denied for a moment that the individual has eyes and ears and hands. It is pointed out, however, that the things at which children look, the sounds to which they listen, and the object which they handle are determined not by individual impulse but primarily by the demands of the social group in the midst of which the individual moves and has his social contacts." [5]

This is not the first time that the suppressive effect of environment has been noted. Jesperson states that singing is found wherever the indoor life of civilization has not killed all open-air hilarity. The following quotation is credited to the Swedish peasant, Jonas Stolt:

"I have known a time when young people were singing from morning till

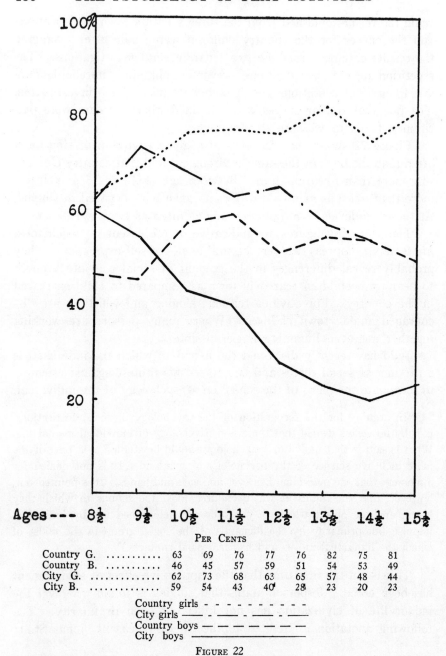

		Per Cents					
Country G.	63	69	76	77	76	82	75	81
Country B.	46	45	57	59	51	54	53	49
City G.	62	73	68	63	65	57	48	44
City B.	59	54	43	40	28	23	20	23

Country girls - - - - - - - - - -
City girls ——— · ——— · ——— · ———
Country boys —— —— —— —— —— ——
City boys ————————

FIGURE 22

Percentages of town and country children who indicated that they had engaged in "Just singing" during the course of one week.

eve. Then they were caroling both out- and indoors, behind the plough as well as at the threshing-floor and at the spinning-wheel. This is all over long ago; nowadays there is silence everywhere; if someone were to try and sing in our days as we did of old, people would term it bawling." [6]

SUMMARY

Rural boys of ages 8½ to 10½ inclusive were found to engage in *fewer* activities than town boys of the same ages. Rural boys older than 10½ in chronological age were found to engage in a *larger* number of play activities than town boys of corresponding ages.

Older country children were found to be less mature than city children in their play interests. Particularly noticeable was this fact when group games were considered. It seems likely that country life affords little opportunity for play in homogeneous age groups. Therefore, play activities must be chosen in terms of the average age of the children in the group. This would militate against choice of more mature plays and games.

City life probably operates to suppress certain natural modes of self-expression (notably whistling and singing). Rural life permits freer expression to certain natural modes of behavior. Such individual activities as whistling and singing are examples thereof. However, rural life affords less opportunity for participation in certain organized mature group activities.

Play behavior is conditioned by many variables. One of these is environment. The play of country and city children shows conspicuous differences directly traceable to environmental opportunity. A survey of play behavior must include therefore more than an invoice of play equipment or observable facilities.

REFERENCES

1. O'Shea, M. V. (Editor). *The Child; His Nature and His Needs.* Valparaiso, Indiana. The Children's Foundation. 1924. Pp. ix-516. (p. 439.)
2. O'Shea, M. V. *op. cit.* (p. 438 f.)
3. Charters, W. W. *Teaching the Common Branches.* New York. Houghton Mifflin Co. 1924. Pp. viii-411. (p. 359.)
4. Curtis, Henry S. "Physical Education . . . Rural and City Aspects." *The Playground.* May, 1925, *19,* p. 106.
5. Judd, C. H. "Types of Learning." *Elementary School Journal.* November, 1924. *25,* p. 183.
6. Jesperson, Otto. *Language; Its Nature, Development, and Origin.* New York. Henry Holt and Company. 1923. 448 pp. (p. 435.)

CHAPTER IX

RACE DIFFERENCES IN PLAY BEHAVIOR (NEGRO AND WHITE CHILDREN)

Numerous investigations have yielded results which show rather conclusively that Negro children do less well than white children in tasks which involve abstract intelligence.[1] Peterson has suggested that certain traits worthy of note may be stronger in Negro than in white children. Peterson mentions specifically "freedom from tension" and "ease of bearing in social situations."

"In a positive way, the Negro probably has certain traits worthy of note which are stronger than those in the white man. These have unfortunately not received as much attention as the deficiencies. It is probable that the Negro has greater freedom from tension and from concern about remote conditions with an ease of bearing in social situations that is due to something more than a lack of realization of remote relations."[2]

Lack of an adequate technique heretofore has militated against objective measurement of the traits mentioned by Peterson. Too, there has been much speculation and little objective measurement of racial differences in other traits of character. Pintner cautiously refrains from speculating about racial differences in social or emotional traits.

"While we cannot conclude dogmatically that there are no qualitative differences between the two races, we may at least say that any marked qualitative difference in intelligence, as measured by the tests under consideration, does not seem to exist. In saying this we must remember that we are restricting ourselves entirely to the type of intelligence which is largely verbal or abstract; that is the sort of thing which is tested most effectively by the Binet and customary group tests. Mechanical intelligence has been much less effectively measured and social intelligence practically not at all. Furthermore we must remember that we have not raised the question as to emotional and moral differences between the two races. Popular opinion assumes large differences in these traits. There are no scientific measures of these as yet, and speculation about possible differences in this regard does not belong in a book devoted to intelligence testing." [3]

The inferiority of the Negro in tasks involving abstract intelligence has been demonstrated by various workers in quantitative psychology. It must be remembered that the tests used in most cases have been the group or individual intelligence examinations in which reading or language mastery play an important part. There is some evidence that Negro children also fall below the standing of white children in mental ability when the test employed is of the performance type and the language handicap is partially eliminated.

The present writers have obtained through the Lehman Play Quiz significant data regarding certain characteristic traits of Negro and white children.

In January, 1926, the Quiz was given to more than 6,000 children of Kansas City, Missouri, schools. The number of Negro children included in five investigations of play behavior is presented in Table XXXII. The Tulsa children included in Table XXXII were given the Play Quiz by Mrs. Thelma Hill Anderson, a graduate student of The School of Education of the University of Kansas. Mrs. Anderson administered the Play Quiz to Tulsa pupils in procuring data for a Master's thesis.** Acknowledgment is herewith made for the use of data obtained from the Tulsa children.

TABLE XXXII

NUMBER OF NEGRO CHILDREN INCLUDED IN FOUR INVESTIGATIONS OF PLAY BEHAVIOR.

Ages	Nov. 1923		Feb. 1924		Apr. 1924		Jan. 1926		Tulsa, Oklahoma Both Sexes
	B	G	B	G	B	G	B	G	
8½	26	26	19	27	*	*	39	48	..
9½	28	28	33	27	29	26	75	90	*
10½	44	32	34	46	32	34	94	123	24
11½	39	37	29	46	33	49	89	114	49
12½	40	77	40	34	26	53	104	110	65
13½	35	60	48	46	51	63	80	91	87
14½	59	43	51	45	34	65	48	71	112
15½	47	70	49	56	51	65	40	34	109
16½	51	51	50	62	58	60	.:	..	72
17½	28	48	23	55	35	53	..	..	25
18½	24	*	22	17	28	19	..	..	*

* Insufficient number of cases for computation of per cents.
** See *The Pedagogical Seminary*, June, 1927.

PLAY ACTIVITIES MOST COMMONLY PARTICIPATED IN BY NEGRO CHILDREN AND BY WHITE CHILDREN

The play activities of the Negro children were found for the most part to be similar to those of white children. Some of the results of the investigation of January, 1926, are given by race in Tables XXXIII to XLIV. The plays that were most frequently participated in are given for the boys and girls of the two races. A form of play is here included for a given age only when it was participated in by at least 20 per cent of the individuals of that age. Table XXXIII is to be read

TABLE XXXIII

RANK IN FREQUENCY OF GAMES AND OTHER PLAY ACTIVITIES MOST COMMONLY ENGAGED IN BY WHITE BOYS EIGHT TO SEVENTEEN YEARS OF AGE. JAN. 1926, KANSAS CITY, MISSOURI.

Activity		Ages									
	8	9	10	11	12	13	14	15	16	17
Looking at the Sunday "funny" paper	1	1	1	1	1	1	1	1	1	2
Reading the newspapers	10	10	5	2	2	2	1	2	2	1
Looking at daily comic strips *	7	10	4	6	2	5	3	3	3	4
Reading books	3	7	3	3	5	4	6	7	9	9
Reading or looking at magazines *	9	4	11	7	6	6	5	6	4	5
Going to the "movies"	11	6	2	4	2	3	4	4	4	6
Chewing gum	11	5	12	9	10	7	7	8	7	13
Coasting on a sled	2	2	7	5	7	9	11	13	25	..
Riding in an auto	14	30	10	11	9	10	10	5	6	3
Helping somebody with his work *	17	11	6	8	12	9	10	11	10	11
Reading jokes or funny sayings	14	18	15	12	8	12	12	10	11	7
Going to Sunday School (and liking it) *	6	15	8	13	15	13	18	14	19	16
Listening to the Victrola	12	16	20	14	26	26	27	20	18	..
Snowball fights	5	3	12	10	11	11	14	18	21	37
Drawing with pencil, pen, chalk, or crayon..	4	14	9	16	17	20	22	37	38	39
Reading other short stories	20	17	21	15	16	16	24	17	12	17
Whistling	18	12	16	20	25	22	19	18	23	23
Driving an auto	..	..	..	..	..	..	..	25	20	10
Playing with pet dogs	25	29	16	22	14	18	19	19	16	17
Using a hammer, saw, nails, etc., for fun...	27	23	26	21	20	17	25	27	29	27
Making something *	23	19	24	17	13	13	22	27	34	..
Looking at pictures	7	20	20	27	22	33	36	29	38	23
Wrestling	28	27	33	25	27	23	28	24	24	25
Listening to the radio	34	35	30	27	22	18	17	12	13	8
Just running and romping	14	7	14	20	19	25	46	..	..	..
Listening to stories	18	28	32	37	34	35	41	39	..	..
Boxing	31	39	53	32	40	35	36	42	40	33
Just singing	21	25	33	30	36	42	34	44	..	..
Watching athletic sports	38	51	77	38	20	23	7	15	14	12
Doing calisthenics	22	32	40	53	53	58	..	..	..	..
Writing letters	35	34	42	58	34	39	40	44	33	33
Going to church or to mass *	38	45	61	69	53	49	..	31	42	22
Having "dates"	..	..	..	..	..	..	..	47	24	37
Fixing or repairing something	51	67	43	44	55	41	30	30	32	39
Basket ball	61	66	45	38	22	15	12	8	8	14
Attending the theater *	69	56	64	18	29	20	15	16	15	21

* Activities thus marked were not included in the Play Quiz list prior to Nov. 1925.

as follows: "Looking at the Sunday 'funny' paper," is the one activity in the entire list of 200 items that was most generally engaged in by the boys from eight to sixteen years of age. "Reading books" was third in frequency for the boys eight, ten and eleven years of age, fourth in frequency for the boys thirteen years of age, and still lower in rank for the boys from fourteen to seventeen years of age. A blank space in the table indicates that the particular activity was engaged in by less than 20 per cent of the pupils of the given age. Tables XXXVII to XLIV indicate the games and other play activities which were liked best by the subjects and to which the subjects thought they

TABLE XXXIV

RANK IN FREQUENCY OF GAMES AND OTHER PLAY ACTIVITIES MOST COMMONLY ENGAGED IN BY NEGRO BOYS EIGHT TO FIFTEEN YEARS OF AGE. JAN. 1926. KANSAS CITY, MISSOURI.

Activity	Ages							
	8	9	10	11	12	13	14	15
Looking at the Sunday "funny" paper	1	1	1	1	1	1	1	1
Reading the newspapers	5	3	5	2	2	3	2	2
Going to the "movies"	7	14	7	4	3	1	3	3
Going to Sunday School (and liking it.) * ..	3	4	2	3	3	5	5	6
Reading or looking at magazines *	8	8	8	8	5	7	5	4
Helping somebody with his work *	8	5	2	7	8	9	9	8
Chewing gum	8	10	9	9	9	8	4	8
Reading books	2	2	3	5	6	6	11	12
Coasting on a sled	25	14	2	6	7	4	5	8
Boxing	13	21	16	20	11	12	8	12
Looking at pictures	13	18	15	19	13	18	19	5
Wrestling	24	29	29	16	9	11	13	5
Whistling	4	6	14	12	12	13	19	20
Drawing with pen, pencil, chalk, or crayon..	12	8	9	13	16	27	34	25
Looking at daily comic strips *	13	19	18	14	22	16	16	16
Reading jokes or funny sayings	29	19	25	20	13	18	11	16
Listening to the Victrola	18	14	12	22	21	22	13	23
Playing with pet dogs	23	32	16	30	16	9	22	16
Writing letters	25	32	45	33	37	30	16	29
Making something *	32	28	38	22	27	28	24	32
Reading other short stories	18	7	18	10	18	15	24	36
Going to church or to mass *	32	26	24	14	23	22	37	28
Using a hammer, saw, nails, etc., for fun	32	26	18	25	19	22	32	16
Just running and romping	8	12	14	11	27	16	38	32
Listening to stories	18	11	21	16	13	28	16	25
Snowball fights	25	22	9	26	20	14	21	41
Riding in an auto	49	51	31	30	23	21	16	20
Just singing	18	24	35	35	37	44	44	29
Attending the theater	104	54	43	50	33	18	8	14
Basket ball	..	..	..	..	53	41	28	23
Listening to the radio	29	54	34	36	49	36	32	25
Doing calisthenics	45	24	21	36	51	46	..	..
Fixing or repairing something *	86	60	56	50	53	48	40	41
Watching athletic sports	86	..	62	..	..	58	47	29
Driving an auto	..	..	..	..	..	..	..	..

* Activities thus marked were not included in the Play Quiz list prior to Nov. 1925.

had given the most time. On the whole, the activities liked best by the boys and girls of both races tend to be those most frequently engaged in and also those to which the greatest amount of time was devoted.

TABLE XXXV

Rank in Frequency of Games and Other Play Activities Most Commonly Engaged in by White Girls Eight to Seventeen Years of Age. Jan. 1926. Kansas City, Missouri.

Activity	8	9	10	11	12	13	14	15	16	17
Looking at the Sunday "funny" paper	1	1	1	1	1	1	1	1	1	1
Reading the newspapers....................	16	9	7	2	2	2	2	2	2	2
Reading books	3	2	2	4	3	3	9	9	12	11
Looking at daily comic strips *	5	6	5	9	4	4	5	4	3	5
Helping somebody with his work *	6	4	4	5	6	7	4	9	6	5
Going to Sunday School (and liking it) * ..	9	7	6	12	6	11	10	6	9	3
Reading or looking at magazines *	10	10	9	3	8	5	6	3	3	9
Going to the "movies"	16	7	3	5	4	6	3	5	7	16
Drawing with pencil, pen, chalk, or crayon..	2	3	7	9	13	16	23	28	33	31
Dolls, doll carriages, doll clothes, etc.	3	4	11	19	23	..	..	..	..	..
Reading jokes or funny sayings	22	15	16	7	9	9	8	6	7	10
Riding in an auto	23	19	13	17	13	13	11	9	5	3
Chewing gum	14	16	10	8	11	10	11	13	16	18
Listening to the Victrola	14	17	12	12	13	13	13	16	13	14
Reading other short stories	7	11	13	16	12	18	16	18	26	5
Looking at pictures	11	13	17	14	20	25	19	29	28	18
Just singing	13	17	13	11	10	12	13	15	27	23
Writing letters	12	24	22	21	19	15	13	8	11	8
Making something *	17	22	22	33	26	30	24	23	24	14
Just running and romping	19	14	19	19	26	48	39	..	..	..
Playing house	8	11	18	29	34	..	..	..	..	..
Playing school	18	36	28	34	..	..	..	..	..	..
Having "dates"	..	..	..	..	..	..	..	32	19	21
Snowball fights	30	31	31	27	21	19	27	38	..	..
Listening to the radio	38	32	33	32	30	23	25	22	16	21
Listening to stories	34	20	26	23	39	38	49	..	..	32
Cutting paper things with a scissors	23	29	26	26	44	38	37	..	..	..
Doing calisthenics	19	26	32	53	46	45	..	..	..	..
Playing with pet dogs	36	41	33	37	30	25	32	34	36	35
Telling stories	43	36	39	37	36	..	..	..	..	38
Whistling	44	45	44	46	..	..	48	..	..	35
Going to church or to mass *	51	53	54	45	40	36	39	17	22	16
Teasing somebody	..	57	42	40	25	27	18	20	21	18
Sewing, knitting, crocheting, etc., for fun ..	49	45	30	24	26	22	21	35	30	26
Watching athletic sports	70	..	..	61	48	36	38	21	18	25

* Activities thus marked were not included in the Play Quiz list prior to Nov. 1925.

TABLE XXXVI

RANK IN FREQUENCY OF GAMES AND OTHER PLAY ACTIVITIES MOST COMMONLY ENGAGED IN BY NEGRO GIRLS EIGHT TO FIFTEEN YEARS OF AGE. JAN. 1926. KANSAS CITY, MISSOURI.

Activity	8	9	10	11	12	13	14	15
Looking at the Sunday "funny" paper	1	1	1	1	1	1	1	1
Reading the newspapers	11	4	2	2	2	2	2	2
Reading or looking at magazines	3	3	7	5	4	8	5	3
Going to Sunday School (and liking it) * ..	4	3	5	5	6	2	4	7
Reading books	19	2	2	3	3	7	8	5
Going to the "movies"	31	9	14	8	8	2	3	3
Helping somebody with his work *	10	7	4	7	5	5	5	5
Chewing gum	14	7	6	4	6	6	5	10
Reading other short stories	17	11	10	10	12	13	17	10
Listening to stories	2	4	11	22	18	21	24	20
Writing letters	17	24	21	12	10	10	9	6
Listening to the Victrola	7	11	9	15	15	12	9	12
Looking at pictures	8	19	20	12	13	9	19	18
Just singing	14	15	14	20	17	16	25	12
Reading jokes or funny sayings	40	26	21	9	9	11	11	9
Drawing with pencil, pen, chalk, or crayon..	11	10	18	12	12	17	36	31
Making something *	20	27	26	22	22	22	25	28
Teasing somebody	30	29	28	26	15	13	12	20
Cutting paper things with a scissors	11	15	19	17	24	29	..	34
Dolls, doll carriages, doll clothes, etc.	6	15	8	15	25	38	..	..
Playing house	9	11	14	24	38	41	..	..
Telling stories	19	15	24	30	20	29	40	20
Looking at daily comic strips	23	24	11	11	14	17	15	28
Having "dates"	..	..	..	..	..	..	32	25
Playing school	4	22	23	20	29	29	38	48
Just running and romping	14	14	25	29	28	25	..	48
Listening to the radio	35	47	33	27	33	28	30	44
Doing calisthenics	20	22	29	35	41	43	..	37
Sewing, knitting, crocheting, etc., for fun ...	48	38	29	31	26	20	18	17
Playing with pet dogs	41	50	31	33	27	25	25	31
Going to church or to mass *	50	28	26	24	19	15	14	12
Watching athletic sports	..	..	..	..	..	..	..	40
Riding in an auto	70	61	36	32	31	32	22	16
Whistling	36	50	62	46	50	..	..	..
Snowball fights	71	54	42	35	32	45	32	50
Fixing or repairing something	..	..	..	..	..	..	..	..

* Activities thus marked were not included in the Play Quiz list prior to Nov. 1925.

TABLE XXXVII

RANK IN FREQUENCY OF GAMES AND OTHER PLAY ACTIVITIES LIKED BEST BY WHITE BOYS EIGHT TO SEVENTEEN YEARS OF AGE. JAN. 1926. KANSAS CITY, MISSOURI.

Activity	8	9	10	11	12	13	14	15	16	17
Coasting on a sled	1	1	2	1	3	4	6	2	8	12
Basket ball	15	12	9	5	4	3	1	1	1	1
Going to the "movies"	3	2	1	2	1	1	2	4	4	5
Swimming	..	..	..	..	5	4	5	2	2	..
Snowball fights	5	12	4	6	6	12	8	..	..	..
Boxing	2	3	4	3	8	6	..	12	11	9
Reading books	4	14	11	3	2	2	4	5	3	2
Looking at the Sunday "funny" paper	6	3	3	7	7	15	10	9	..	..
Playing cowboy	7	6	7	12	..	..	..	..	..	..
Going to Sunday School (and liking it) *	7	6	12	12	..	..	..	..	15	..
Wrestling	9	8	12	7	..	7	..	..	12	..
Football	10	5	11	11	9	10	..	10	6	15
Driving an auto	..	..	..	..	..	15	10	5	5	3
Having "dates"	..	..	..	..	..	..	..	5	6	7
Listening to the radio	..	..	..	..	..	..	8	13	..	9
Ice-skating	..	14	14	7	11	..	7	10	10	12
Watching athletic sports	..	..	..	..	..	..	..	3	8	12	16
Hunting	..	..	..	..	..	..	10	10	15	7
Playing with pet dogs	11	..	..	12	13	12	..	16	..	..
Checkers	15	10	..	..	..	..	..	..	..	..
Social dancing	..	..	..	..	..	..	..	..	15	5
Attending the theater	..	..	..	..	..	..	..	..	15	12
Making or assembling a radio or other electrical apparatus	..	..	..	..	..	..	..	..	16	14	4
Using a hammer, saw, nails, etc., for fun	..	..	..	..	13	8	..	..	..	..

* Activities thus marked were not included in the Play Quiz list prior to Nov. 1925.

TABLE XXXVIII

RANK IN FREQUENCY OF GAMES AND OTHER PLAY ACTIVITIES LIKED BEST BY NEGRO BOYS EIGHT TO FIFTEEN YEARS OF AGE. JAN. 1926. KANSAS CITY, MISSOURI.

Activity	8	9	10	11	12	13	14	15
Going to the "movies"	5	2	2	3	3	1	1	1
Coasting on a sled	5	1	1	1	1	2	3	10
Going to Sunday school (and liking it) *...	7	2	6	4	2	5	3	..
Playing cowboy	1	2	3	4	9	..	..	..
Boxing	3	6	3	7	3	4	5	8
Football	4	..	3	7	3	4	10	5
Sleigh-riding	2	9	7	9	12	13	10	14
Wrestling	7	..	10	11	3	8	11	3
Riding in an auto	7	6	..	4	14	9	5	10
Looking at the Sunday "funny" paper	12	5	10	13	8	9	11	8
Going to church or to mass	..	10	14	..	14	13	17	5
Riding a bicycle	..	13	9	9	14	7	5	14
Basket ball	..	..	..	12	6	6	2	2
Coasting on a wagon	7	10	8	7	..	..	..	..
Reading books	..	..	..	13	..	11	11	..
Ice-skating	13	..	14	..	9	13	4	5
Baseball with a hard ball	7	..	10	13	..	..	..	..
Driving an auto	..	..	..	..	..	9	11	10
Watching athletic sports	..	..	..	..	..	..	..	13
Playing Indian	7	6	..	..	..	..	..	..
Snowball fights	13	..	..	..	..	..	..	..

* Activities thus marked were not included in the Play Quiz list prior to Nov. 1925.

TABLE XXXIX

RANK IN FREQUENCY OF GAMES AND OTHER PLAY ACTIVITIES LIKED BEST BY WHITE GIRLS EIGHT TO SEVENTEEN YEARS OF AGE. JAN. 1926. KANSAS CITY, MISSOURI.

Activity	Ages									
	8	9	10	11	12	13	14	15	16	17
Dolls, doll carriages, doll clothes, etc.	1	1	3	5	..	..	..	..	..	..
Going to the "movies"	4	3	1	1	1	1	1	1	3	3
Reading books	8	10	5	4	2	2	1	2	2	1
Looking at the Sunday "funny" paper	3	4	4	3	3	12	7	..	..	16
Going to Sunday school (and liking it) *.....	6	2	2	8	4	10	9	10	7	9
Attending the theater *....................	..	..	..	11	13	6	4	6	5	4
Social dancing	..	..	..	15	13	6	5	4	1	2
Playing house	8	9	6	..	..	..	..	..	..	..
Playing the piano (for fun)	..	8	10	5	10	9	6	6	7	4
Watching athletic sports	..	..	..	..	..	..	..	9	4	4
Playing school	5	..	..	..	..	..	..	..	..	..
Helping somebody with his work *	8	5	10	2	5	11	..	..	14	..
Roller skating	7	5	9	11	..	..	..	..	..	..
Coasting on a sled	2	5	6	7	5	4	..	15	14	..
Sewing, knitting, crocheting, etc., for fun ..	..	..	6	11	12	12	11	..	..	..
Having "dates"	..	..	..	..	..	..	11	8	6	9
Social clubs, or being with the gang	..	..	..	..	..	..	11	11	10	7
Riding in an auto	16	..	13	10	..	..	..	11	..	15
Sleigh-riding	..	..	15	..	..	..	11	12	..	..
Checkers	8	13	15	..	..	..	..	..	..	..
Visiting or entertaining company	..	..	..	..	..	..	..	..	12	9
Card games, such as authors, bridge, whist..	18	..	..	14	..	15	..	14	..	..
Listening to the radio	..	..	..	..	..	8	..	..	14	9
Going to church or to mass	..	..	..	..	..	..	17	..	14	9

* Activities thus marked were not included in the Play Quiz list prior to Nov. 1925.

TABLE XL

RANK IN FREQUENCY OF GAMES AND OTHER PLAY ACTIVITIES LIKED BEST BY NEGRO GIRLS EIGHT TO FIFTEEN YEARS OF AGE. JAN. 1926. KANSAS CITY, MISSOURI.

Activity	Ages							
	8	9	10	11	12	13	14	15
Going to the movies	12	3	1	2	2	1	1	1
Going to Sunday School (and liking it) * ..	2	1	2	1	1	2	1	2
Dolls, doll carriages, doll clothes	1	2	2	3	4	13	..	..
Reading books	4	..	6	8	4	3	4	3
Looking at the Sunday "funny" paper	3	8	8	6	7	5	6	..
Reading or looking at magazines	..	..	..	..	..	..	6	6
Social dancing	..	..	..	..	..	..	..	3
Card games, such as authors, bridge, whist.	..	..	..	..	7	..	6	9
Playing house	6	5	6	14	..	..	..	..
Helping somebody with his work *	6	4	5	6	11	11	13	15
Playing school	5	9	11	..	17	..	..	..
Playing the piano (for fun)	12	7	4	8	3	4	3	10
Attending the theater	..	..	..	..	14	13	4	5
Roller skating	..	10	5	11	4	7	..	..
Sewing, knitting, crocheting, etc., for fun	..	..	..	5	11	6	10	6
Riding in an auto	..	..	8	14	..	7	10	6
Going to church or to mass *	..	..	13	10	6	7	8	9
Coasting on a sled	6	..	10	10	14	..	..	..
Sleigh-riding	6	..	14	12	7	..	..	..
Checkers	..	..	14	13	14	13	..	9
Listening to the Victrola	..	..	..	..	..	13	15	9
Listening to the radio	..	..	..	14	..	11	..	15

* Activities thus marked were not included in the Play Quiz list prior to Nov. 1925.

TABLE XLI

RANK IN FREQUENCY OF GAMES AND OTHER PLAY ACTIVITIES TO WHICH WHITE BOYS OF AGES EIGHT TO SEVENTEEN GAVE THE LARGEST AMOUNT OF TIME. JAN. 1926. KANSAS CITY, MISSOURI.

Activity	8	9	10	11	12	13	14	15	16	17
Reading books	..	3	5	1	1	1	1	1	1	1
Coasting on a sled	1	1	2	2	2	2	2	5	4	9
Going to the "movies"	1	2	..	3	3	2	2	5	4	9
Helping somebody with his work *	..	..	2	..	5	..	7	..	4	7
Boxing	3	5	..	4	..	4	..	..	..	..
Basket ball	..	7	..	..	..	..	3	3	2	5
Using a hammer, saw, nails, etc., for fun	..	5	..	..	..	..	7	5	..	9
Driving an auto	..	..	..	..	..	..	..	5	3	3
Making or assembling a radio or other electrical apparatus	..	..	..	..	..	4	..	..	4	2
Playing cowboy	3	..	4	..	..	..	..	..	..	..
Toy trains, ships, autos, wagons, etc.	3	7	..	..	..	..	..	..	..	..
Building snow men, snow forts, snow houses	..	..	1	5	..	..	..	..	..	..
Having "dates"	..	..	..	..	..	..	..	..	..	4
Playing other musical instruments than the piano	..	..	..	..	..	..	..	..	..	4

* Activities thus marked were not included in the Play Quiz list prior to Nov. 1925.

TABLE XLII

RANK IN FREQUENCY OF GAMES AND OTHER PLAY ACTIVITIES TO WHICH THE NEGRO BOYS OF AGES EIGHT TO FIFTEEN GAVE THE LARGEST AMOUNT OF TIME. JAN. 1926. KANSAS CITY, MISSOURI.

Activity	8	9	10	11	12	13	14	15
Coasting on a sled	1	2	1	1	4	2	2	4
Playing cowbody	1	4	3	4	..	..	..	..
Helping somebody with his work *	4	1	4	2	2	2	6	2
Going to the "movies"	4	3	5	..	4	5	5	2
Basket ball	..	7	..	..	..	2	1	1
Sleigh-riding	8	4	1	3	8	..	2	4
Going to Sunday School *	..	7	..	5	1	1	..	8
Going to church or to mass *	..	..	7	..	8	..	..	8
Boxing	1	6	..	..	..	..	..	..
Reading books	..	..	..	..	4	6	6	..

* Activities thus marked were not included in the Play Quiz list prior to Nov. 1925.

TABLE XLIII

RANK IN FREQUENCY OF GAMES AND OTHER PLAY ACTIVITIES TO WHICH WHITE GIRLS OF AGES EIGHT TO SEVENTEEN GAVE THE LARGEST AMOUNT OF TIME. JAN. 1926. KANSAS CITY, MISSOURI.

Activity	8	9	10	11	12	13	14	15	16	17
Reading books	3	8	2	2	1	1	1	1	1	1
Dolls, doll carriages, doll clothes, etc.	1	1	5	..	..	..	..	..	..	..
Helping somebody with his work *	1	3	4	1	2	3	3	4	3	3
Going to the "movies"	8	2	1	3	4	2	2	5	9	..
Playing the piano (for fun)	5	4	5	4	6	..	8	2	9	..
Coasting on a sled	4	..	8	6	5	..	..	..	..	..
Visiting or entertaining company	..	..	8	..	8	8	6	5	5	2
Sewing, knitting, crocheting, etc., for fun	..	..	5	6	6	4	7	..	..	..
Having "dates"	..	..	..	..	..	..	..	3	2	..
Making something *	..	..	..	..	..	..	8	..	5	4
Going to Sunday School *	5	6	..	..	..	..	..	..	..	..
Playing house	8	6	..	..	..	..	..	..	..	..

* Activities thus marked were not included in the Play Quiz list prior to Nov. 1925.

TABLE XLIV

RANK IN FREQUENCY OF GAMES AND OTHER PLAY ACTIVITIES TO WHICH NEGRO GIRLS OF AGES EIGHT TO FIFTEEN GAVE THE LARGEST AMOUNT OF TIME. JAN. 1926. KANSAS CITY, MISSOURI.

Activity	8	9	10	11	12	13	14	15
Reading books	2	..	5	3	1	1	1	2
Playing the piano (for fun)	1	..	4	5	3	3	4	8
Helping somebody with his work *	2	1	2	1	3	7	6	..
Going to the "movies"	4	3	8	4	2	2	1	6
Going to Sunday School *	..	5	5	8	6	5	3	8
Dolls, doll carriages, doll clothes, etc.	4	2	1	1	5	..	..	..
Sewing, knitting, crocheting, etc., for fun	..	..	..	6	8	5	6	1
Coasting on a sled	..	5	5	8	8	..	..	..
Going to church or to mass *	..	4	..	8	6	..	10	..
Visiting or entertaining company	..	..	..	8	..	3	10	..

* Activities thus marked were not included in the Play Quiz list prior to Nov. 1925.

RACE DIFFERENCES IN PARTICIPATION IN GROUP ACTIVITIES *

In addition to indicating those activities in which they had engaged during the preceding week, the children were asked to mark the activities in which they had participated *alone*.

For each child the total number of play activities engaged in during the preceding week was ascertained. The number participated in with one or more additional children was next determined. The percentage of the total activities that the social activities represented was

* See *The Journal of Applied Psychology*, Dec., 1926.

designated the index of social participation. Thus, an index of social participation of 80 indicates that 80 per cent of the activities engaged in by the child were ones in which one or more additional children took part. By this method of reckoning a high index of social participation signifies that the child is relatively social in his play behavior. Conversely, a lower index of social participation means that the child is relatively solitary in his play.

Figure 23 and Table XLV show the mean indices of social participation for the four groups of children. It will be noted from Table XLV that the Negro children are distinctly more social in their play than either of the white groups.

Table XLVI shows the percentages of Negro children whose indices of social participation reach or exceed the median of the white children of corresponding chronological ages. In Table XLVI comparison is made of two groups only, namely, the Negro children of Kansas City, Missouri, and the white children of the same city.

Particularly salient is the fact that in every age interval (8½ to 15½) Negro children are more social in their play than white children. The differences are *marked* and *consistent* from year to year. From the data it is apparent that a conspicuous difference exists between the races in the extent to which sociability is manifested.

TABLE XLV

MEAN INDICES OF SOCIAL PARTICIPATION FOR EACH OF FOUR GROUPS OF CHILDREN.

C. A.	Negro Children Tulsa, Ok.	Negro Children Kansas City Missouri	White Children Kansas City Missouri	White Children Rural (Kansas)
8½	*..	68.4	61.8	59.3
9½	*..	67.4	60.6	59.9
10½	68.3	65.5	58.9	55.1
11½	65.3	64.5	56.1	55.9
12½	62.4	63.0	53.7	54.4
13½	60.5	61.9	54.4	55.5
14½	60.2	59.0	52.1	52.5
15½	54.8	59.5	51.4	*..

* Data lacking.

TABLE XLVI

PERCENTAGES OF NEGRO CHILDREN WHOSE INDICES OF SOCIAL PARTICIPATION REACH OR EXCEED THE MEDIANS OF WHITE CHILDREN AT EACH AGE LEVEL.

C. A.	8½	9½	10½	11½	12½	13½	14½	15½
	68%	63%	61%	67%	68%	63%	65%	64%

Index of Social
Participation

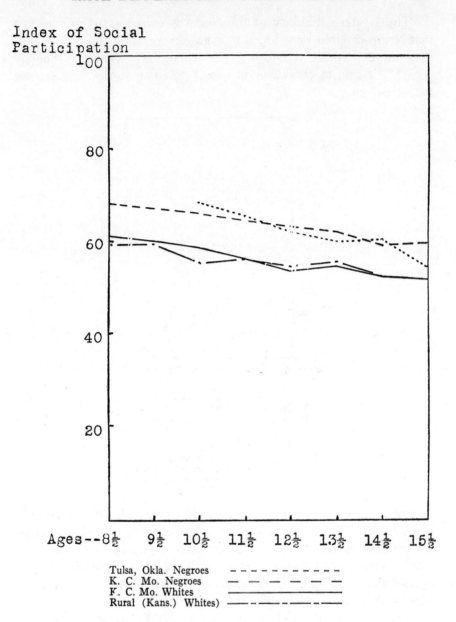

Ages--8½   9½   10½   11½   12½   13½   14½   15½

Tulsa, Okla. Negroes	– – – – – – – – – –
K. C. Mo. Negroes	– – – – – – – –
F. C. Mo. Whites	————————
Rural (Kans.) Whites)	—– —–— —– —

FIGURE 23

Relationship between C.A. and the Index of Social Participation. Racial differences in
the Index of Social Participation also shown. See Table XLV, p. 142.

The greater sociability of the Negro is corroborated by the fact that Negro children were found to engage more often than white children in such social activities as the following: "Going to Sunday school," "Going to church or to mass," "Telling stories," "Listening to stories," etc.

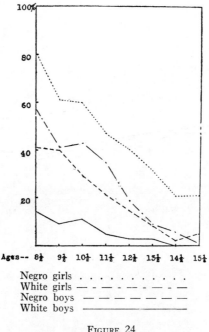

FIGURE 24

Percentages of Negro children versus white children who engaged in playing school during the course of one week. See Table XLVII, p. 146.

Speculation regarding the Negro child's relatively great sociability is interesting. There appears to be no means of ascertaining whether the extreme socialibility of the Negro child is a cause or a result of other racial characteristics. How much social participation is consonant with well-balanced development is unknown. It is entirely possible that over-participation in social activities may result in neglect of certain individual activities essential to well-balanced development. It is therefore impossible to say whether the Negro child's excessive sociability is a handicap or an asset.

In a later chapter it will be shown that children retarded in school progress are considerably more social in their play behavior than are children who make normal progress in school (p. 203 ff). It will be shown further that gifted children (I. Q. 140 or above) are less social than are unselected children (p. 211 ff). In an unpublished Master's thesis in which a study was made of two groups of Negro children, one group consisting of children having high indices of social participation, the other consisting of children having very low indices of social participation, it was found that the solitary group was superior to the extremely social group in scholarship.[4]

These data indicate that an exceedingly high index of social participation is likely to coexist with inferior scholarship. Whether much social participation posits also "freedom from tension" and "ease of bearing in social situations" is a matter of speculation.

Hollingworth asks, "What does quantitative psychology teach with respect to the combination of performances in a given personality?"[5] She concludes, "It will be seen that there is no law of compensation in human ability, however much we may long to find it there."

Again Hollingworth states: "There is found to be a quality of the individual which results in general superior, mediocre, or inferior performance in his case a *positive coherence in the amounts of all traits possessed* extending even to appreciable coherence between mental and physical."[6] (Italics ours.)

It seems reasonable to conclude from the data presented in this chapter that decision in reference to compensation or correlation of desirable traits must be reserved until definitions of "desirable and undesirable" have been formulated and agreed upon.

RELATIVE EXTENT TO WHICH NEGRO AND WHITE CHILDREN ENGAGE IN "PLAYING SCHOOL" *

Table XLVII and Figure 24 show the percentages of boys and girls of each race who engaged in "Playing school," during the course of one week preceding the investigation of January, 1926. As the results of this investigation corroborate the earlier findings, data are presented only for the study of January, 1926. The following facts are revealed: (a) Girls of both races engage in this activity much more

* See *Psychological Review* for Nov. 1926.

frequently than boys; (b) Negro children participate in playing school more frequently at all ages than white children; (c) Both race groups participate less often in this activity as chronological age increases.

Witty and Decker found that Negro children were educationally retarded in all subjects at all ages when comparisons were made with the educational achievement of white children.[7]   As Negro children are conspicuously unsuccessful in academic behavior, it seems paradoxical that they should play school more frequently than their more successful classmates.   One would naturally expect the Negro to turn during his leisure hours to activities in which he can best succeed and to avoid those for which he manifests restricted ability.   What explanation is there for the relatively great frequency with which Negro children relive school activities by playing school?   The following is offered as a likely hypothesis in this regard.

TABLE XLVII

PERCENTAGES OF WHITE AND OF NEGRO BOYS AND GIRLS WHO INDICATED THAT THEY HAD BEEN "PLAYING SCHOOL" DURING THE COURSE OF ONE WEEK. JAN., 1926.

Ages	Negro Girls	White Girls	Negro Boys	White Boys
8½	81	57	41	13
9½	61	41	40	9
10½	60	43	29	11
11½	47	35	21	5
12½	41	19	15	3
13½	32	9	8	3
14½	21	6	2	0
15½	21	1	5	0

Probably none would deny that the Negro is cognizant of his inferior social status.   Negro children doubtless are aware of their lack of social and intellectual prestige from very early ages.   The writers suggest that Negro children engage in playing school more commonly than white children because this activity symbolizes to them knowledge, power, and prestige, which they are unable to achieve in the world of actuality.   This form of make-believe play may be a compensatory activity.

Various writers have emphasized the compensatory nature of the day-dream or fantasy.   Robinson insists that conscious shamming or make-believe play is essentially a compensatory mechanism having the same origin and impetus as the day-dream or fantasy.[8] Every normal child must play because childhood is primarily a period of incomplete adjustment.

"The child is driven by many inherited and acquired impulses, some of which are adequately and easily expressed, and some of which find no direct outlet. These latter create a situation demanding compensation, and this compensation is as a rule secured through make-believe activities. Most common among such activities are play and fantasy. A child would fight, hunt, and make a home as particular stimuli arouse him. He is seldom in such an environment, however, and he is practically never so organized by inheritance or training that these undertakings can be fully carried out. There are inexhaustible inhibitors around him and within him which check free expression. And so he plays at, or has day-dreams of fighting, hunting, and home-making. I have no desire at this time to say which of the unsatisfied impulses of childhood are inherited and which acquired; but, however they arise, we find that they are many and urgent, and consequently that every normal child must find compensation for their inhibition." [9]

Full of impulses to do actual things, the child is equipped with a physique and surrounded by an environment which are constant obstacles to success. In such cases we are apt to have a mimicry of feats of strength and daring. The satisfactoriness of the resultant make-believe play is sometimes increased by muscular overt accompaniments. Robinson illustrates this fact by drawing upon his own boyhood experience:

"As a child I was full of baseball fantasies. Although I played baseball a great deal, these games did not satisfy certain standards set up by reading athletic stories and watching older and more skillful players. But the fantasies, too, often became unsatisfactory on account of their intangibility. As a result I formed the habit of laying out a diamond upon the lawn and there, without ball or playmates, carrying out the overt movements of an heroic baseball performance. Many a time, I pitched nine long innings to baffled athletes who swung immaterial bats at my imaginary curves. Here was fantasy improved and made realistic by the actuality of its muscular accompaniments." [10]

Common observations make evident the fact that fantasy is sometimes improved and made more realistic by the presence of playmates.

Reaney holds that organized group games may have a compensatory function.[11]

The compensatory function of make-believe play is not ordinarily evident to the performer. Consciousness of inferiority is the very thing that the performer seeks to avoid. Success crowns the individual's efforts only when he forgets the unpleasant actuality which has given rise to the compensatory activity.

It is probable that Negro children play school as a compensatory mechanism. How then is one to explain the fact that boys engage less frequently than girls in this activity?

It has been shown that girls' play does not extend over so wide a geographical radius as boys' play. Girls are not permitted to roam as far from home at the earlier ages as are boys. Girls must adjust their play activity to the indoor situation in which they find themselves. The differences between the sexes in native equipment plus the environmental restrictions to which girls are subjected offer a plausible explanation of the sex difference revealed in this regard.

With increased maturity both sexes and both races engage less frequently in playing school. This may be due to the fact that the satisfaction which is derived from compensatory behavior is dependent upon the extent to which the activity is reconcilable with the child's own credulity. It is likely further that increase in chronological age brings progressively greater opportunity to participate in diverse plays and games, some of which are intrinsically more satisfying than playing school. This would account in part for the decrease in participation in this activity with increase of maturity.

CHURCH AND SUNDAY SCHOOL ATTENDANCE OF NEGRO CHILDREN *

Table XLVIII shows the percentages of boys and girls of each race who went to Sunday school (and liked it) during the course of one week preceding the investigation of January, 1926.

Data are presented separately for the sexes in Figures 25 and 26. It is of interest that Negro children of both sexes exceeded white children in frequency of Sunday school attendance. It is further significant that *boys* of both races participated less frequently in this

* See *Journal of Religious Education* for Jan. 1927.

activity as chronological age advanced.   Girls, however, exhibited interest in this activity at all of the age levels investigated.   It is of interest further that *rural* children engaged less frequently in all the various church activities than city children.

Table XLIX presents data in reference to church attendance.   The facts presented in Figures 25 and 26 are corroborated here.   The Negro

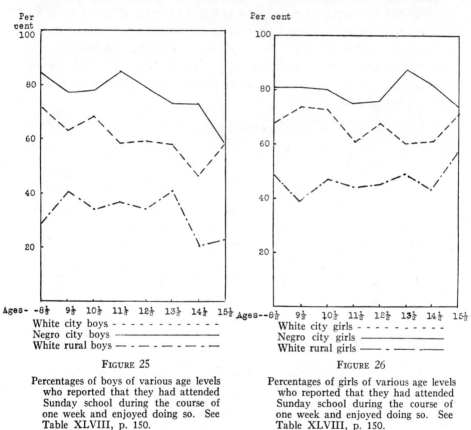

FIGURE 25

Percentages of boys of various age levels who reported that they had attended Sunday school during the course of one week and enjoyed doing so. See Table XLVIII, p. 150.

FIGURE 26

Percentages of girls of various age levels who reported that they had attended Sunday school during the course of one week and enjoyed doing so. See Table XLVIII, p. 150.

children attended church more frequently than white children.   It is of interest that all of the children attended Sunday school more frequently than church.

In addition to checking each activity that he had voluntarily engaged in during the preceding week, each child was asked to designate also his three favorites.   A large percentage of the Negro girls mentioned activity No. 44, "Going to church or to mass," as one of their three favorites. The only activities of the entire list of 200 that were as popular as "Going to church or to mass," are "Playing with dolls, doll clothes, doll carriages, etc.," and "Going to the moving-picture show." Several activities preceded "Going to church or to mass," in order of popularity among white girls. Data are presented in Table L showing the percentages of boys and girls of various age levels who mentioned "Going to church or to mass," as one of their three favorite activities. Table LI shows how this activity ranked in reference to popularity among white girls and Negro girls. It is clear that "Going to church or to mass," is much more popular among Negro girls than among white girls.

TABLE XLVIII

PERCENTAGES OF BOYS AND GIRLS OF VARIOUS AGE LEVELS WHO REPORTED THAT THEY HAD GONE TO SUNDAY SCHOOL DURING THE COURSE OF A WEEK.

Ages	Nov. 1925 (Rural)	Jan. 1926 (White)	Jan. 1926 (Negro)	Nov. 1925 (Rural)	Jan. 1926 (White)	Jan.1926 (Negro)
		Boys			Girls	
8½	29	71	84	49	68	81
9½	40	63	77	39	74	81
10½	34	68	78	47	73	80
11½	37	58	85	44	61	75
12½	34	59	79	45	68	76
13½	41	58	73	49	60	87
14½	20	46	73	43	61	82
15½	23	58	58	57	71	74

TABLE XLIX

PERCENTAGES OF BOYS AND GIRLS OF VARIOUS AGE LEVELS WHO REPORTED THAT THEY HAD GONE TO CHURCH OR TO MASS DURING THE COURSE OF ONE WEEK.

Ages	Nov. 1925 (Rural)	Jan. 1926 (White)	Jan. 1926 (Negro)	Nov. 1925 (Rural)	Jan. 1926 (White)	Jan. 1926 (Negro)
		Boys			Girls	
8½	11	33	49	31	30	32
9½	29	31	50	24	28	51
10½	18	27	53	25	24	50
11½	28	21	58	33	28	44
12½	20	28	48	23	24	54
13½	26	25	48	35	27	54
14½	12	19	31	23	24	56
15½	5	30	38	29	49	62

The popularity of an activity is well indicated by the extent to which it affects other activities. The extent to which the children studied play "Church" and "Sunday school," is presented in Tables

LII and LIII. The conspicuous fact herein presented is that *simulation* of church-going activities is more popular among Negro children than among white children.

It is perhaps needless to remind the reader that the foregoing data reveal nothing in reference to the effect of church-going activities upon Negro children's moral conduct. Odum maintains that the Negro's religion is not a religion of daily application.

"The church has been called the central point around which all Negro life revolves. It is certainly a great influence in the life of the Negroes and furnishes them with the greater part of their better life and the outlet for much of their energy. The function of the Negro church is rather to give expression and satisfaction to social and religious emotions than to direct moral conduct." [12]

In a Master's thesis, Scruggs points out that the nearest approach to unanimity of interest among Negro children in types of reading material was elicited in response to Bible stories.[13]

TABLE L

PERCENTAGES OF BOYS AND GIRLS OF VARIOUS AGE LEVELS WHO MENTION ACTIVITY
No. 44, "GOING TO CHURCH OR TO MASS," AS ONE OF THEIR THREE FAVORITE ACTIVITIES.

Ages	Nov. 1925 (Rural)	Jan. 1926 (White)	Jan. 1926 (Negro)	Nov. 1925 (Rural)	Jan. 1926 (White)	Jan. 1926 (Negro)
		Boys			Girls	
8½	0	9	8	17	10	19
9½	0	9	13	4	20	24
10½	0	6	15	8	24	24
11½	8	5	12	6	9	26
12½	3	2	21	3	14	29
13½	0	4	20	2	8	33
14½	0	4	10	0	7	31
15½	..	2	18	..	10	32

TABLE LI

HOW ACTIVITY No. 44, "GOING TO CHURCH OR TO MASS," RANKED AMONG
200 ACTIVITIES IN REFERENCE TO POPULARITY.

Ages	Rank	Rank
8½	2	6
9½	1	3
10½	1½	2
11½	1	8
12½	1	4
13½	2	10
14½	2	9½
15½	2	10

TABLE LII

PERCENTAGES OF BOYS AND GIRLS OF VARIOUS AGE LEVELS WHO REPORTED THAT THEY HAD BEEN "PLAYING CHURCH" DURING THE COURSE OF ONE WEEK.

Ages	Nov. 1925 (Rural)	Jan. 1926 (White)	Jan. 1926 (Negro)	Nov. 1925 (Rural)	Jan. 1926 (White)	Jan. 1926 (Negro)
		Boys			Girls	
8½	6	5	26	15	6	33
9½	2	2	20	18	3	39
10½	1	1	18	16	6	29
11½	3	0	12	11	6	17
12½	3	2	7	6	2	22
13½	2	2	4	7	1	9
14½	0	2	0	3	1	13
15½	1	1	3	4	0	21

TABLE LIII

PERCENTAGES OF BOYS AND GIRLS OF VARIOUS AGE LEVELS WHO REPORTED THAT THEY HAD BEEN "PLAYING SUNDAY SCHOOL" DURING THE COURSE OF ONE WEEK.

Ages	Nov. 1925 (Rural)	Jan. 1926 (White)	Jan. 1926 (Negro)	Nov. 1925 (Rural)	Jan. 1926 (White)	Jan 1926 (Negro)
		Boys			Girls	
8½	4	2	18	12	7	42
9½	3	1	12	8	7	30
10½	4	2	15	9	12	25
11½	1	0	15	3	10	18
12½	3	2	7	2	2	17
13½	1	4	4	0	2	8
14½	1	0	4	1	0	8
15½	2	0	0	0	0	21

"Among the kinds of stories chosen Bible stories first demand attention, not because of sentiment, but because more pupils evince an interest in this type of reading matter than any other type." [14]

"In expressing their best liked types of stories boys at age 9 years prefer, first, funny stories; second, Bible stories; third, bedtime stories. At age 10 years preference is shown for Bible stories first, bedtime stories second, and funny stories third. At age 11 to 14 years, inclusive, Bible stories are first, adventure second, and how to make things, third. At ages 15 and 16 years inclusive, Bible stories lead, adventure ranks second, and information, third." [15]

It is clear that Negro children and adults demonstrate conspicuous interest in religious acts.

Seashore has mentioned the fact that religious faith provides for extension of the personality. It is possible that religion to the Negro is an escape mechanism, a device by means of which he frees himself from environmental inhibitions and feeling of inferiority.

"The sense of freedom is prominent in religious life—the self-expression of the soul set free. We play when we are free; religion has always been a breaking away from the bonds and cares of this world. . . . We play when we are in need of recreation; religion is not only a haven of rest but a fountain for the renewal of life's energies. The freedom which in ordinary life comes from a sense of freedom in movement is limited in comparison with that freedom which comes to the devout in taking hold of the Infinite by faith." [16]

"The feeling of extension of personality finds its fullest expression in the religious attitude. . . . Faith is power; in a very real sense we are what we believe ourselves to be." [17]

The writers make no pretense of being able to "explain" in any ultimate or final sense, the Negro's interest in religious activities. It seems reasonable to suppose, however, that the church and the Sunday school give expression and satisfaction to the Negro's social and religious emotions. It may be that the Negro's relatively inferior status (social, intellectual, educational, and economic) produces in him a felt need for extension of his personality. It may be that in some instances the Negro's religion is a compensatory mechanism having the same origin and impetus as the day-dream or fantasy.

RACE DIFFERENCES IN REFERENCE TO "BOXING"

Thus far, the writers have emphasized race differences in frequency of participation in certain activities primarily social in nature. The greater sociability of the Negro seems to be verified by these findings.

There are racial differences in activities not markedly *social in nature* that merit attention. Conspicuous among these activities is "Boxing."

Table LIV and Figure 27 present, for the first three of the studies that were made, the percentages of Negro boys and the percentages of white boys that participated in "Boxing." It will be noted that the curves for the Negro boys are distinctly above those of the white boys in each of the three investigations. This difference was found likewise to exist in the subsequent investigation of January, 1926. Figure 28 presents averages for the several investigations.

Is the Negro boys' excessive indulgence in "Boxing" a compensatory device? It is obvious that in "Boxing" one attempts to

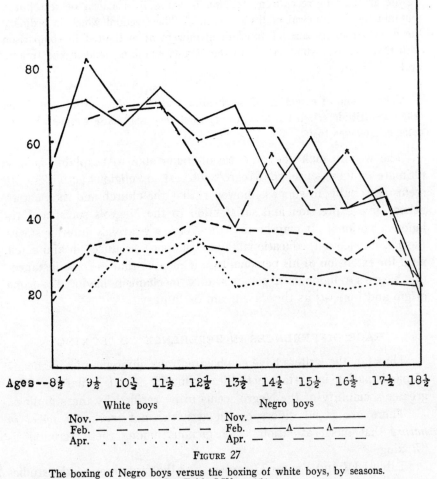

FIGURE 27

The boxing of Negro boys versus the boxing of white boys, by seasons.
See Table LIV, p. 156.

reveal physical superiority. Moreover, physical prowess and success in "Boxing" are at once apparent and unmistakable. The fact has been mentioned that the Negro is inferior to the white in numerous ways; intellectually, educationally, socially, and economically.* He does not appear, however, to be physically inferior to the white man.

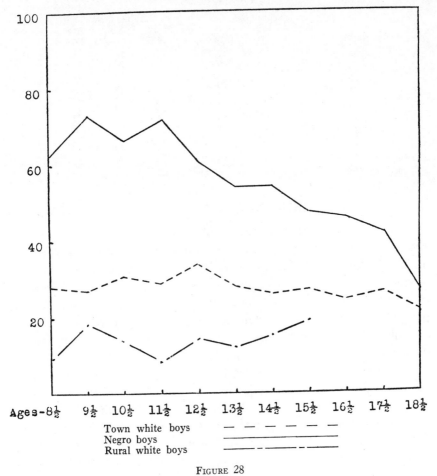

| Ages-8½ | 9½ | 10½ | 11½ | 12½ | 13½ | 14½ | 15½ | 16½ | 17½ | 18½ |

Town white boys   — — — — — —
Negro boys
Rural white boys   ——— - ——— - —

FIGURE 28

The boxing of Negro boys versus the boxing of white boys. Average of results obtained from three separate investigations of town children and one study of rural children. See Table LIV, p. 156.

It may be, therefore, that this activity affords the Negro an opportunity of equality in competition that is denied him in other realms.

* It is of course possible that certain of these race differences may be due to environmental rather than to hereditary differences. However, to b˙ treated as an inferior is in itself sufficient to produce attempts on the part of the Negro to compensate.

TABLE LIV

PERCENTAGES OF NEGRO BOYS AND WHITE BOYS WHO INDICATED THAT THEY HAD PAR-
TICIPATED IN "BOXING" DURING THE COURSE OF ONE WEEK PRECEDING
A GIVEN INVESTIGATION.

| | Negro boys | | | White boys | | |
| | Nov. | Feb. | Apr. | Nov. | Feb. | Apr. |
Ages	1923	1924	1924	1923	1924	1924
8½	69	53	*	25	18	*
9½	71	82	66	30	32	20
10½	64	68	69	28	34	32
11½	74	69	70	26	34	30
12½	65	60	54	32	39	34
13½	69	63	37	30	37	21
14½	46	63	56	24	36	23
15½	55	45	41	23	35	22
16½	41	56	41	25	28	20
17½	44	39	46	21	35	21
18½	20	41	18	20	22	22

* Insufficient data for the computation of percentages.

THE NEGRO CHILD'S INTEREST IN WRITING POETRY

Table LV shows the percentages of Negro and white boys and girls who indicated that they had written poems during the week preceding the administration of the Quiz. Marked seasonal differences are not revealed in these data. This fact is best shown by the data obtained from the investigations of Nov., 1923, Feb., 1924, and Apr., 1924, these three investigations having been made among identical groups of children. The similarity of the results obtained from each race in the three investigations is striking.

Sex differences were found to be relatively slight, the girls writing poems only slightly more frequently than the boys of the same ages. This tendency was consistent in each of the three studies.

The data presented in Table LV show further that the older individuals included in the study wrote poems less often than the younger ones. The transition from age to age is, however, gradual.

The Negro children wrote poems much more commonly than the white children during *each* season of the year and at *all age levels*. The difference is clearly revealed in Figure 29, and in Table LVI which present the composite results obtained from the several investigations.

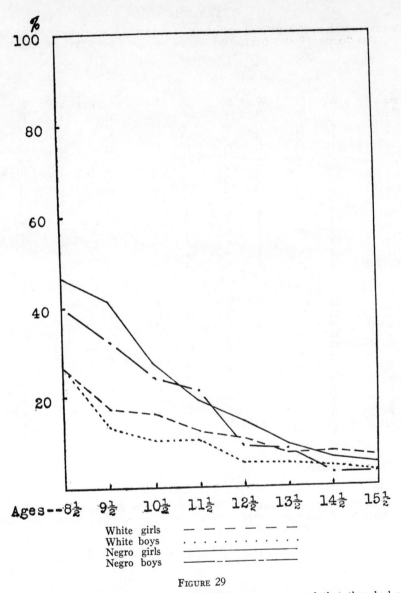

FIGURE 29

Percentages of white children and of Negro children who reported that they had engaged in "Writing Poems" during the course of one week.   Composite results of
four different studies of play behavior.   See Table LV, p. 158.

TABLE LV

PERCENTAGES OF BOYS AND GIRLS OF VARIOUS AGE LEVELS WHO INDICATED THAT THEY HAD WRITTEN POEMS DURING THE COURSE OF ONE WEEK "JUST FOR FUN."

Boys

Ages	Nov. 1923 W.	Nov. 1923 N.	Feb. 1924 W.	Feb. 1924 N.	Apr. 1924 W.	Apr. 1924 N.	Nov. 1924 (Rural) (White)	Nov. 1925 (Rural) (White)	Jan. 1926 W.	Jan. 1926 N.
8½	27	61	34	56	*	*	11	6	19	33
9½	20	45	12	46	9	11	14	13	8	33
10½	11	25	7	30	10	22	20	9	14	21
11½	12	41	11	11	12	12	12	18	9	20
12½	4	5	4	5	4	5	21	6	9	15
13½	4	9	5	4	3	3	9	5	10	16
14½	6	0	5	8	3	0	6	4	2	2
15½	2	3	5	4	3	0	13	9	1	3
16½	2	*	4	*	2	*	*	*	2	*
17½	3	*	4	*	3	*	*	*	*	*
18½	3	*	2	*	2	*	*	*	*	*
19½	3	*	5	*	1	*	*	*	*	*
20½	2	*	1	*	3	*	*	*	*	*
21½	6	*	4	*	4	*	*	*	*	*
22 and up	3	*	8	*	4	*	*	*	*	*

Girls

Ages	Nov. 1923 W.	Nov. 1923 N.	Feb. 1924 W.	Feb. 1924 N.	Apr. 1924 W.	Apr. 1924 N.	Nov. 1924 (Rural) (White)	Nov. 1925 (Rural) (White)	Jan. 1926 W.	Jan. 1926 N.
8½	35	66	22	37	*	*	18	6	22	40
9½	27	42	17	59	14	23	26	20	8	39
10½	19	24	18	20	13	15	32	21	14	37
11½	14	28	11	20	9	8	28	22	13	21
12½	10	18	9	12	14	6	10	5	6	15
13½	8	2	8	17	7	6	9	7	5	11
14½	6	0	8	6	6	5	7	0	6	10
15½	6	1	8	11	5	0	7	0	4	6
16½	4	*	5	*	6	*	*	*	1	*
17½	3	*	8	*	3	*	*	*	*	*
18½	6	*	8	*	4	*	*	*	*	*
19½	2	*	6	*	2	*	*	*	*	*
20½	4	*	2	*	7	*	*	*	*	*
21½	2	*	4	*	3	*	*	*	*	*
22 and up	0	*	5	*	2	*	*	*	*	*

* No data assembled.

TABLE LVI

PERCENTAGES OF WHITE CHILDREN AND OF NEGRO CHILDREN WHO INDICATED THAT THEY HAD ENGAGED IN "WRITING POEMS" DURING THE COURSE OF ONE WEEK. COMPOSITE RESULTS OF FOUR DIFFERENT INVESTIGATIONS.

Ages	Whites Girls	Whites Boys	Negroes Girls	Negroes Boys
8½	26	26	46	40
9½	17	13	41	32
10½	16	10	27	24
11½	12	10	19	21
12½	10	5	14	9
13½	7	5	9	8
14½	7	4	6	3
15½	6	3	5	3

It is of interest to attempt to account for the racial difference revealed in the above data.

Kerlin maintains that the Negro possesses certain poetic traits by original nature. In a survey of contemporary Negro poetry in which quotations are made from sixty odd Negro writers of verse he makes the following statement:

"It comes not within the scope of this anthology to include any of these folk-rhymes of the elder day, but a few specimens seem necessary to indicate to the young Negro who would be a poet his rich heritage of song and to the white reader what essentially poetic traits the Negro has by nature." [18]

Kerlin then cites a few examples of Negro folk-rhymes of earlier times.

Jesperson holds that poetry is a more primitive mode of expression than prose and that poetry is found in every country to precede prose:

"Just as in the literature transmitted to us poetry is found in every country to precede prose, so poetic language is on the whole older than prosaic language; lyrics and cult songs come before science. . . ." [19]

The greater interest in poetry-writing demonstrated by the Negro may be due to the state of development which he exemplifies. It is, however, possible that the interest is due to the markedly emotional nature of the Negro.

"The Negro might well be expected to exhibit a gift for poetry. . . . It will readily be admitted that the Negro nature is endowed above most others, if not above all others, in fervor of feeling, in the completeness of self-surrender to emotion. Hence we see that marvelous display of rhythm in the individual and in the group." [20]

Additional evidence of the Negro's fondness for rhythm is apparent from the following facts: Negro boys engage somewhat more generally than white boys in "Playing the piano (for fun)," and both the boys and the girls participate more commonly than white children in "London Bridge," and "Other singing games."

THE NEGRO CHILD'S PLAY—A FUNCTION OF HIS ECONOMIC AND SOCIAL STATUS

Opportunity for participation is a potent factor in effecting certain differences in the play behavior of Negro and white children. Several examples will follow of activities in which Negro and white children differ conspicuously because of what appears to be inequality of opportunity.

(a) Riding in an auto

Race difference in reference to "Riding in an auto," is marked. About twice as many white girls as Negro girls were found to have ridden in an auto during the course of one week preceding the investigations. Economic conditions doubtless had much to do with the above findings in reference to riding in an auto.

(b) Making or Assembling a Radio or Other Electrical Apparatus

Negro boys were found to engage less frequently than white boys in "Making or assembling a wireless or other electrical apparatus." The economic status of the parents was probably a causal agent in effecting this difference also.

(c) Watching Athletic Sports

In general, Negro children participated in "Watching athletic sports," less often than did white children. This finding is probably due in part to the fact that Negro children are not urged to attend athletic contests to the extent that white children are. Too, they probably do not find themselves so much at home at an athletic contest as do the white children. It is usually white children who compete in athletic contests and it is only the exceptionally competent Negro who is permitted to take part.

(d) Playing Basket ball

White children were found to play basket ball more frequently than Negro children. The writers found that where equal opportunity was provided for participation in this activity (in schools for Negroes only), Negro children took part with equal or greater frequency than white children.

The four activities discussed above exemplify clearly the potency of economic or social factors in effecting racial differences in play behavior.

SUMMARY

Lack of adequate technique heretofore has militated against the measurement of the races in regard to certain traits of character. Conspicuous differences are often assumed. The present writers have developed a technique by which certain outstanding differences are demonstrated and expressed quantitatively.

Particularly salient is the fact that Negro children are more social in their play than white children. The differences are marked and consistent from year to year. About 65 per cent of the Negroes studied have indices of social participation which reach or exceed the medians of white children of various ages.

Negro children were found to participate more frequently than white children in such social activities as: "Going to Sunday school," "Going to church," "Telling stories," etc.

There appears to be no means of ascertaining whether the extreme sociability of the Negro is a cause or a result of other racial characteristics.

The writers have demonstrated that a high index of social participation is likely to coexist with inferior scholarship. It is impossible at present to say whether the Negro child's excessive sociability is a handicap or an asset. It is entirely possible that over-participation in social activities may result in neglect of certain individual activities essential to well-balanced development.

Although Negro children are relatively unsuccessful in academic endeavor, they play school more frequently than do white children. It appears likely that Negro children engage in playing school more frequently than white children because this activity symbolizes knowledge, power, and prestige which they are unable to achieve in the world of actuality. This form of play may be a compensatory activity.

It is significant that Negro children of both sexes exceed white children in frequency of Sunday school and church attendance. It seems reasonable that church and Sunday school attendance permit expression and subsequent satisfaction in the Negro of certain strong social and emotional drives. It may be that the Negro's relatively inferior status (social, intellectual, educational, and economic) produces in him a felt need for extension of his personality. It may be that the Negro's religion is a compensatory mechanism having the same origin and impetus as the day-dream or fantasy.

There are racial differences in activities not markedly social in nature that merit attention. "Boxing" is a case in point It may be that this activity affords the Negro an opportunity of equality in competition that is denied him in other realms.

Very conspicuous is the race difference in frequency of participation in writing poems. The Negro children write poems much more commonly than white children at all age levels. It is impossible to state the cause of this condition. Various writers have emphasized the excessive display of rhythm by the Negro.

Certain race differences in play behavior are obviously a function of the social and economic status of the parents. Particularly noticeable are these forces in effecting differences in such activities as:

> Riding in an auto.
> Assembling a radio.
> Watching athletic sports, and
> Playing basket ball.

REFERENCES

1. Pintner, Rudolf. *Intelligence Testing.* New York. Henry Holt and Company. 1923. Pp. v-406. (pp. 337-48.)

2. Peterson, Joseph. "The Comparative Abilities of White and Negro Children." *Comparative Psychology Monographs.* Vol. I, Serial No. 5, July, 1923. 141 pp. (p. 137 f.)

3. Pintner, Rudolf. *op. cit.* p. 345.

4. Anderson, Thelma Hill. Trait Ratings Received by Sociable and Unsociable Groups of Boys. Unpublished Master's Thesis on file in Watson Library. The University of Kansas. 1926. 93 pp.

5. Hollingworth, Leta S. *Special Talents and Defects.* New York. The Macmillan Co. 1923. Pp. xix-215. (p. 9.)

6. Hollingworth. Leta S. *op. cit.* p. 33 f.

7. Witty, Paul A. and Decker, Albert I. "Educational Attainment of Negro and White Children in the Elementary School." *Journal of Educational Psychology.* (Forthcoming article.)

8. Robinson, E. S. "The Compensatory Function of Make-Believe Play." *Psychological Review.* 1920, 27. Pp. 429-39.

9. Robinson, E. S. *op. cit.* p. 429 f.

10. Robinson, E. S. *op. cit.* p. 437.

11. Reaney, Mabel Jane. "The Psychology of the Organized Group Game." *The British Journal of Psychology. Monograph Supplements*, No. I.   Cambridge at the University Press. 1916. Quoted by Robinson, E. S. *op. cit.* p. 429.

12. Odum, Howard W. "Social and Mental Traits of the Negro." A Ph.D. dissertation printed in *Studies in History, Economics, and Public Law.* Edited by the Faculty of Political Science of Columbia University. Vol. 37, No. 3. New York; Columbia University. Longmans Green and Co. Agents. 1910. pp. 302. (p. 54.)

13. Scruggs, Sherman Dana. *Reading Interests of Negro Children.* Unpublished Master's Thesis on file in Watson Library. The University of Kansas. 1925.   62 pp.

14. Scruggs, Sherman Dana. *op. cit.* p. 13.

15. Scruggs, Sherman Dana. *op. cit.* p. 18.

16. Seashore, Carl. *Psychology in Daily Life.* New York. D. Appleton and Company. 1916. Pp. xvii-225. (p. 25 f.)

17. Seashore, Carl. *op. cit.* p. 26.

18. Kerlin, Robert T. *Negro Poets and Their Poetry.* Washington, D. C. Associated Publishers. 1923. Pp. xv-285. (p. 13.)

19. Jesperson, Otto. *Language; Its Nature, Development, and Origin.* New York. Henry Holt and Company. 1923. 448 pp. (p. 432.)

20. Kerlin, Robert T. *op. cit.* (p. 4.)

CHAPTER X

SOME OTHER VARIABLES WHICH INFLUENCE PLAY

Varied and subtle forces are active agents each year in producing changed behavior. Difficult to identify, they often elude analysis. One is able to recognize only the changed behavior, not the active agents. Particularly true is this of play, a phenomenon of so many variables, subject to such numerous environmental influences that it is often impossible to isolate the causal agents that effect the obvious change.

The student of human behavior is concerned primarily with behavior data *per se*. The play data of utmost interest to him are those which are revealed through human behavior. It is of course true that behavior data often reveal little as to causes. Although the causes are sometimes apparent they are more often obscure or unidentifiable.

A phenomenon of so many variables as play, based upon a number of innate trends and environmental influences, *must* be subject to continuous change. Data gathered for one *decade* should not be taken to represent permanent or characteristic features of play behavior for all time. The present play activities are to a large extent temporary; they will be modified or given up in subsequent years. Certain writers in psychology and education have failed sometimes to take cognizance of the fact of eternal change. Unjustifiable generalizations have been formulated from the results of specific investigations; these results are often merely temporary modes of expression of a given group. Nowhere is the principle of eternal change better illustrated than in the play manifestations of children from year to year or decade to decade.

THE PRESENT STATUS OF THE TENDENCY TO COLLECT AND HOARD *

The student of psychology or education is cognizant of the various attempts to characterize certain periods in the child's development.

* See *Psychological Review* for Jan. 1927.

Team play and social participation in play behavior have been emphasized as characteristic of certain periods of development. Individualistic play too has been designated to be characteristic of other periods of development. Collecting and hoarding are individualistic activities often regarded as instinctive and characteristic of particular periods of development. Thorndike says:

"There is originally a blind tendency to take portable objects which attract attention, and carry them to one's habitation. There is the further response of satisfaction at contemplation and fingering them there. These tendencies commonly crystallize into habits of collecting and storing certain sorts of objects whose possession has additional advantages, and abort as responses to other objects whose possession brings secondary annoyance." [1]

The writers will avoid raising the question of the instinctive character of collecting and hoarding. They have observed certain clear evidence of *less* marked interest in these activities among present-day children than was reported a few decades ago. Other activities seem to have become vastly more popular than these. The emphasis upon these activities by educational theorists makes it desirable to estimate their present importance in the development of the child.

The writers will present data showing: (1) The frequency with which children now engage in collecting and hoarding activities at various ages, (2) Comparative results of data obtained now in those obtained in previous decades.

One of the items included in Play Quiz was No. 38 "Collecting stamps, birds' eggs, etc." From responses to this item, the writers hoped to secure significant data in regard to the extent to which pupils now engage in such activities.

FREQUENCY OF PARTICIPATION IN COLLECTING AND HOARDING ACTIVITIES

Figure 30 shows the percentages of boys and girls of various age levels who indicated that they had engaged in the above activity during the course of one week. The curves in Figure 30 were made after averaging the results obtained from the investigations which have been previously described. Figure 30 shows that interest in collecting stamps, birds' eggs, etc., was not especially marked among the children included in the several investigations. Figure 30 shows also that the transition from age to age was very gradual. It brings out clearly the fact that there are no *age levels at which the interest in collecting or hoarding suddenly decreases or increases by spurts.*

Table LVII shows the percentages of boys and girls of various age levels who indicated that they had engaged in making collections during the course of a week preceding each of the several investigations. Marked seasonal differences are not revealed in regard to frequency of participation in these activities. There are obviously differences in the types of collections made at various times in the year. It is important, however, that universality of the collecting interest is *not* revealed by the data. Further, it is significant that the rural children studied did not engage more frequently in these activities than city children. The curves for the rural and city children are strikingly similar.

COMPARISON WITH OTHER INVESTIGATIONS

It is of interest to compare the above findings with those obtained by C. F. Burk almost thirty years ago.[2] Burk makes the following statements:

". . . the children were asked to make out a list of all the things they had ever collected, tell when they began and when they stopped any collection, give the number of objects in each, and tell also various things about them, as will be discussed later. The results proved so fertile that a set of questions was made out and given to most of the teachers in the city to be filled out by the children, and a similar set was gathered from school children of Santa Rosa. Several days were allowed in order that they might have time carefully to think up, look up and count up their collections, and jog the memory of their mammas, also, as to their past collections. In some cases, as when an enterprising youth of ten years recorded sixty-six collections, fifty-five of them still continuing, the teacher herself consulted the mother and made sure that all were verified.

"Records were obtained from 510 Santa Barbara children and 704 Santa Rosa children, in all 607 boys and 607 girls, or 1,214 children.

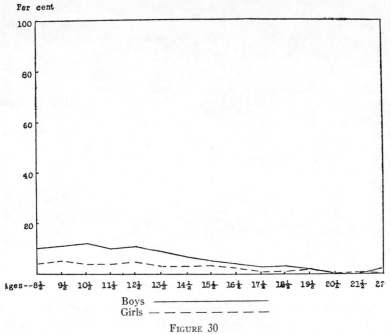

Per cent

Ages--8½ 9½ 10½ 11½ 12½ 13½ 14½ 15½ 16½ 17½ 18½ 19½ 20½ 21½ 2?

Boys ——————————
Girls — — — — — — —

FIGURE 30

Percentages of boys and girls who collected stamps, birds' eggs and so on during the course of a week. Average of results obtained from six separate investigations. See Table LVII, pp. 167-8.

TABLE LVII-a

PERCENTAGES OF BOYS OF VARIOUS AGE LEVELS WHO COLLECTED STAMPS, BIRDS' EGGS, ETC., DURING THE COURSE OF ONE WEEK.

				Boys			
Ages	Nov. 1923	Feb. 1924	Apr. 1924	Nov. 1924 (Rural)	Nov. 1925 (Rural)	Jan. 1926 (White)	Jan. 1926 (Negro)
8½	10	4	29	7	7	9	8
9½	11	11	17	8	10	9	4
10½	12	15	21	7	11	8	5
11½	11	8	21	2	6	11	1
12½	9	12	20	8	8	11	3
13½	9	10	14	2	6	16	1
14½	7	7	11	6	7	9	0
15½	6	4	5	7	3	6	3
16½	7	3	3	*	*	3	*
17½	3	4	3	*	*	3	*
18½	3	5	1	*	*	4	*
19½	2	2	2	*	*	*	*
20½	0	0	2	*	*	*	*
21½	0	0	0	*	*	*	*
22 and up	3	4	0	*	*	*	*

TABLE LVII-b

PERCENTAGES OF GIRLS OF VARIOUS AGE LEVELS WHO COLLECTED STAMPS, BIRDS' EGGS, ETC., DURING THE COURSE OF ONE WEEK.

Girls

Ages	Nov. 1923	Feb. 1924	Apr. 1924	Nov. 1924 (Rural)	Nov. 1925 (Rural)	Jan. 1926 (White)	Jan. 1926 (Negro)
8½	10	4	4	4	13	1	0
9½	7	1	7	5	8	3	3
10½	5	5	4	10	6	2	2
11½	6	3	4	5	12	0	1
12½	6	6	6	9	12	1	3
13½	1	2	6	4	9	5	0
14½	3	3	4	4	0	0	6
15½	2	2	5	0	0	3	3
16½	2	1	2	*	*	1	*
17½	0	0	2	*	*	2	*
18½	2	1	1	*	*	*	*
19½	3	3	1	*	*	*	*
20½	0	0	0	*	*	*	*
21½	0	0	0	*	*	*	*
22 and up	0	0	0	*	*	*	*

* No data assembled.

"The universality of the collecting interest was strikingly brought out. Only ten per cent of the boys and nine per cent of the girls were not actively making collections at the time. . . ."[3]

Although Burk studied children living in a different locality and employed a technique differing from that employed by the present writers, it is questionable that these variables alone are sufficient to account for the difference in the findings. Burk found ninety per cent of the children actively making collections.[4] The present writers found hardly more than ten per cent doing so. Nor were Burk's subjects restricted in their interests:

"That the children on the average were in process of making from three to four actual collections bespeaks a considerable amount of energy being drained off through the channels of this instinct."[5]

It is of course true that in the present study interest in stamps and birds' eggs might be revealed more readily than interest in other activities since mention of these two items in the list would probably serve as a memory aid. Comparison of Burk's findings for these two items with the results of the present investigations, therefore, will operate to make the techniques employed more comparable. According to Burk's charts more than 40 per cent of the boys of ages 7 to 14 inclusive were actively engaged in collecting stamps. At ages 9 and 11 the per cent rose almost to 60. The children's interest in collecting birds' eggs was not quite so great. However, between ages 8 to 16 inclusive, more than 15 per cent of the boys of each age level were collecting birds' eggs, and from ages 12 to 14 inclusive the per cent was above 30 at each age.

In contrast to Burk's data, this study shows that at no age level were as many as 15 per cent of boys making collections *of any kind*. To what is this large difference due? It seems reasonable to assume that interest in collecting differs from decade to decade. But Burk seemed to be oblivious to the fact that the only permanent phenomenon is that of eternal change. Note the following conclusions:

"The marble collection begins at least by six years, with a small number of followers, and reaches its height from seven to ten years, but especially at eight and nine years. After this age it declines, and from thirteen years on plays a small part. Stamps hold their own from seven to fifteen years, declining thereafter. The prominent ages are from nine to fourteen years. Cigar-tags are rather full-fledged at as early an age as six years. The craze increases, reaching its greatest intensity at twelve years, and then diminishes, dying out practically at sixteen years. This collection is prominent through a greater number of years than any other collection. The bird egg fever begins mildly at seven years and increases, reaching its height from twelve to fourteen years." [6]

A further generalization from data such as Burk's is made by Norsworthy and Whitley:

"The strength of this tendency (collecting) in childhood and the fact that it is still present in so many adults—witness the collections of string pieces, bottles, boxes, corks, bags, hats, etc., as well as those of hunting trophies, stamps, coins, rugs, china, art objects, etc.,—suggest that the schools would do well to use the instinct more." [7]

The implications revealed by the data herein presented are in sharp contrast to those presented above. Older children became less and less interested in making collections. It may be that present-day conditions present opportunities to use leisure that are more pleasing to young people than are activities such as collecting and hoarding. Activities such as moving-picture theater attendance, dancing, listening to the radio, etc., seem to be vastly more attractive to the youth to-day than activities such as collecting. Deductions based upon studies of children's interests need to be made with much caution since interests are often temporary. Both children and adults displayed much interest in "cross-word puzzles" during the winter of 1923-24. Conclusions based upon a study of this interest would be applicable only to the time at which the study was made. The parallel with respect to collecting and hoarding activities is obvious.

In one point only does Miss Burk's study and the present study show marked agreement, namely, the age at which the collecting tendency reaches its maximum intensity. Miss Burk found the largest number of collections was made by ten-year-old boys. The present writers find that a *slightly* larger percentage of boys of this age level was engaged in making collections. However, as mentioned above, the transition from age to age is very gradual. Certainly, a difference of one or two per cent is not enough to justify the assumption that age ten is an age of "individualism" and that ages nine and eleven are to be characterized differently.

VARIATION IN PLAY BEHAVIOR FROM YEAR TO YEAR— FASHIONS IN PLAY ACTIVITY

(a) Turning Handsprings, Cartwheels, Etc.

Table LVIII presents the findings of January, 1926, in reference to "Turning handsprings, cartwheels, etc." The data are given by sex and by race. It is noticeable that the white girls of ages 8½ to 11½ inclusive, participated in this activity much more frequently than did boys of the same chronological ages. This situation is contrary to that which would be expected ordinarily, and it is also contrary to the findings in previous studies, namely, those of November, 1923, February, 1924, and April, 1925. It is also contrary to the findings for the rural children. It is noticeable further from Table LVIII that only a very small percentage of Negro girls of ages 8½ to 11½ engaged in "Turning handsprings, cartwheels, etc." It is evident that Table LVIII requires explanation.

Investigation of the situation at Kansas City, Missouri, in January, 1926, revealed that many of the younger white girls, who were included in the study of that year, were taking private lessons in æsthetic dancing. The æsthetic dancing lessons involved the turning of hand-springs, cartwheels, etc.

TABLE LVIII

PERCENTAGES OF WHITE CHILDREN AND OF NEGRO CHILDREN WHO INDICATED THAT THEY HAD ENGAGED IN "TURNING HANDSPRINGS, CARTWHEELS, ETC.," DURING THE COURSE OF ONE WEEK. JAN., 1926.

	Whites		Negroes	
Ages	Girls	Boys	Girls	Boys
8½	41	22	6	20
9½	43	22	7	20
10½	34	26	8	12
11½	40	15	1	12
12½	19	22	4	12
13½	21	14	3	10
14½	8	14	7	6
15½	9	15	0	5

It became evident that this activity was very popular among certain of the younger white girls and that they tended to practice these stunts whenever they found opportunity to do so. It is obvious that opportunity was provided whenever they chanced to find themselves dressed for gymnasium work. The example of these girls apparently aroused emulation on the part of their classmates. In consequence, fully 40 per cent of the white girls of Kansas City, Missouri, ages 8½ to 11½ inclusive, were participating in turning handsprings, cartwheels, etc., in January, 1926.

The Negro children of Kansas City, Missouri, do not attend school with the white children. The Negro girls therefore would be uninfluenced by the white girls' interest in æsthetic dancing. This probably explains the very large discrepancy in the extent to which white girls and Negro girls engaged in this activity.

It is improbable that similar results would be obtained invariably were the investigations to be repeated from year to year. As previously mentioned, the only permanent phenomenon is that of eternal change. At the time this chapter is being written (1926) much interest is being manifested in the "Charleston." Time alone will tell whether this interest will continue or whether it will prove to be transitory.

LOCAL PLAY MANIFESTATIONS—THE NEIGHBORHOOD "CRAZE" *

(b) Marbles

Figure 31 presents the percentages of town boys of various ages who played "Marbles" during the course of one week. The curve in Figure 31 was made by use of the average of the findings obtained from the first three studies.

Figure 32 reveals the curves obtained when the seasonal results are treated separately. Figure 32 shows that, contrary to popular opinion, "Marbles" was played almost as commonly during the autumn and winter as during the spring of the year. The above findings were verified both by the testimony of teachers and school principals, and also by personal observation on the part of one of the writers.

The principal of a Kansas City, Kansas, elementary school stated in February, 1924, that the majority of the boys of her school had been playing "Marbles" throughout the fall of the preceding year and as late as the beginning of the Christmas vacation of 1923. A Lawrence teacher also testified that she had observed numerous Lawrence boys playing "Marbles" in February, 1924, at a time when the weather was particularly warm for a few days. A similar observation was made by one of the present writers at the time that he was delivering copies of the Play Quiz preliminary to making the second investigation of play, February 20, 1924. There is reason to believe that the results pictured in Figure 32 are indicative of a more or less general tendency in this regard.

Figure 33 shows the percentages of town boys and the percentages of country boys of various age levels who participated in playing "Marbles" in November. In Figure 33 the curve for the town boys was made by using the average of the results that were obtained from the first three investigations while the curve for the rural boys was made by using data obtained in November, 1924. Data for the first three investigations of town children were averaged for purposes of com-

* Most of the graphs presented in this chapter appeared in *The Pedagogical Seminary*, Sept., 1926.

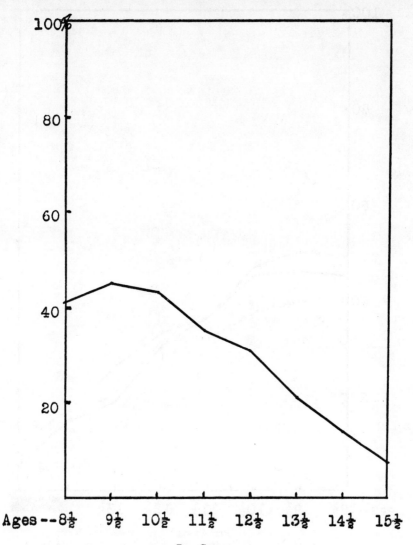

Ages -- 8½   9½   10½   11½   12½   13½   14½   15½

PER CENTS

Average of three investigations....   41   45   43   35   31   21   14   7

FIGURE 31

Percentages of town boys of various age levels who indicated that they had played
marbles during the course of a week.

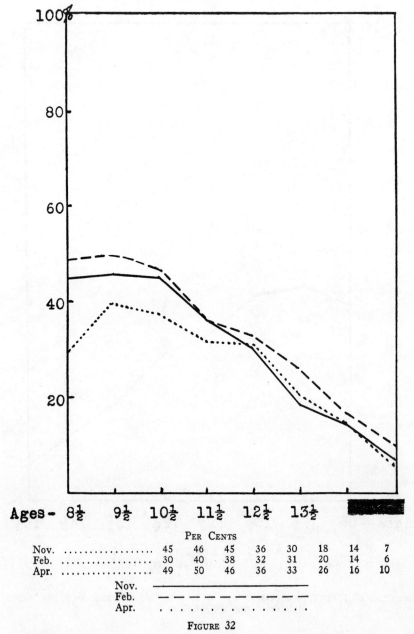

	PER CENTS							
Nov.	45	46	45	36	30	18	14	7
Feb.	30	40	38	32	31	20	14	6
Apr.	49	50	46	36	33	26	16	10

Nov.	————————————
Feb.	— — — — — — — —
Apr.	. . . .

FIGURE 32

Percentages of town boys of various age levels who indicated that they had played marbles during the course of a week. Results of three different investigations.

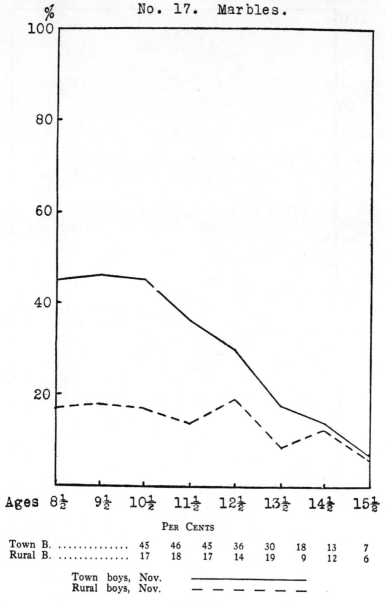

No. 17. Marbles.

	Ages 8½	9½	10½	11½	12½	13½	14½	15½
				PER CENTS				
Town B.	45	46	45	36	30	18	13	7
Rural B.	17	18	17	14	19	9	12	6

Town boys, Nov. ————
Rural boys, Nov. — — — — —

FIGURE 33

Percentages of town boys versus rural boys who indicated that they had played marbles during the course of one week.

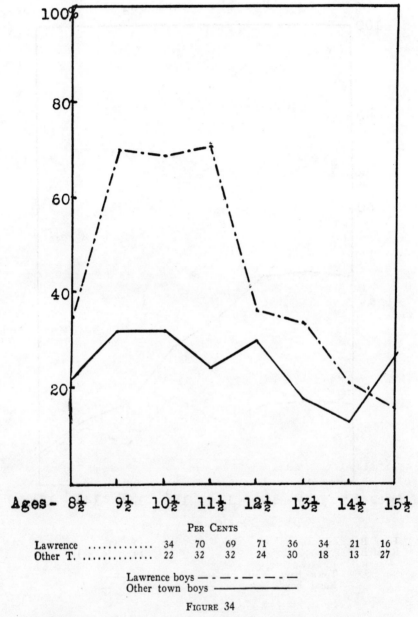

		Per Cents						
Lawrence	34	70	69	71	36	34	21	16
Other T.	22	32	32	24	30	18	13	27

Lawrence boys — - — - — - — -
Other town boys ——————

FIGURE 34

Percentages of Lawrence boys versus percentages of other town boys who played marbles during the course of a week.

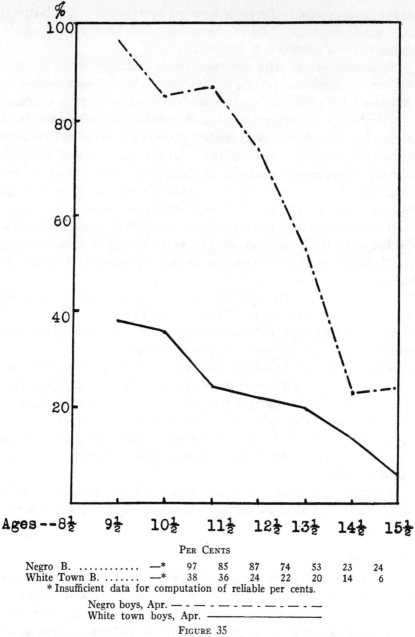

Ages --	8½	9½	10½	11½	12½	13½	14½	15½

PER CENTS

Negro B.	—*	97	85	87	74	53	23	24
White Town B.	—*	38	36	24	22	20	14	6

* Insufficient data for computation of reliable per cents.

Negro boys, Apr. — - — - - — - — - - — - — - —
White town boys, Apr. ————————————

FIGURE 35

Percentages of Negro boys versus percentages of white boys who played marbles during the course of the week preceding April 30, 1924.

parison since seasonal differences were not conspicuous. A subsequent investigation of rural children made one year later yielded results similar to those described in Figure 33.

Treatment of the data for the various communities as a whole obscures one important feature of these data. Within each community "Marbles" was played by various neighborhoods at various times.

"Marbles" was being played with considerable frequency in at least one of the neighborhoods studied during each of the three seasons of the year but at no one time was "Marbles" being played generally in every neighborhood studied. In November, 1923, "Marbles" was being played by the boys of the Lowell, Hawthorne, Riverview and Morse elementary schools, all of them located in Kansas City, Kansas. In February, 1924, this game was being indulged in by the boys of the Pinckney and the Quincy schools of Lawrence, and in April most frequently by the boys of the Douglass elementary school of Kansas City, Kansas.

Figure 34 shows the relative extent to which Lawrence boys and the other town boys played "Marbles" in February, 1924. A few warm, midwinter days probably account for the fact that marble playing became popular during the month of February.

Figure 35 shows the relative extent to which Negro boys of Kansas City, Kansas, and white town boys played "Marbles" in April, 1924. It is probable that the difference herein revealed is not a characteristic race difference. This difference between Negroes and whites was not revealed in November, 1923, or in February, 1924. Nor was any racial difference found in the study of Kansas City, Missouri, children in January, 1926.

Playing marbles appears to be subject to environmental demands, not so much a product of seasonal change as of the whims of a community.

(c) Jacks

Figure 36 reveals the percentage differences in the extent to which the Negro girls played "Jacks" during the week preceding April 30, 1924. It is clear that Negro girls participated in this activity much more frequently than white girls. Significant differences between the two races were not found in this regard in November, 1923, or Feb-

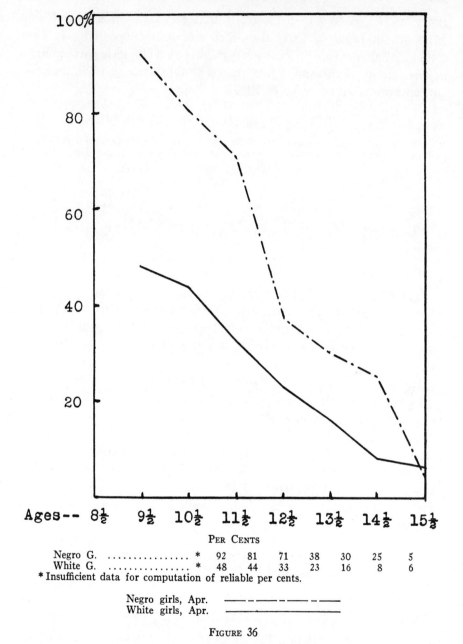

Ages--	8½	9½	10½	11½	12½	13½	14½	15½

PER CENTS

Negro G.	*	92	81	71	38	30	25	5
White G.	*	48	44	33	23	16	8	6

*Insufficient data for computation of reliable per cents.

Negro girls, Apr.   — — — — — — — —
White girls, Apr.   ————————————

FIGURE 36

Percentages of Negro girls versus percentages of white girls who played jacks during the course of the week preceding April 30, 1924.

ruary, 1924. However, in the study that was made in Kansas City, Missouri, in January, 1926, the differences again appeared. It was found that almost twice as many Negro girls as white girls participated in this activity at this time. The results of the January, 1926, investigations are presented in Table LIX.

TABLE LIX

PERCENTAGES OF WHITE CHILDREN AND OF NEGRO CHILDREN WHO INDICATED THAT THEY HAD ENGAGED IN PLAYING "JACKS" DURING THE COURSE OF ONE WEEK. JAN., 1926.

Ages	Whites		Negroes	
	Girls	Boys	Girls	Boys
8½	22	3	48	13
9½	17	2	38	11
10½	17	3	33	10
11½	13	0	21	7
12½	4	0	20	6
13½	3	0	12	5
14½	2	0	10	2
15½	2	0	6	0

These fluctuations in play behavior are difficult to explain. Figures 35 and 36 probably are illustrative of what happens when a so-called craze appears in a particular neighborhood. When such a craze occurs, almost every member of a given group temporarily participates in the craze.

In some instances a game seems to appear only for a brief time in a given neighborhood and then suddenly disappears. Such activities are not markedly seasonal but seem to depend rather upon what may be called neighborhood whims. These activities do not seem to depend upon social conditions, playground equipment, season, or size of school grounds, for their actuation. The writers do not pretend to be able to explain their occurrence. Possibly they are one aspect of the general fact of variation which is represented by the normal distribution surface.

THE LOCAL SITUATION OR THE ADULT INTERESTS WITHIN A GIVEN COMMUNITY

Athletics

Figure 37 shows the percentages of Lawrence boys who indicated by their responses that they had engaged in playing basket ball during the week preceding the investigation of February 20, 1924. Data are

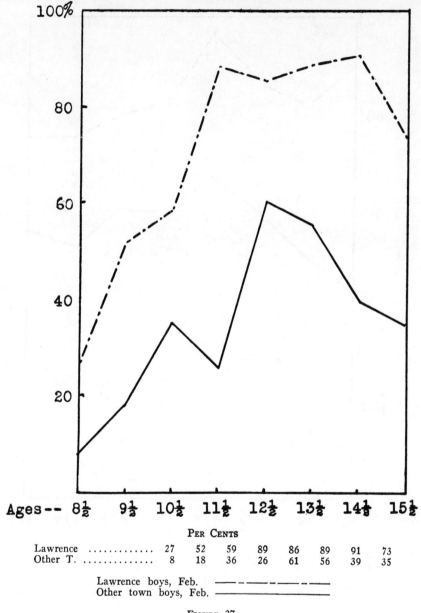

| Ages -- | 8½ | 9½ | 10½ | 11½ | 12½ | 13½ | 14½ | 15½ |

PER CENTS

	8½	9½	10½	11½	12½	13½	14½	15½
Lawrence	27	52	59	89	86	89	91	73
Other T.	8	18	36	26	61	56	39	35

Lawrence boys, Feb.   — — — — — —
Other town boys, Feb. ———————————

FIGURE 37

Percentages of Lawrence boys who were found to engage in basket ball in February versus the percentages of other town boys who were found to engage in basket ball during the same week.

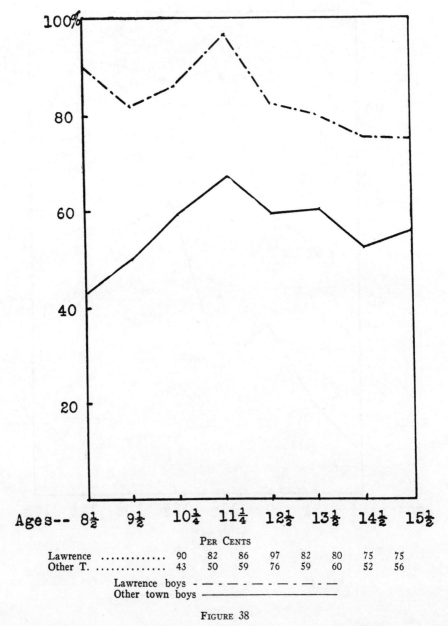

FIGURE 38

Percentages of Lawrence boys who were found to engage in football in November versus the percentages of other town boys who were found to engage in football during the same month.

presented also for the boys of like chronological ages who lived in other towns. Evidently, basket ball is much more frequently participated in by Lawrence boys than by boys in certain other towns and cities.

Figure 38 shows an analogous situation with respect to "Football."

The differences displayed by Figures 37 and 38 may be accounted for by the fact that Lawrence is the seat of the University of Kansas. Since Lawrence has a population of 12,000 persons, the community is dominated to a considerable degree by university life. Similar differences, though less marked than those given in Figures 37 and 38, were found for such activities as "Running races," "Jumping for height," "Jumping for distance," "Pole vaulting," etc., etc., the Lawrence boys participating more frequently than boys of certain other towns in these activities.

Small boys attempt to play football much more frequently than basket ball. This fact is clearly shown in Figures 37 and 38 for boys of ages 8½ to 9½. Numerous factors probably combine to bring about this situation. One important factor is that greater opportunity is provided for small boys to attend football games than to attend basket ball contests. The general conditions under which basket ball games are played are such that few boys of ages 8½ to 9½ are permitted to witness them. They are obviously not so restricted in witnessing football games.

Small boys probably play basket ball less frequently than football because of the relatively greater ease with which certain elements of football may be simulated. Playing basket ball demands dribbling of the ball. Basket ball dribbling requires smooth surfaces not often available out-of-doors. Football, on the other hand, may be played on almost any vacant lot or neighborhood lawn.

Other factors also enter in. It is difficult to procure suitable basket ball goals or their substitutes. The regulation basket ball is too large for the small boy to handle successfully and smaller ones are apparently not generally manufactured.

This detailed attempt to account for the difference in the relative extents to which small boys participate in football and basket ball reveals many variables that may condition play behavior.

HOME TRAINING

It was found that book reading is more frequently engaged in by Lawrence girls than by the girls of certain other towns and villages. Similar results were found for the boys and the results are similar for the various seasons. It was likewise found that Lawrence girls participate in chewing gum less frequently than girls of other towns.

The preceding facts seem to be illustrative of the effect of the social status of a given environment upon play behavior. It seems likely that Lawrence children are afforded greater opportunity and given greater encouragement to read than are children in certain other towns.

The difference between Lawrence and certain other towns in reference to gum-chewing may be due to the difference in the social status of the various communities.

PLAYGROUND SPACE AND EQUIPMENT

Figure 39 presents the findings for activity No. 4, "Playing ball with an indoor or playground ball," for November, 1923. Lawrence boys of ages 10½ and 11½ played with an indoor or playground ball much more frequently than boys of corresponding chronological ages of certain other towns. Beyond age 11½ the curve for Lawrence boys drops suddenly. Similar data were secured for Lawrence girls.

The sudden decrease in participation in this activity is not consistent with what has been said previously in reference to continuity of variation. This sudden waning, however, was found only in a very few instances. This phenomenon may be due to the fact that the Lawrence children under age 12½ were selected from elementary schools (Quincy, and Pinckney schools) which have abundant out-of-door playing space. These younger children are provided with balls, bats, and other equipment and they are encouraged to play out-of-doors.

The Lawrence children of age 12½ to 15½ were for the most part, pupils of the Lawrence Junior High School. The Lawrence Junior High School has no playground adjacent to the school building. Hence the pupils have no opportunity to play ball with an indoor

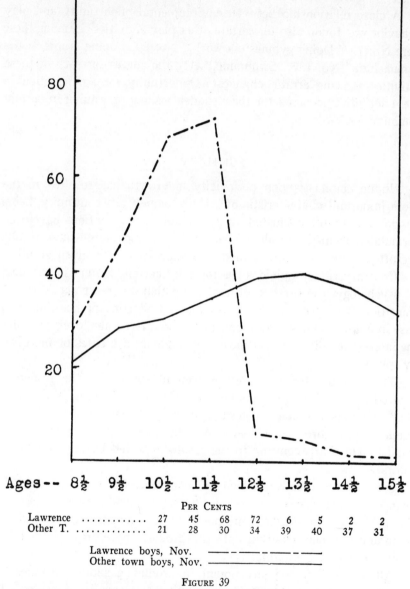

Ages --	8½	9½	10½	11½	12½	13½	14½	15½
Per Cents								
Lawrence	27	45	68	72	6	5	2	2
Other T.	21	28	30	34	39	40	37	31

Lawrence boys, Nov.   — — — — — —
Other town boys, Nov. ——————

FIGURE 39

Percentages of Lawrence boys versus the percentages of other town boys who played baseball with an indoor or playground ball.

ball when they are at school. The result of this lack of playground space is clearly shown in Figure 39.

A close relationship between environmental opportunity and play behavior was found also for certain other play activities. Among these were No. 79, "Doing gymnasium work," No. 80, "Doing stunts in the gymnasium," No. 137, "Swimming," etc., the curves for each of these activities showing erratic changes. Opportunity for participation in these activities accounts for their sudden waxing or waning in certain communities.

SUMMARY

Undue emphasis upon periodicity in growth has resulted in the more important characteristic of growth, namely, its continuity, being obscured and underestimated. Unjustifiable generalizations have been formulated from the results of particular investigations—these results are often merely temporary modes of expression of a given group.

Contrary to the opinions set forth by certain writers in the field of psychology, the present writers found that for most activities the transition from year to year is gradual. Collecting or hoarding is a case in point. The writers found that there are no age levels at which the interest in collecting and hoarding suddenly decreases or increases by spurts.

The fact of eternal change is well illustrated by the responses secured by the writers to item No. 38, "Collecting stamps, birds' eggs, etc." Universality of the collecting interest was not revealed. At no age level was more than 15 per cent of boys making collections. This finding is in sharp contrast to the results reported by earlier investigators.

Some of the variables which influence play behavior and produce change are: age differences, racial differences, sex differences, seasonal change, prevailing fashions in play, adult interests within a given community, social environment, playground space, material equipment for playing, etc., etc.

All of these factors are potent in producing sudden changes in play manifestations in certain communities. Generalizations regarding play behavior must be made, therefore, with extreme care.

TABLE LX

NUMBER OF LAWRENCE, KANSAS, CHILDREN INCLUDED IN THREE INVESTIGATIONS OF PLAY BEHAVIOR.

Ages	Nov. 1923 B	Nov. 1923 G	Feb. 1924 B	Feb. 1924 G	Apr. 1924 B	Apr. 1924 G
8½	30	27	*	24	*	32
9½	40	25	33	22	36	31
10½	28	38	29	36	33	36
11½	32	37	28	23	31	27
12½	34	41	36	30	37	39
13½	62	53	35	28	49	45
14½	53	45	33	33	39	57
15½	40	51	62	44	32	60

* Insufficient number of cases for computation of per cents.

TABLE LXI

NUMBER OF INDIVIDUALS INCLUDED IN THE INVESTIGATION OF JAN., 1926, WHOSE DATA WERE TABULATED AND USED IN THE CONSTRUCTION OF 200 GRAPHS OF PLAY BEHAVIOR.

Ages	Whites B	Whites G	Negroes B	Negroes G
8½	100	100	39	48
9½	100	100	75	90
10½	100	100	94	123
11½	100	100	89	114
12½	100	100	104	110
13½	100	100	80	91
14½	100	100	48	71
15½	100	100	40	34
16½	100	100	..	..
17½	68	50	..	..

REFERENCES

1. Thorndike, E. L. *Educational Psychology.* In Three Volumes. New York. Teachers College, Columbia University. 1913. Vol. I. p. 53 f.

2. Burk, Caroline Frear. "The Collecting Instinct." *Ped. Sem.* July, 1900, 7. Pp. 179-207.

3. Burk, Caroline Frear. *op. cit.* p. 180.

4. Burk, Caroline Frear. *ibid.*

5. Burk, Caroline Frear. *op. cit.* p. 181.

6. Burk, Caroline Frear. *op. cit.* p. 190.

7. Norsworthy, Naomi, and Whitley, Mary T. *The Psychology of Childhood.* New York. The Macmillan Co. 1922. Pp. xix-375. (p. 54.)

CHAPTER XI

INDIVIDUAL DIFFERENCES IN PLAY BEHAVIOR

Educational psychology teaches the fact of individual differences with respect to every trait that has been measured or estimated.

"Individuals of the same age differ greatly in every trait that has been measured or estimated. In height, weight, and strength; in susceptibility to disease, nervous stability and mental balance; in intellect, character, and skill; and in aptitudes for special subjects, arithmetic, spelling, music, or athletics individual variations are found." [1]

For obvious reasons the amount of individual difference was first ascertained for those traits which are most easily measured. For example, differences in height, weight, strength, etc., were among the first to be recognized and measured quantitatively. The gradual development of measurement of intellect followed. Fairly precise tools for the measurement of ability and educational attainment have been constructed. Some of the more elusive traits of character are as yet unmeasured. The desirability of quantitative expression of deviation in these regards, however, is recognized.

"The fact has long been recognized that objects of interest determine conduct and that there are great differences among individuals in this respect. Some children show early in life definite leanings toward music or games or mechanical appliances or books. The marked cases are easily observed, but we have had slight technique for the exact determination of fundamental preferences which are often too deeply hidden for even the individual himself to recognize. He does not see himself as different from others, and teachers have vague standards with which to compare him." [2]

It seems reasonable to suppose that the activities in which children spontaneously and voluntarily participate represent their genuine interests. If the teacher can identify those activities to which different children turn "just because they want to," he will doubtless have discovered fundamental individual differences of interest. Such discovery is of the utmost importance both to the school and to the individual. It is important for the teacher to know in what respects a given child differs from other children.   It is even more important for the individual child to identify the ways in which he is different from others.   Such discovery squares with the Socratic dictum, "Know thyself."

The most striking fact that has come to light as a result of the present series of investigations is the enormously wide range of individual differences with respect to those activities which are frequently participated in, those which are best liked, and those to which individuals reported that they had given the largest amount of time.

It was found that each of the 200 activities listed in the Play Quiz had been participated in by one or more individuals during the course of a week, but that no activity of the list was engaged in by all individuals of any age level.   In the investigation that was made in Kansas City, Missouri, in January of 1926, almost 100 per cent of the younger children indicated that they had looked at the Sunday "funny" paper.   For the whole series of investigations approximately 50 per cent of the younger children were found to have participated in this activity.   It is possible that lack of opportunity rather than lack of interest accounts for the fact that some few children failed to check this activity.

There are, however, few activities in which anything approaching unanimity of interest was demonstrated.   In most instances, less than 50 per cent of the children of a given age participated in a given activity.   Since lack of unanimity of play interest was repeatedly found even when such factors as age, sex, race, season, neighborhood, etc., were kept constant, it seems logical to infer that a chief factor in play behavior is that of individual difference of interest.   As compared with individual differences, such differences as age, sex, race, season, and neighborhood are relatively insignificant and unimportant.

NUMBER OF ACTIVITIES ENGAGED IN

Figure 1, and Table IX (pages 58 and 59) present the median number of play activities and the middle fifty per cent range of the number of activities participated in by boys and girls of various ages.   Figure 1, and Table IX, reveal the following facts: (a) The typical boy of age 8½ participated in approximately 40 different play activities during the coures of one week; (b) 25 per cent of boys of this age engaged in less than 27 different play activities during the course of one week; (c) 75 per cent of boys of age 8½ engaged in more than 53 different play activities during the course of one week.

Table LXII presents the percentages of boys of various ages who engaged in a given number of play activities. Table LXII is to be read as follows: Four per cent of boys of age 8½ participated in 6-10 play activities during the course of one week. Five per cent of boys of this age engaged in 11-15 activities. One per cent engaged in more than 95 activities. Table LXIII presents similar information for girls.*

Tables LXII and LXIII reveal the fact that the most active child of eight years participated in approximately 100 different play activities during the course of one week. The child having the least versatility of play interest participated in less than half a dozen different play activities during the same time. These tables show that with respect to versatility of play interest, age differences and sex differences pale into insignificance when compared to individual differences.

It is of interest that as chronological age increases individual differences in number of play activities are less conspicuous. Maturity seems to effect a restricting influence in this regard.

TABLE LXII

PERCENTAGES OF BOYS OF VARIOUS AGE LEVELS ENGAGING IN A GIVEN NUMBER OF PLAY ACTIVITIES.

No. of Activities Engaged in	Ages														
	8½	9½	10½	11½	12½	13½	14½	15½	16½	17½	18½	19½	20½	21½	22
5 or less	..	1	1	1	..	1	1	2	2	..	2	2	1	1	1
6-10	4	2	2	3	3	4	7	8	10	12	11	13	15	9	8
11-15	5	4	6	6	8	13	13	21	18	19	18	18	22	18	30
16-20	5	9	11	11	12	16	18	16	22	21	22	24	25	27	31
21-25	8	11	10	14	13	15	15	17	16	19	20	18	18	19	16
26-30	13	9	11	12	13	13	13	12	13	11	12	13	10	15	9
31-35	9	9	9	12	11	10	12	8	9	8	7	7	4	5	2
36-40	10	10	10	9	11	8	7	5	5	4	2	2	2	3	2
41-45	8	8	8	7	10	6	6	3	3	2	1	2	2	2	1
46-50	7	7	6	7	6	4	4	3	1	1	3	..	..	1	..
51-55	8	6	5	5	3	4	2	1	1	1	..	..	1	1	..
56-60	5	3	6	4	2	1	2	1	..	1	..	1	..	..	..
61-65	4	4	5	2	2	2	1	1	1	..	..	..	..	..	
66-70	3	2	3	2	2	1	1	1	..						
71-75	2	4	2	2	1	1	..	..	..						
76-80	2	2	2	1	1	1	..	..	..						
81-85	2	3	1	1	..	..	..	..							
86-90	3	2	1	1	1	1	..	..	..						
91-95	2	1	1	1	1	..	..	..							
Over 95	1	2	1	1	..	..	..	..							

* See *The Pedagogical Seminary*, June, 1927.

TABLE LXIII

PERCENTAGES OF GIRLS OF VARIOUS AGE LEVELS ENGAGING IN A GIVEN NUMBER OF PLAY ACTIVITIES.

No. of Activities Engaged in	8½	9½	10½	11½	12½	13½	14½	15½	16½	17½	18½	19½	20½	21½	22
5 or less	2	..	..	..	..	..	1	1	2	2	2	1	1	..	2
6-10 ..	3	3	3	3	3	4	6	4	10	13	11	14	11	7	14
11-15 ..	8	7	6	7	9.	10	13	18	22	24	16	19	26	18	30
16-20 ..	11	10	11	11	14	17	19	24	21	24	27	29	25	34	25
21-25 ..	10	10	10	16	16	16	17	18	21	15	22	17	19	22	17
26-30 ..	9	12	12	13	16	15	15	14	13	8	13	11	11	8	7
31-35 ..	10	11	11	10	9	11	9	7	5	6	5	5	5	7	4
36-40 ..	11	9	14	9	9	8	8	7	3	4	3	2	2	2	..
41-45 ..	9	7	6	7	6	5	4	3	1	2	1	2	1	2	..
46-50 ..	7	6	6	6	4	4	3	2	1	1	1	..	..	..	..
51-55 ..	4	4	5	6	4	2	1	1	..	1	..	..	..	..	..
56-60 ..	3	5	5	3	2	2	1	..	..	..	..	..	..	..	..
61-65 ..	4	3	3	1	2	1	..	..	..						
66-70 ..	1	3	2	2	1	2	1	..	..						
71-75 ..	2	3	3	3	1	1	..	..	..						
76-80 ..	2	3	2	1	1	1	..	..	..						
81-85 ..	2	1	1	..	..	..	..	..	..						
86-90 ..	..	1	1	..	..	..	..	..	..						
91-95 ..	1	1	1	..	..	..	..	..	..						
Over 95	2	1	..	..	..	..	..	..	..						

SOCIAL PARTICIPATION*

Table LXIV shows the indices of social participation for the children studied. Sex differences in this regard were found to be so slight that the data were given composite treatment. Table LXIV is to be read as follows: Two per cent of children of age 8½ had indices of social participation of less than 5. This means that less than five per cent of the activities engaged in by these children were ones in which one or more other children also took part. It is evident that these two per cent of children are relatively solitary in their play behavior.

Table LXIV shows that nine per cent of children of age 8½ were found to have indices of social participation of 95 or above. This means that 95 per cent or more of the activities which they participated in were ones in which one or more other children also took part. Evidently these latter children were not inclined to take part in solitary plays and games.

* Social participation was studied only in the rural investigation that was made in Nov. 1925, and in the Kansas City, Mo., study made in Jan. 1926.

It is quite possible that in the case of a given child a high degree of solitariness may be due to illness, to a peculiar environmental situation, etc. The consistency with which these differences appear at various age levels suggests that the deviations displayed are not due merely to chance or accident. The child's withdrawal from his fellows may be a deliberate withdrawal or a blind trial-and-error outcome of an attempt to avoid unpleasant social contacts. In either case it is indicative of a lack of social adjustment and demands the attention of the educator.

TABLE LXIV

PERCENTAGES OF CHILDREN OF VARIOUS AGE LEVELS HAVING VARIOUS INDICES OF SOCIAL PARTICIPATION.

Cases	464	721	775	814	902	914	767	802
Ages	8½	9½	10½	11½	12½	13½	14½	15½
Indices of Social Participation								
Less than 5	2	1	1	1	1	..	..	1
5-9	1	1	1	1	1	..	1	1
10-14	1	1	1	1	1	1	2	2
15-19	1	1	2	1	1	3	3	2
20-24	2	2	4	3	2	4	4	4
25-29	2	3	3	3	4	3	4	4
30-34	4	4	3	3	5	5	6	6
35-39	4	4	4	5	5	7	8	7
40-44	5	4	7	8	9	8	9	9
45-49	7	7	7	9	8	10	8	9
50-54	6	7	8	9	10	10	9	10
55-59	6	7	9	9	11	9	9	9
60-64	9	6	8	8	10	9	9	12
65-69	8	10	8	8	8	8	9	7
70-74	9	10	8	6	6	6	8	7
75-79	7	5	6	6	5	6	4	3
80-84	6	5	6	4	5	6	4	3
85-89	7	7	6	6	4	3	3	3
90-94	4	6	5	3	2	2	1	2
95 and above	9	7	6	5	3	3	2	2

It is entirely possible that overparticipation in group activities may result in neglect of certain individual activities essential to well-balanced development. It is, therefore, of importance that thorough-going case studies be made of children of extremely low or high indices of social participation. Table LXIV enables one to identify these children for further study.

The following quotations are illustrative of noteworthy attempts at corrective play adjustments:

"At the Institute whatever is attempted recreationally is done in accordance with the psychiatrist's interpretation of the behavior problem. For example, a child may appear extremely self-centered; the actual cause may not be a desire to show off but rather a deep sense of inferiority for which he is unconsciously compensating. Here the objective is to place him in a situation in which there will be relatively few possibilities of having his feeling of inferiority played upon. The shy, timid child usually needs a small group in which he may receive considerable attention from the leader without being conspicuously singled out. The child who lacks persistence and gives up easily is placed in a group where individual accomplishment is not especially clear-cut, otherwise he may become discouraged from the very start; and so we might go on piling up illustrations." [3]

"The problem involved in the recreational placement of the child diagnosed 'psychopathic personality, egocentric type' is to find for him a means of self-expression with special opportunities for 'showing off.' Clubs with facilities for dramatic expression fit this need for girls of practically all ages and for boys until the adolescent age. While it is possible that the egocentric boy of adolescent age may benefit by dramatic expression, few organizations have found such recreation feasible because the 'average' boy develops a self-consciousness at that age that makes him reluctant to take part in dramatic work.

"Organizations such as the Boy Scouts, Girl Scouts, and Camp Fire Girls with their definite system of ranks and promotion, may prove a worthwhile experiment for the egocentric child provided he is interested in the duties that are included in the various tests. When his interest is not aroused, the experiment is likely to prove a failure because he is brought face to face with a clear-cut issue between accomplishment and failure. Unable to obtain the recognition he craves, he soon becomes discouraged from making any effort to fulfill the requirements." [4]

"In the recreational placement of children of the opposite type—'psychopathic personality, inadequate type'—the emphasis is also placed upon recognition, but in this case the efforts are directed toward stimulating a desire for it in the child. If possible, the inadequate child should be placed in small groups, where competition is not keen, and where he will receive a great deal of attention from the recreation leader. No opportunity to give praise and encouragement for duties well performed should be lost. The nature of the activity will depend to a great extent upon the intelligence of the child, but possibly the 'trial and error' method of selection is indicated in this type more than with the others. An associate with decided play interests who will supply the necessary motive force may prove a decided asset in carrying out this treatment. Whatever is attempted should be regarded as a 'splint method,' and the support should be withdrawn as the child progresses." [5]

It is, of course, true that the data presented in this study are partial in regard to the play function. There is a *quality* as well as a quantity of social paricipation. It may be that significant differences with respect to social participation and solitariness in play are to be found by qualitative analyses. These differences can be discerned by the method of detailed psychological analyses of *how* persons of various ages participate in their recreational activities.

The subjective nature of such analyses makes them difficult and of questionable validity. Too, the enormous individual differences that exist among the members of a group of the same chronological age make doubtful the advisability of a program to discover such tendencies. The writers have contented themselves, therefore, with quantitative statement showing the wide variability which exists among school children in respect to social participation in plays and games.

The writers feel that the technique herein presented will prove particularly useful in identifying extremely solitary children in order that remedial work may ensue.

SUMMARY

The technique used in the present investigations of play life of children reveals enormous individual differences.

Few activities were isolated in which anything approaching unanimity of interest was demonstrated. In most instances, less than 50 per cent of the children of a given age participated in a given activity.

As compared with individual differences, such differences as those associated with age, sex, race, etc., are relatively unimportant and insignificant.

Early childhood is a period of exploration, a period of self-discovery, experimentation, etc. The tendency on the part of small children toward manifold physical and mental activity results in great versatility of play interests. This tendency decreases with increase of maturity. Hence, the play behavior of adults tends to become relatively conservative.

There are conspicuous individual differences in respect to the extent to which children take part in plays and games with other children. Two per cent of children of age 8½ were found to have indices of participation less than 5. This means that less than 5 per cent of the activities engaged in by these children were ones in which one or more other children took part. Nine per cent of children of the same age were found to have indices of social participation of 95 or above. This signifies that 95 per cent or more of the activities in which they participated during the week preceding the examination were ones in which other children also took part.

The writers have emphasized the need of identification of children who are extremely solitary or extremely social in their play life. The technique herein presented affords a method of more complete child accounting.

REFERENCES

1. Gates, A. I. *Psychology for Students of Education.* New York. The Macmillan Company. 1923. Pp. xvi-489. (p. 398.)

2. Haggerty, M. E. Character Education and Scientific Method. *Journal of Educational Research.* Apr. 1926. *13*, p. 244.

3. Wannamaker, Claudia. "The Relation of the Individual Problem Child to Recreation." *The Playground.* July, 1925. *19*, p. 204.

4. Wannamaker, Claudia. "Methods of Recreational Adjustment as a Form of Social Case Treatment." *Mental Hygiene.* Vol. VII, No. 4, October, 1923. Pp. 744-754. (p. 750.)

5. Wannamaker, Claudia. *op. cit. Mental Hygiene.* Pp. 744-754. (p. 752.)

CHAPTER XII

PLAY ACTIVITY AND THE SEASONS OF THE YEAR

It has been emphasized previously that when human traits are measured objectively, continuity of variation is found. Attempts to differentiate certain chronological age periods in terms of differences in play behavior manifested therein are likely to prove spurious. The play behavior which characterizes a given group seems to be the result of gradual changes occurring during the growth period. These changes have been shown to be gradual and contingent, not sudden and sporadic.

Of the 200 play activities listed in the Lehman Play Quiz, few are subject to seasonal variation to a marked degree. Table LXV gives a list of activities which are little affected by seasonal changes. A cursory examination of these activities will convince the reader that the bulk of the play life of the child is not subject to marked variation effected by seasonal changes.

TABLE LXV

PLAY ACTIVITIES WHICH SHOW PRACTICALLY NO SEASONAL CHANGE

Visiting or entertaining company.
Going to the movies.
Chewing gum.
Smoking.
Having "dates."

Listening to the victrola.
Playing the piano (for fun).
Playing other musical instruments for fun.
Looking at the Sunday "funny" paper.
Reading jokes or funny sayings.

Reading the newspaper.
Reading short stories.
Reading books.
Writing letters.
Whistling.

Teasing somebody.
Just singing.
Drawing with pencil, pen, chalk, or crayon.
Cutting paper things with scissors.
Sewing, knitting, crocheting, etc., for fun.

Using a hammer, saw, nails, etc., for fun.
Looking at pictures.
Playing with pet kittens.
Doing gymnasium work.

HIGHLY SEASONAL ACTIVITIES

Everyone is aware that the frequency of participation in certain plays and games is conditioned largely by seasonal variation. Such activities make up a relatively small part of the total play life of the child. They are important nevertheless.

The activities which showed the most marked variation in frequency of participation therein during the various seasons are listed in Table LXVI.

TABLE LXVI

SEASONAL PLAY ACTIVITIES

Activities most frequently participated in, November, 1923.

Boys	Girls
Football.	Basket ball.
Basket ball.	Gathering nuts.
Gathering nuts.	Going to parties or picnics.
Going to parties or picnics.	
Hunting.	

Activities most frequently participated in, February, 1924.

Boys	Girls
Basket ball.	Basket ball.
Checkers.	Checkers.
Coasting on a sled.	Coasting on a sled.
Ice-skating.	Ice-skating.
Sleigh-riding.	Sleigh-riding.
Snowball fights.	Snowball fights.
Building snow men, snow forts, snow houses, etc.	Building snow men, snow forts, snow houses, etc.

Activities most frequently participated in, April, 1924.

Boys	*Girls*
Baseball with a hard ball.	Baseball with a hard ball.
Ball with an indoor or playground ball.	Just playing catch.
	Tennis.
Just playing catch.	Excursions to the woods, parks, country, etc.
Golf.	
Tennis.	Gathering flowers.
Swimming.	Going to entertainments, concerts, and so on.
Excursions to the woods, parks, country, etc.	
	Jumping or skipping rope.
Gathering flowers.	Jacks.
Fishing.	Swimming.
Running races.	
Jumping for height.	
Jumping for distance.	
Pole vaulting.	
Flying kites.	

In the spring many of the children studied engaged in certain activities in which participation was rare during the other seasons. These activities may be thought of as seasonal ones. The frequency of such seasonal activities was found to be largest for spring. There were few activities characteristically autumn ones. Winter had a considerable number of such activities. The largest number of such activities, however, was found in the spring.

ACTIVITIES SOMEWHAT SUBJECT TO SEASONAL CHANGE

Graphs were made for the 200 items of the Play Quiz showing frequency of participation in each activity at various ages during each season. Some of the graphs showed marked change from season to season. The activities that showed marked variation have been listed. Some activities, however, showed practically no seasonal variation. Between these two extremes every shade of seasonal difference was found. It is, therefore, not an easy matter to draw a line between seasonal and non-seasonal activities.

Following is a list of activities which are somewhat influenced by season but which are not ordinarily regarded as seasonal activities.

TABLE LXVII

ACTIVITIES SOMEWHAT MORE FREQUENTLY PARTICIPATED IN
DURING MIDWINTER

Boxing.
Roller skating.
Card games, such as authors, bridge, whist.
Listening to the radio.

ACTIVITIES SOMEWHAT LESS FREQUENTLY PARTICIPATED IN
DURING MIDWINTER

Riding a bicycle.
Horseback riding.
Riding in an auto.
Driving an auto.
Just hiking or strolling.

Building or watching bonfires.
Climbing porches, trees, fences, posts, etc.
Pitching horseshoes.
Mumbly peg.
Throwing rocks or stones.

Playing in the sand.
Wading in the water.
London bridge.
Drop the handkerchief.
Three deep.

Other ring games.
Making mud pies, mud dolls, etc.
Walking on stilts.

It will be noted that many activities are somewhat *less* frequently participated in during midwinter and that only a few activities are somewhat *more* commonly engaged in during midwinter. Perusal of the preceding list is sufficient explanation of this fact.

Such winter sports as ice-hockey, skiing, snow-shoeing, and tobogganing are practically unknown in Kansas, and even so common a winter sport as ice-skating is a very uncertain winter sport. The seasonal differences revealed in the communities included in the present series of investigations are therefore probably less marked than would be revealed by studies in other geographical areas. In Kansas it is possible to be out-of-doors almost the entire year, the winters being relatively mild. The relatively mild winter weather probably accounts for the fact that "Riding in an auto," shows only slight seasonality. It is possible to drive a car at all seasons of the year in the communities studied but there is less temptation to do so in midwinter than during the spring. Since one is apt to be indoors more during the winter than during the autumn or spring, there is increased opportunity to take part in certain indoor activities as "Card games, such as authors, bridge, whist," "Boxing," etc. Frequent participation is found therefore in these activities during the winter season.

Football was found to be more seasonal than any other of the 200 activities. Basket ball is not nearly so seasonal as football. Basket ball is played almost as commonly during the fall of the year as in midwinter. Boys under 12½ play basket ball fully as much during the autumn as in midwinter. It is of interest further that adolescent boys (ages 12 to 18) play basket ball only slightly less during the fall than during the winter.

"Marbles" is considered a spring pastime. It is traditional that the appearance of marbles is a token of spring. In the present studies the game was found to be participated in almost as frequently during one season as another.

SEX DIFFERENCES AS REGARDS SEASONAL PLAY ACTIVITIES
SUMMARY

It is readily noticeable in Table LXVI that there is a greater seasonal variation in the play of boys than of girls. Girls seem to be more conservative than boys. It was found that the girls showed less variation than the boys in frequency of participation in certain highly seasonal games. They also varied less in the number of favorite activities and in those consuming the largest amount of time. (See Chapter VII on Sex Differences.) The girls engaged in fewer of such transitory activities as "Walking on stilts," "Flying kites," "Playing blackman," etc. The girls' conservatism was further revealed by comparison of the play behavior of groups of children. Certain strictly community games were engaged in more often by boys than by girls.

Certain writers have maintained that the male shows greater variability than does the female. It has been said that women are less variable than men in reference to numerous traits. Hollingworth found practically no difference in the variability of the sexes when several thousand measurements of infants of both sexes were made.[1] Comprehensive and reliable data must be at hand before valid generalizations regarding the relative variability of the sexes may be made. It is possible that lack of precise measuring instruments may account for certain of the contradictory findings.

It would be a superficial explanation to maintain that girls show less seasonal fluctuation in their play life because of the fact that fewer seasonal activities are open to them. The real question is: Why have the girls not developed a larger variety of seasonal games and other play activities?

It is possible that girls are inherently more conservative than boys and that this conservatism is manifested in their play life. There is, however, no conclusive evidence in support of this hypothesis. The following hypothesis is advanced by the writers by way of explaining the boys' greater variability.

Data in possession of the writers seem to show that girls' play activities are usually of a type that does not take them far from home or out-of-doors so frequently. Boys, being more frequently out-of-doors, have had either to adapt their play activities to seasonal changes, or to withdraw from out-of-door activities. Apparently, they have resorted to the first alternative. Girls, being indoors much more commonly than boys, have not been obliged to develop seasonal play activities to the degree which boys have.

SUMMARY

In a number of extensive investigations of play, it was found that *few* activities are subject to seasonal variation to a marked degree. The bulk of the play life of the child is not subject to marked variation effected by seasonal change.

In the spring, many of the children engaged in certain activities in which participation was rare during the other seasons. The frequency of such seasonal activities was found to be greatest in the spring.   There are few activities characteristically autumn ones. Winter was found to have a considerable number of such activities but by far the largest number was found in the spring of the year.

Some of the activities showed tremendous seasonal variation; some practically no variation from season to season.   Between the two extremes every shade of seasonal difference was found.   It is difficult, therefore, to draw a line between seasonal and non-seasonal activities.

Greater seasonal variation was found in the play of boys than that of girls.   Girls seem to be more conservative than boys.   It was found that the girls showed less variation than the boys in the frequency of participation in highly seasonal games.

The greater conservatism of the girl in play may be due to the lesser variability of the female.   Certain writers have maintained that the male shows greater variability than does the female.   Conflicting data have been secured in this regard.   It is possible that girls are inherently more conservative than boys, this conservatism being manifested in their play life.   It may be, however, that girls are supervised in their play to a greater extent than boys, the restriction operating to keep them indoors more, preventing participation in many outdoor seasonal games.

REFERENCES

1. Hollingworth, Leta S. "The Comparative Variability of the Sexes at Birth." *American Journal of Sociology*. 1914-15, XX, Pp. 335-70.

CHAPTER XIII

PLAY ACTIVITY AND SCHOOL PROGRESS *

Educational writers have emphasized repeatedly the fact that normal play life is essential if the child is to develop to his maximum.[1] Within recent years there has been much discussion regarding the advisability of separating the gifted child from companions of his own age in order that he may progress in his school work at a rate consonant with his mentality. Prominent writers have taken opposite stands on this question. Holmes has argued that the gifted child should not be allowed to "run the dangers of a forced pace during the earlier years."

"Something should be said for normality. Health, companionship, and happy participation in the activities of his companions are considerations which should all be taken into account in dealing with every individual case. Education is a means whereby the individual may have full development among his fellows and for the common good. No short-sighted view of what individual development means should lead us to separate a bright child from the companions with whom he can be happiest and from whom he can learn most through common work and play.

". . . Nature has a program in the development of children of which we must also take account, and it may be far better to curtail or telescope the higher stages of education, which come after natural development is more nearly completed, than to run the dangers of a forced pace during the earlier years.

". . . Before we assume that they (gifted children) ought . . . to be encouraged to complete their work in the grades and in the high school in less than the usual time, we ought at least to experiment with the plan allowing them, instead, to use the time they have on school routine in freer, happier, and more rewarding ways."[2]

Klapper, too, has insisted that the gifted child should not be separated from his companions. He states that maladjustments re-

* See *The Journal of Educational Psychology,* May, 1927.

sult when a child is permitted to progress through the grades too rapidly.

"The junior high-school graduate of eleven is a maladjusted child. Child life is more than mere school study. The eleven-year-old graduates cannot play with children eleven years old, nor can they play safely with those fourteen-year-old children who are their mental equals. The high-school senior of fourteen finds few friends among his classmates of seventeen. He is decidedly a maladjusted adolescent and the school has unwittingly become a party in producing his problem. . . . Would it not be wiser to keep the superior child in school longer and to enrich its education by the addition of a variety of manual and trade experiences, by music, by physical activities, by club life, by visits to museums, and by extensive reading of fiction, of current events, and of biography? Where is the enriched curriculum that is so frequently promised?" [3]

The preceding assertations are interesting but their subjective nature renders them of questionable validity.

Freeman, on the other hand, has emphasized that acceleration as a means of adjustment has advantages not generally recognized or accredited to it; that grade skipping as a regular practice is not as detrimental as we have been inclined to think, its results being dependent upon the ability of the pupil. He states:

". . . we have in the past emphasized the distinction between acceleration and enrichment. In so doing we have made a false distinction. The real distinction is between the adjustment which merely aims at saving time and the adjustment which aims at securing for the gifted an opportunity to do work at a higher intellectual level. We have further assumed that enrichment implies keeping the pupil engaged in the work in which the pupil of average classification of the same age is engaged. This assumption is, I believe, incorrect. Acceleration actually provides enrichment. The work of the advanced grades is intellectually superior because the method which is pursued and the content are superior to those of the lower grades. From the point of view of intellectual adjustment, then, acceleration accomplishes both the saving of time and the enrichment of the instruction. The difficulties with this mode of adjustment are not of an intellectual nature but of a social nature. These difficulties may be met by proper forms of organization, and they are being progressively diminished by the very increase in the frequency of acceleration itself." [4]

The above quotations give evidence of conflicting opinions regarding the effect of acceleration upon the child's adjustment. Data in this regard are scant. The present writers have attempted to obtain salient data in respect to the effect of retardation or acceleration upon the play life of the child.

The data herein presented disclose: (1) The relationship between school progress and the number of play activities participated in by representative school children of Kansas City, Missouri, and (2) The extent to which retarded and accelerated pupils engage in social play activities.

It will be remembered that the children included in the investigation of January, 1926, were asked: (1) To indicate among the activities of the Play Quiz *only those* in which they had engaged *during the preceding week*, and (2) To designate the activities in which they had participated *alone*. The activities in which the children engaged without companionship will be designated solitary activities when alluded to in the discussion following.

Progress quotients were obtained by dividing the mean chronological age in months of Kansas City pupils of a given grade by the chronological age in months of each child in that grade.

For each child the total number of play activities participated in during the preceding week was ascertained. The number participated in in company with one or more additional children was next determined. The percentage of the total activities that the social activities represented was designated the index of social participation.

The data were assembled for 6,886 children. These were grouped according to increasing chronological age in six month intervals. Table LXVIII presents the following data for the children in each age interval: (1) Frequency, (2) Mean number of activities engaged in, and (3) Mean index of social participation. The first significant finding was the fairly consistent tendency for the number of play activities to diminish as chronological age increased. This fact is shown in Figure 40.

The relationship between chronological age and the index of social participation is revealed in Figure 41. The older groups engaged in a larger number of solitary games than the younger groups. This tendency was not especially marked but was consistent in the indices

No. of activities

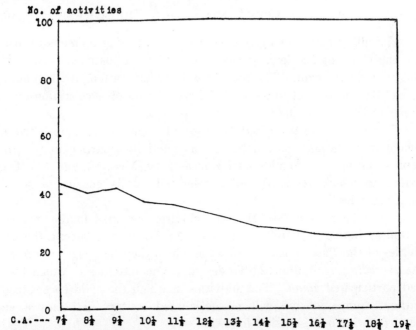

FIGURE 40. Relationship between C. A. and mean number of play activities in which
children engage. See Table LXVIII, p. 207.

Index of
Social Participation

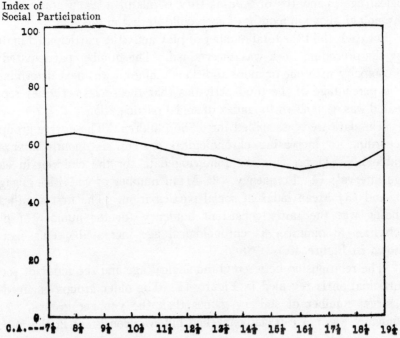

FIGURE 41. Relationship between C. A. and Index of Social Participation. See Table
LXVIII, p. 207.

of children of chronological ages 8½ to 16½. The slight rise of the curve at the extreme right (chronological ages 17½ to 19½) may be due to the small number of cases involved. On the other hand it may be due to the fact that the oldest children were pedagogically retarded children.

TABLE LXVIII

Play Data for 6,886 Children.

C. A.	Frequencies	Mean Index of Social Participation	Mean No. of Activities Engaged in
7½	84	62.01	44.26
8½	468	63.25	40.56
9½	935	61.70	42.37
10½	981	60.58	37.67
11½	748	58.12	36.86
12½	903	55.69	34.01
13½	946	55.65	31.52
14½	848	52.92	28.58
15½	573	52.28	27.45
16½	288	50.56	25.91
17½	82	52.04	24.93
18½	25	52.32	25.50
19½	5	57.50	25.50
Total	6886		

Table LXIX presents the frequency of progress quotients for 6374 children. The progress quotients ranged from 65-135. A quotient of 65 indicates that the child so designated is retarded 35 per cent of his chronological age; a quotient of 135 indicates that the child is accelerated 35 per cent of his age beyond the norm for Kansas City, Missouri, school children.

Table LXIX reveals a striking uniformity in the number of activities engaged in by all the children regardless of their varying rates of school progress. There seems to be little variation in the *number* of activities engaged in by children who vary widely in rate of progress in school. Between the intervals represented by progress quotients 80-120 there was found striking regularity. The extremes (progress quotients 120-135) also adhered rather closely to the general trend.

There are too few cases to permit generalization in regard to the extremes. The meager evidence in reference to them corroborates, however, the results of the more complete body of data, namely, the educationally retarded and accelerated children engaged in *approxi-*

TABLE LXIX

Play Data for 6,374 Children

Progress Quotients	Frequencies	Mean Index of Social Participation	Mean No. of Activities Engaged in
65-69	8	75.31	33.20
70-74	31	73.95	32.19
75-79	75	68.86	37.81
80-84	195	62.64	35.36
85-89	363	61.82	36.07
90-94	663	59.11	33.49
95-99	999	58.67	34.87
100-104	1427	56.05	34.50
105-109	1482	57.53	34.38
110-114	868	55.89	34.10
115-119	182	54.28	34.66
120-124	62	57.82	38.15
125-129	12	57.50	36.43
130-134	7	61.08	36.67
Total	6374		

mately the same number of play activities as do children who are making normal progress in their school work.

Acceleration does not exact its toll in reduction in the number of activities engaged in by the child after it has occurred. Nor does the child who progresses normally in school engage in more play activities than the retarded one. The data herein presented seem to show the falsity of the traditional view that the accelerated school child demonstrates a conspicuous lack in reference to the number of plays and games in which he participates.

The foregoing data reveal no appreciable difference in versatility of play interest exhibited by children of widely varying progress quotients. The next important consideration is concerned with the types of play in which these children participated. Particularly salient is the analysis of play in reference to the extent to which social participation is permitted. This relationship is made evident in the indices of social participation.

Table LXIX presents the relationship between indices of social participation and progress quotients. In contrast to the slight differences found in the social characteristic of play for children of increasing chronological age, there existed a rather marked tendency for pupils having very low progress quotients to turn to social play activities. It will be noted from Table LXIX that the index of social participation decreases as the progress quotient increases. This tendency was particularly noticeable with children of progress quotients 65-100. Fifty-six per cent of the activities engaged in by children of progress quotient 100, and seventy-five per cent of the activities participated in by those of progress quotient 65 were social ones. No appreciable difference was discernible in the type of play in which children of progress quotients 100-135 take part.

Robinson pointed out that it is unsafe to assume a causal relationship just because a correlation is found. Referring to the negative correlation that is always found between smoking and school marks, he expresses the following:

"Certain correlations have . . . been pointed out between tobacco smoking and such measures of intelligence as school marks. With practically no exceptions groups of non-smoking students make better marks than groups of smokers. But the earlier disposition to interpret this fact as a sign that tobacco smoking had a detrimental effect upon intelligence has been checked by more careful analysis. It is quite possible that where small boys take up smoking they do so because they lack certain social inhibitions, and the lack of these same, or closely related inhibitions may also be a cause of their disregarding scholastic duties. Among older boys perhaps the socially more intelligent are in a position where the tobacco habit is more easily cultivated. And they may also be in a position where there are a maximum number of distractions from purely scholastic activities. Thus, one aspect of intelligence might be the cause of both tobacco smoking and low scholarship. In other words the true state of affairs is far more complex than that suggested by the statement of a single causal relationship between tobacco smoking and intelligence or even tobacco smoking and scholarship."

It is difficult to account for the fact that the pupils of lowest progress quotients are found to be most social in their play. It is possible that the very environment that provides choice companionship also offers a maximum number of distractions from purely scholastic activities.

SUMMARY

Play data were assembled for 6886 children grouped according to their varying rates of progress in school. The number of activities engaged in and the mean indices of social participation were obtained for the various groups. The following facts were revealed from a study of these children:

There was no appreciable difference revealed in the studies made by the present writers in the number or diversity of play activities engaged in by children of widely varying progress quotients.

There was considerable variation among children of varying progress quotients with respect to the *type* of play activity engaged in.

Pedagogically retarded children participated in a considerably larger number of social play activities than did children who had progressed normally in school. It seems reasonable to assume that the type of activity which the child spontaneously and voluntarily participates in is a reflection of his felt need. The pedagogically retarded child then demonstrated a conspicuous need for and active interest in plays and games which provide social contacts. It is of course possible that the pedagogically retarded child's felt need is an inadequate criterion. The question is one that cannot be answered until further studies have been made. There is need for careful studies of the personality development of the pedagogically retarded child. Such studies will need to follow the child's development, and his success as an adult in the game of life will need also to be taken into account. It is possible that the retarded child's social development compensates somewhat for his pedagogical retardation; the validity of this assumption will need to be substantiated by subsequent investigation.

Pedagogically accelerated children showed little variation from children who had progressed normally in school in reference to the social quality of their play behavior. They did not engage in a larger number of solitary plays and games. On the contrary, there was a tendency for pedagogically accelerated children to engage in a slightly larger number of social play activities than children who had progressed normally. The difference between the two groups, however, was not marked in this regard. The significant fact is that acceleration did not effect a reduction either in the *number of different activities engaged in or the extent to which the child participated with others in recreational activities.*

REFERENCES

1. See Chapter I.
2. Holmes, H. W. "Intelligence Tests and Individual Progress in School Work." *Twenty-First Yearbook of the National Society for the Study of Education.* Bloomington, Illinois. The Public School Publishing Company. 1922. Pp. ix-275. (pp. 121-2.)
3. Klapper, Paul. "The Experimental Study of Education with Special Reference to the Elementary School." *Journal of Educational Research.* Sept. 1925. *12*, pp. 126-7.
4. Freeman, Frank N. "The Treatment of the Gifted Child in the Light of Scientific Evidence." *Elementary School Journal.* May, 1924. Pp. 652-661. (p. 661.)
5. Robinson, E. S. and Robinson, Florence Richardson. *Readings in General Psychology.* Chicago. The University of Chicago Press. 1923. Pp. xvi-674. (p. 655 f.)

CHAPTER XIV

PLAY AND INTELLIGENCE

In the preceding chapter it was pointed out that pedagogically retarded children are inclined to turn more frequently to social plays and games than pedagogically normal or accelerated ones. One logically inquires whether the tendency to turn frequently to social plays and games is a function of low intelligence, for it seems reasonable to assume that the children of low progress quotients are likewise of low I. Q. Dickson maintains that the chief cause of over-ageness is inferior mentality.[1]

It seems reasonable also to assume then that the intelligence of children who are accelerated in school is above the average. However, acceleration is less closely associated with mental superiority than is retardation with mental inferiority. This is proven by the fact that, although there are equal numbers of inferior and superior mentality respectively, the over-age children outnumber the under-age ones by a ratio of 7:1.[2] *

The selection of accelerated school children does not afford an adequate sampling of mentally superior children since many of mental superiority are not permitted to progress in school at a rate commensurate with their capacities for achieving. Hollingworth has stated that "nearly all children of I. Q. above 150 could enter high school at eleven years of age, and college at fifteen years or earlier. They could be graduated from college at an age not far from that at which adolescents ordinarily enter."[3]

The objections to the plan suggested by Hollingworth are based chiefly upon the discrepancies between intellectual maturity on the one hand and social maturity on the other. Before acceleration is adopted as a feasible means of providing educational opportunity for superior children, it is desirable to estimate the social adjustment of

---

* In 1925 the per cents of over-ageness and under-ageness in Kansas City, Missouri, were 23.0 and 9.4 respectively.

children whose mental ability is above average. It is necessary, therefore, to examine not only the exceptionally gifted but also groups of
children of all degrees of intelligence above I. Q. 100. The relatively
superior need adequate educational opportunity as well as the exceptionally gifted.

The present writers have secured extensive data regarding the play
behavior of several thousand children of I. Q.'s ranging from 70-145,
and of mental ages ranging from 7½ to 18½.* The Lehman Play
Quiz was employed to secure the play data. The children were asked
to indicate among a comprehensive and catholic list of 200 activities
only those in which they had participated *during the preceding week.*
They were later asked to indicate the three activities enjoyed most,
ranking them in order of merit. They were then instructed to designate
that activity which consumed the greatest amount of time, and they
were finally asked to mark *all* of the activities in which they had
participated *alone.* Data regarding intelligence were secured by the
use of the National Intelligence Test and the Terman Group Test.

Table LXVIII presents the mean number of play activities participated in and the mean indices of social participation for 6886
children arrayed by chronological age. The index of social participation was obtained in the following manner: Each child was asked to
indicate those activities in the Play Quiz in which he had participated
alone. Those participated in in company with one or more other children will be designated *social* activities in the following discussion.
The percentage of the total activities that the social activities represented was designated the index of social participation. Thus an index
of social participation of 80 indicates that 80 per cent of the activities
engaged in by the child were ones in which one or more other children
also took part. From Table LXVIII it is apparent that with increase
in *chronological age* there existed a *marked narrowing* of the play interests of the child and a *slight restriction* in his participation in social
plays and games.

Table LXX displays the mean number of activities participated in
and the mean indices of social participation for the children assembled
according to mental age. Table LXX shows clearly that the children
of higher mental ages engaged in fewer activities than those of lower

* The writers are indebted to Miss Edith Lewis for assistance in assembling these data.

mental ages. The table shows too that with increase in mental age, participation in social activities was lessened.

When Table LXX is compared with Table LXVIII it is at once apparent that the index of social participation diminishes slightly *more rapidly* with increase in mental age than with increase in chronological age.*

TABLE LXX

PLAY DATA FOR 3,176 CHILDREN

M.A.	Frequencies	Mean Index of Social Participation	Mean Number of Activities
7½	22	71.47	49.33
8½	68	67.38	43.78
9½	144	61.66	41.35
10½	222	62.17	41.09
11½	380	58.26	39.11
12½	414	55.36	32.42
13½	463	53.77	30.63
14½	410	54.28	27.99
15½	461	52.62	30.13
16½	423	51.48	32.26
17½	146	50.73	32.10
18½	23	46.41	30.54
Total	3176		

Intensive study of mentally retarded children revealed a tendency for such children to engage more frequently than normal children in *social* plays and games. It is true of course that feebleminded children are unlikely to engage in *any* type of play unless urged to do so. The conspicuous tendency to turn to social activities therefore holds only for those children of I. Q. 70-100.

In Chapter XIII (Table LXIX, p. 208) data were presented showing that pedagogcially retarded children evince also marked interest in plays and games in which others participate. Analysis of the data reveals further that the dull child tends to avoid certain individual activities, notably those involving reading, an ability in which he is conspicuously weak.

* As this chapter goes to press, but too late to make corrections in the text, the authors have secured data which seem to indicate that, when chronological age is held constant, mental age is less potent than chronological age in influencing play behavior except at the extremes of the distribution of intelligence. The figures presented in Table LXXI are correct but the youngest mental age group is not a random mental age sampling since it contains no children less than 7½ years in chronological age. Similarly, the oldest mental age group is not a random sampling since it contains few, if any, individuals more than 18½ years in chronological age.

It appears from these data that increase in mental age has relatively little effect upon versatility of play interest; that children of widely varying mental ages engage in *approximately the same number* of activities as do children with the same range of chronological ages. It is interesting, however, that participation in *social* plays and games decreases more rapidly with increase in mental age than with increase in chronological age. The mean indices of social participation for the children of three different age levels is shown in the following table:

TABLE LXXI

		Index of Social Participation
C.A.	7½	62.01
M.A.	7½	71.47
C.A.	11½	58.12
M.A	11½	58.26
C.A.	18½	52.32
M.A.	18½	46.41

How can one account for the fact that with increase in mental maturity, there exists such a decrease in participation in social activi- ties? Two hypotheses are presented by the writers as possible ones for explaining this phenomenon.

First, it seems likely that many group activities are of such a nature that low mentality does not preclude equal opportunity for success therein. On the other hand, inferior mental ability militates against success in many individual or solitary activities, particularly in reading activities. Therefore, group activities may furnish escape mechanisms through which the child of restricted ability is able to compensate for his lack of success in certain solitary activities.*

In this regard, too, it seems probable that the expression of intelligence as gauged by the group mental test is an expression of the reading ability of the individual to a large degree. It seems probable then that the very nature of the group intelligence test would posit an inordinate interest in reading activities on the part of those who succeed well upon such a test. The individual reading activities are the very

---

* It would perhaps be more logical to regard reading activities as escape mechanisms. It might then be asserted that certain children of exceptional mentality use reading as an escape mechanism to compensate for their lack of success in certain social activities.

ones best liked and most frequently engaged in by the children of advanced mental ages who were studied by the writers.

The assertion may be made with some fairness that the mental age rating of the child is but an expression of his *reading* ability and that the findings herein reported are simply corroborative evidence of the inadequacy of the group intelligence test in gauging the true mental ability of the child. The validity of such a charge will depend upon the ultimate decision as to what the group intelligence test actually measures.

The following discussion of 50 gifted children reveals certain significant differences between normal children and gifted ones in their play life.

THE PLAY BEHAVIOR OF FIFTY GIFTED CHILDREN *

There has been a great deal of speculation regarding the play behavior of gifted children. One of the most recent studies of the play of gifted children was made by Terman.[4][5] The subjects rated 90 play activities with respect to their interest in them, their knowledge of them, and the time devoted to them. Terman concluded that "The gifted are somewhat less interested than the control pupils in the more active plays and somewhat more interested in intellectual and sedentary games." [6]

The present writers secured extensive play data from fifty children of I. Q. 140 or above (Stanford Revision of Binet-Simon Test Rating). It was felt that intensive study of a relatively small group would lead to salient results.** Forty-two of these children were identified in grades 3-7 of the public schools of Kansas City, Missouri; eight were chosen from neighboring towns. Each gifted child was paired with a mentally average child (I. Q. 90-110) of like age, sex and environment. Effort was made to secure average children in reference to mental age, educational age, and school progress. The study was conducted in Jan., 1926. Nine months previous a similar study was made by the writers, using practically the same group of gifted children. In the first study the pairing device was not utilized. Comparisons were made with general standards obtained from large groups of

* The term "gifted" as here employed posits I.Q. of 140 or above (Stanford Revision of Binet-Simon Test Rating). No other implications are intended by the writers.
* See *The Journal of Educational Psychology,* April, 1927.

unselected children. It was found, however, that the two studies tended to corroborate each other.

The Stanford Achievement Test, Form A, was employed to measure educational attainment of the gifted children. The mean subject quotient (subject age divided by chronological age) was computed for each section of the test. The means ranged from 128-153. The highest mean was for reading, the next highest language usage, the lowest spelling. The children indicated that reading was the best-liked subject and spelling the least-liked. The mean educational quotient was 132.8. This signifies that the typical child in the group studied had already mastered the subject matter 32.8 per cent of his age beyond the norm for his age. The progress quotient for the group was 114. The typical child in the group was accelerated, therefore, 14 per cent of his age. The difference between 32.8 per cent and 14 per cent is 18.8 per cent. The typical gifted child in this group was under-promoted 18.8 per cent of his actual educational age. He was held back redoing work that he already knew and pursuing methods already mastered. Such findings corroborate those of Terman and De Voss.[7]

VERSATILITY OF PLAY INTEREST

The gifted group was compared with the control in reference to the number of activities in which the two groups took part. The median for the gifted group was 56. For the control group the median was also 56. When the data were assembled by sex it was found that the gifted girls engaged in a somewhat larger number of play activities than average girls, but that the gifted boys engaged in a slightly smaller number of activities than average boys. The writers feel that the differences are insignificant as the differences were small.

When the group of gifted children was considered as a whole, it was found that the median number of activities participated in was exactly the same as the median for the control group. The two groups of widely varying I. Q. did not differ in *the number* of play activities in which they engaged. The individual differences in this regard, however, were conspicuous.

SOCIAL PARTICIPATION

Indices of social participation were assembled for the two groups. The median for the gifted group was 32.0. For the control group the median was 41.67. The significance of the difference becomes more evident when it is stated that only 26 per cent of the gifted group reached or exceeded the median of the control group. Similar differences between the gifted and the average children were found when the data were partitioned for the sexes. A significant difference appears to exist between gifted and average children in the *kind* of activities engaged in. The gifted children engaged *less frequently* than average children in *social plays and games.**

ACTIVITIES IN WHICH GIFTED CHILDREN MOST FREQUENTLY TAKE PART

The indices of social participation gave evidence of the tendency of gifted children to turn frequently to solitary games and plays. One logically asks: What are the games and plays in which the gifted group participated more frequently than the average group? The writers found the percentages of each group which took part in the various plays and games. Data were assembled by sex. The gifted children engaged more frequently in every play or game listed in which reading was required. The following table shows the percentages of the two groups of boys taking part in five activities, each of which involves reading. It will be noted that 100 per cent of the gifted boys engaged in each of the activities during the week preceding the examination.

TABLE LXXII

PERCENTAGES OF THE TWO GROUPS OF BOYS WHO TOOK PART IN FIVE
ACTIVITIES, EACH OF WHICH REQUIRED READING

Name of Activity	Gifted Boys	Control Boys	Per Cent Difference
Looking at the Sunday "funny paper"....	100%	96%	4
Reading the newspapers...............	100%	88%	12
Looking at the daily comic strips.......	100%	83%	17
Reading or looking at magazines........	100%	75%	25
Reading jokes or funny sayings.........	100%	67%	33

* See P. 141 f for the discussion of the Negro Child's index of social participation, and p. 205 for a discussion of indices of social participation of children having various progress quotients.

Table LXXIII shows the activities in which the two groups of boys differed most in respect to frequency of participation. Data are presented showing the percentages of each group which participated in a given activity, and the differences between the two groups.

TABLE LXXIII

ACTIVITIES IN WHICH THE TWO GROUPS OF BOYS DIFFER MOST IN RESPECT TO PARTICIPATION

A. Activities *more* frequently engaged in by the gifted boys.

Name of Activity	Gifted Boys	Control Boys	Per Cent Difference
Reading jokes or funny sayings........	100%	67%	33
Going to entertainments, concerts, etc.....	50%	21%	29
Reading or looking at magazines........	100%	75%	25
Doing stunts in the gymnasium.........	46%	29%	17
Looking at the daily comic strips........	100%	83%	17
Watching athletic sports..............	75%	58%	17

B. Activities *less* generally engaged in by the gifted boys.

Name of Activity	Gifted Boys	Control Boys	Per Cent Difference
Chewing gum........................	50%	88%	38
Using hammer, saw, nails, etc., for fun...	42%	75%	33
Running races	46%	79%	33
Jumping for height..................	13%	46%	33
Boxing	13%	42%	29
Hide and seek......................	4%	25%	21
Baseball with a hard ball.............	21%	42%	21

Although the gifted boys engaged in approximately the same number of activities as the average boys, they chose more often games which are comparatively solitary and sedentary in nature. Particularly noticeable is the sedentary nature of five of the six activities in which the gifted boys more often engaged than average boys. Those activities in which gifted boys participated less commonly are predominantly of a motor type—active, vigorous plays and games.

One of the activities less commonly engaged in by the gifted than by the control group is No. 11 "Boxing." The following tabulation

* See p. 13 f for a discussion of the relative extents to which white children and Negro children engage in boxing.

indicates that the gifted boys were found to box less frequently than average boys.*

TABLE LXXIV

PERCENTAGES OF THE TWO GROUPS OF BOYS THAT ENGAGED IN BOXING

	Present Study	Previous Study
Unselected boys..............................	42%	31%
Twenty-four gifted boys (I.Q. 140 or above)......	13%	19%

These findings do not justify the generalization that gifted boys find less interest in most activities which are motor in nature. Some active, vigorous plays and games were engaged in more often by the gifted boys than by the control boys. "Tennis," "Playing ball with an indoor or playground ball," "Doing stunts in the gymnasium," and "Doing gymnasium work," are physical activities in which the gifted group exceeded the control in frequency of participation.

It is, however, particularly noticeable that, although the gifted child engaged in some vigorous plays, he most often turned in his leisure to sedentary activities or to moderately active games. It is especially significant that he turned much more frequently to activities which involved reading.

Another significant characteristic of gifted children is revealed by the play data. The gifted children chewed gum less frequently than unselected children. In the present study 38 per cent less of the gifted boys than of the control boys engaged in this activity.

"Teachers testify that gifted children obey rules with less urging, that very little 'police duty' is necessary, that *the problem of discipline disappears* with the segregation of the gifted pupils, that in comparison with normal children, they are more sensitive to criticism and more susceptible to correction. By way of example, a Detroit teacher states that the remark 'Refined people do not chew gum in public,' made once to a group of gifted pupils was sufficient, while in a class composed of normal children, exposed to the same suggestion, no fewer than fifteen pupils in the period of one week were asked to remove gum from their mouths." [8]

Miss Davis' conclusion is corroborated by the teachers' judgments of the gifted group studied by the present writers. The teachers reported that 98 per cent of the group respond well to discipline. Only one child seemed to provide difficulty in the classroom in this regard.

BEST LIKED ACTIVITIES AND ACTIVITIES CONSUMING MOST TIME

The data were assembled in reference to "best liked activities." For both boys and girls in the gifted group "Reading books" was the activity which was best liked. Eighteen of the 26 gifted girls mentioned reading as the activity most liked. The next most popular activity was mentioned only three times. Only five of the 26 control girls indicated reading books to be a favorite activity. Aside from the general agreement upon reading, there was no unanimity among the gifted as to their choices. Versatility of interest and tremendous individual differences were displayed. When the activities involving reading were eliminated, there was little difference between the groups in regard to favorite activities.

Data were obtained in regard to "activities consuming the most time." For both the boys and the girls of the gifted group, "Reading books" was mentioned most frequently. Nineteen of the gifted girls and ten of the gifted boys cite "Reading books" as the activity consuming more of their leisure time than any other one activity, while only three girls and one boy in the control groups so responded.

The writers attempted to classify the activities in which the two groups spent the greatest share of their time in five groups from very active plays and games to sedentary ones. When reading activities were eliminated from the list, there were no conspicuous differences between the two groups of children in respect to types of activities consuming the greatest amount of time.

The number and the diversity of the gifted group's favorite play activities and the wide range in the activities reported as consuming the largest amount of time give convincing evidence that mental superiority does not manifest itself exclusively in an inordinate fondness for reading. The gifted child is interested in reading but he has other interests also.

SUMMARY

Over 3,000 elementary school children in Kansas City, Missouri, were given the Lehman Play Quiz and either the National or the Terman Intelligence Test. The data were assembled according to mental age and I. Q. and the play data examined.

It was found that with increase of mental age, there existed a tendency for the children to engage in fewer activities. The change was gradual and the differences in the number of activities from age to age were not especially large. With increase in mental age, there was a tendency for the children to engage progressively in smaller numbers of *plays and games of a social nature.* The children of lower mental ages were found to be considerably more social in their play than those of the higher levels.

These data are corroborated by other findings of the present writers who found that pedagogically retarded children turned to social plays and games more frequently than normal or accelerated ones. (See Chap. III.) Collectively, the data give evidence of a consistent tendency for the dull or retarded school child to evince an unusual interest in games in which others take part. They show further that the dull or retarded child *avoids* certain individual activities, notably those involving reading, an ability in which he is conspicuously weak.

Fifty children of I. Q. 140 and above were selected for intensive study. Each gifted child was paired with a mentally average child of like age, sex and environment. The two groups were compared and the following facts disclosed:

The gifted group and the control group of children demonstrated the same versatility of interest in play and engaged in the *same number* of activities.

The gifted children included in this study were found to be *more solitary* in their play than average children.*

The gifted group engaged more frequently in, and spent more time upon, and preferred to a greater extent than the control group, activities involving reading.

The gifted children tended to avoid certain types of vigorous phys-

* The solitariness of the gifted children was *not* due to the fact that they had few brothers and sisters, for the only child is but *slightly* less social than the average child.

ical play. However, the gifted group participated more often than the control group in certain active plays and games although on the whole less frequently in the extremely active plays and games.

Although the gifted group devoted much more time than the control group to reading, the number of activities in which both groups took part was the same. Normal versatility of play interest may be pointed to, therefore, as a characteristic of the group of gifted children.

REFERENCES

1. Terman *et al. Intelligence Tests and School Reorganization.* Yonkers-on-the-Hudson. World Book Co. 1923. Pp. viii-111. Chap. II.

2. McCall, William A. *How to Measure in Education.* New York. The Macmillan Co. 1922. Pp. xii-416. (p. 23.)

3. Hollingworth, Leta S. *Gifted Children.* New York. The Macmillan Company. 1926. Pp. xxii-374. (p. 298.)

4. Terman, Lewis M. "The Physical and Mental Traits of Gifted Children." *Twenty-Third Yearbook of the National Society for the Study of Education.* Bloomington, Illinois. The Public School Publishing Company. 1924. Part I. 443 pp. (pp. 155-169.)

5. Terman, Lewis M., *et al. Genetic Studies of Genius.* Palo Alto, California. Stanford University Press. Vol. I. 1925. pp. xv-648. (pp. 437-9.)

6. Terman, Lewis M. *Twenty-Third Yearbook of the National Society for the Study of Education. op. cit.* p. 163 f.

7. Terman, Lewis M. and De Voss, James C. *Twenty-Third Yearbook of the National Society for the Study of Education. op. cit.* Part I. Chapter 10.

8. Davis, Helen. "Personal and Social Characteristics of Gifted Children." *Twenty-Third Yearbook of the National Society for the Study of Education.* Bloomington, Illinois. The Public School Publishing Company. 1924. Part I. 443 pp. (pp. 134 ff.)

CHAPTER XV

PLAY IN RELATION TO EDUCATION AND VOCATIONAL GUIDANCE

SUPERVISION OF PLAY

It has been emphasized repeatedly throughout this book that the teacher must accept the responsibility for supervising the play life of the child. In order that intelligent supervision may ensue, it is necessary of course to have fairly complete data at hand regarding the play behavior of each child.

There are several reasons for supervising carefully the total play life of the child. In the first place, it is essential that the educator identify the extremely solitary child, plan remedial measures, and devise an accounting system by which the success of remedial work may be gauged. That some evaluation of the play life of children is essential in estimating their adjustment is evidenced by the following quotation:

"They (psychopathic children) do not play contentedly. Other children are not safe always with them. They do not get along well with children of their own age." [1]

Morgan in discussing the characteristics of the introvertive type of person states:

"*He is of seclusive disposition.* He prefers to play and work alone. He can be found by himself when the rest are all heartily entering into some community activity." [2]

There is need also of supervision in the case of the child who plays too much, who neglects some essential phases of personality development in order that he may turn frequently to certain plays and games.

There has been no adequate technique which the supervisor or teacher might use in evaluating the amount and the character of play.

The technique described by the writers in Chapter IV enables the teacher to identify easily and quickly those children who deviate markedly in their play behavior. It enables the teacher to identify the child who takes part in a conspicuously small number of activities. It permits identification of the child who takes part in an excessively large number of plays and games. It is obvious that the child who is lacking in diversity of play interests will need to be actuated in this regard. Similarly, the child whose play life is excessive in diversity will need to be directed properly.

The use of the index of social participation* permits the identification of the child who is solitary in his play life. A complete case study of such a child is essential; however, one form of adjustment must come through redirection of his play. Particularly important is the identification of certain children who during adolescence tend to avoid social contacts and develop "turned in" personalities. The first step in proper adjustment is diagnosis. The technique described by the writers may be employed in securing salient data in this regard.

The technique may be utilized similarly in identification and diagnosis of the child who takes part too frequently in social plays and games, neglecting thereby essential features of maximum individual development.

Modern educators are becoming increasingly aware of the need of direct supervision of play. Certain modern schools are providing limited types of supervision. Mr. R. L. Lyman makes the following statement regarding play supervision in Atlanta, Georgia:

"Supervised play is a regular part of the school program for all physically capable children. Physical education for boys begins with a ten-minute period of military tactics followed by ten minutes of formal gymnastics in groups and a twenty-minute play period. The instructor makes certain that the boys play all sorts of games, although the formal side is not stressed." [3]

The question immediately arises as to whether the supervision of the boys' play ceases with the ending of the twenty-minute period. Most persons will agree readily that really adequate supervision of play must take into account much more than a child's activity during a twenty-minute period spent on the school playground. However, the

* Described in Chap. IX, pp. 132 ff.

problem of adequate supervision of play is by no means a simple one. It is possible to rob play activity of its spontaneity by means of unwise supervision. The following quotation evidences this danger.

"Valuable as supervision is, not all play should be supervised. . . . When play is supervised there are some serious dangers which must be avoided if it is to be a truly educational factor . . . it is often the case that the teacher or supervisor introduces plays for which the children are not ready. . . . Perhaps the greatest danger of all in supervised play is that the initiative will come from the adult instead of from the child. When this is true, even though children seek the direction and guidance, one of the greatest values of play is gone. The initiative, the motive force must come from the children if their play is to them really natural. When there is too much direction the essential character of the activity may be changed for children, and what in form is play may be work; when this happens, the value of both play and work is diminished. The very fact that the supervisor or teacher is an adult, and that the players are children, makes educative supervision very difficult. Adults must efface themselves more, they must play the rôle of observers more effectively, the doctrine of 'hands off' must be applied more often in dealing with children both in their work and in their play if they are to reap the full benefit of their activity." [4]

Most persons would agree that it *is* sometimes best for the play supervisor to adopt the doctrine of "hands off." However, it is none the less desirable for him to make careful studies of the child's play behavior. These studies should provide extensive factual data regarding the play life of each child.

CURRICULUM CONSTRUCTION *

The importance of utilizing the play life of the child in choosing materials of instruction has been emphasized by many thoughtful educators. According to Bobbitt, the first step in curriculum construction is that of analyzing the broad range of human experience into its major fields. The major fields of human action having been defined, the second step is that of analyzing these major fields into their more specific activities. [5] After this work has been done, evaluation of the worth of

* For a more complete discussion of this subject see Chap. 14 of *Supplementary Educational Monograph*, No. 31, "Curriculum Investigations." Chicago, The University of Chicago Press. 1926.

the specific activities proceeds. Bobbitt suggests that that part of the curriculum which has to do with training for the profitable use of leisure be made up of the worthwhile activities to which human beings spontaneously turn. The plan posits, of course, concentrated attack upon the elimination of various undesirable activities.

Professor Bobbitt's procedure for making curricula is based upon the assumption that education is a matter of human *experience* rather than a matter of textbook memorization followed by lesson hearing. [6]

The evaluation of the play life of the child is therefore a requisite in the construction of one part of the curriculum. The devices employed by the present writers have revealed those activities to which individuals spontaneously turn. It seems important that effort be made to enable children most profitably to engage in those activities in which they will take part ultimately.

Professor Briggs has asserted that the school should teach the child to do better the things that he will do whether he be instructed or uninstructed regarding them.[7] It seems logical that the duty of the school is to so train a child that he will be equipped not only to take part in the experiences of the world of actuality but will be prepared to modify these experiences so as to promote human welfare.

Curriculum construction approached from such a point of view posits a marked revision in educational objectives. At the present time the progressive teacher seeks not only to teach informational material but to develop also desirable ideals and attitudes. The value of non-functioning knowledge is being questioned seriously. Classroom instruction must be evaluated in terms of its power to modify pupil-conduct.

It is clear that in such an educational program the first step must be to ascertain what pupils of various ages actually do outside the classroom. One part of such an accounting requires a careful compilation of the activities to which children spontaneously turn in their leisure. These activities constitute their play life. To make desirable modifications in conduct it is necessary first to know what children actually do now.

It may be noted from the tables presented in this book that one of the activities in which the children studied most frequently participated was "Reading the newspapers." It is significant and vital that the school recognize this fact and utilize it in curriculum construction. It seems sensible that the school should educate children to engage *more profitably* in this activity.

Another activity of high frequency was "Going to the movies." Over 50 per cent of individuals of ages 9½ to 22½ reported that they had gone to the cinema at least once during the week preceding each of the several investigations. It is obvious that there is a danger as well as a possibility of value accruing from moving-picture show attendance. The school should turn this activity to good account.

Another important result of the investigation was the conspicuous fact that children *at particular ages* tend to engage very frequently in certain activities. One example only of this phenomenon will be given and the implications for education pointed out.

One of the activities included in the list was "Playing with hammer, saw, nails, etc., for fun." Marked seasonal differences were not revealed by the data secured in response to this item. The similarity of the results obtained from each of the investigations was striking.

Sex differences were large, the girls using a hammer, saw, nails, etc., for fun, much less frequently than boys of the same ages.

It was found that the older individuals included in the study used a hammer, saw, nails, etc., for fun, much less often than the younger ones. The transition from age to age, however, was *gradual*. The relatively slight extent to which the older individuals engaged in this activity may have been due in part to the fact that the older persons were university students.

The conspicuous and vital fact is that fully fifty per cent of the boys of ages 8½ to 13½ used a hammer, saw, nails, etc., just for fun, during the course of the single week preceding each of the several investigations. Boys older than 13½ engaged somewhat less frequently in this activity. It seems, if education is to be life, and not a preparation therefor, that this activity should be *stressed* in the curriculum at ages 8½ to 13½. The values of such procedure are apparent. Boys *will* use tools at these ages. They probably find considerable pleasure in so doing. Unguided use and lack of preparation for use may result in waste of materials, deleterious habits, and undesirable attitudes. To utilize this spontaneous tendency profitably *at the time when it is most conspicuous* is, therefore, the obligation of the educator.

The writers offer this one example in the utilization of a spontaneous tendency at certain age levels to illustrate a necessary consideration in curriculum construction.

THE PROBLEM OF INTEREST IN REFERENCE TO CLASSROOM INSTRUCTION

A problem of first import to the maker of curricula is the interest factor. It is conceded that interest in classroom work is essential for maximum efficiency. Various writers are cognizant of the need of utilizing the interests of the child.

"Many a teacher's time and patience spent trying to make the boy or girl learn could be better spent trying to find out what the boy or girl has a will to learn. *Will* being a human engine that goes best with certain fuel and in certain directions." [8]

Educational writers have long emphasized the need of utilizing children's interests in order to teach most efficiently.

"The essence of mental hygiene is then—interest for efficiency; and for protection, sleep!" [9]

"The resistance which blocks mental work may be diminished by supplying interest and motive." [10]

". . . it is a fact easily verifiable that interest *does* add to, and repugnance *does* subtract from, the amount of work done." [11]

The problem for the educator becomes one of supplying abundant interesting material in classroom activities. More specifically, the problem may be stated: What are the factors or conditions which make activities interesting to the *child?*

"The children of a school class may work with doubled efficiency simply from learning the significance of the work to their wants, and associating the work with sociability, cheerfulness, and achievement." [12]

"The genuine principle of interest is the principle of the recognized identity of the fact to be learned or the action proposed with the growing self; that it lies in the direction of the agent's own growth, and is, therefore, imperiously demanded, if the agent is to be himself. Let this condition of identification once be secured, and we have neither to appeal to sheer strength or will, nor to occupy ourselves with making things interesting. . . ." [13]

Genuine interest then results from the felt needs of the children for particular forms of activities.

A crucial problem for the teacher is that of identifying the needs of the children and allowing these needs expression in the self-initiated activities of the classroom. It seems reasonable to assume that the activities in which children spontaneously and voluntarily participate represent their felt needs. If the teacher can identify these activities to which the children turn "just because they want to" he will have a core of genuinely interesting activities which can be used as basic elements in curriculum construction and project planning.

The activities to which children turn just because they want to may be considered their play behavior. As educative forces, it is apparent that these activities are vital and indispensable tools to the modern educator.

PITFALLS TO BE AVOIDED

Another important finding of the survey merits emphasis. There is danger that curricula will be based upon the results of investigations in which past generations have been used as subjects. The case of collecting and hoarding is in point. Writers insist upon the utilization of this proclivity in curricula plannng. The investigation of C. F. Burk is cited. Burk's investigation was made in 1900. The writers have found that children engage much less frequently in this activity *now* than in 1900. According to Burk's data, 90 per cent of the boys and 91 per cent of the girls were actively making collections at the time of her investigation.[14] The present writers found barely 10 per cent of children of either sex doing so at the present time. It is important, therefore, that makers of curricula ascertain by some technique the actual interests of present-day children. The writers feel that the technique employed in the investigations herein reported is a usable one for obtaining one essential type of reasonably accurate information.

THE PROBLEM OF INTEREST AND VOCATIONAL GUIDANCE

A problem of first import to the vocational counselor is the interest factor. It is evident that interest alone is an insufficient criterion upon which to base the selection of one's life work. Individual aptitude and ability must be taken into account also. It was formerly hoped that the measurement of intelligence would afford an adequate criterion for vocational counseling. This criterion has been found to be inadequate. Analysis of the army test scores showed that although the *median* scores of the various occupational groups differed, the *overlapping of ability* among members of the various occupational groups was so great that it would be unjustifiable to attempt to use the intelligence score singly as a criterion for vocational guidance. It is probable that intelligence scores may be used to determine the *range* of occupations to which the child may aspire with a reasonable chance of success. However, the specific occupation chosen by a given child should be based upon his intrinsic interests.

The term "intrinsic interest" must not be confused with the child's passing fancy or temporary whim. The vocational counselor must evaluate the various interests of the child in terms of his ability and in terms of the *individual* or social values, accruing from utilization of these interests in further endeavor. It is, of course, true that some of the interests manifested by children are the result of undesirable motives. For example, an occupation may prove fascinating to a child solely because it offers large financial returns, or social prestige, or an opportunity to exercise authority over others. These contingencies must be recognized and safeguarded. It is the function of the vocational counselor to seek out the various interests of the child, redirect or eliminate the undesirable ones, and turn the desirable ones to good account.

In a general way, interests may be said to reveal abilities. This is another reason why the vocational counselor needs to study the child's interests.

"Interests are also shown to be symptomatic, to a very great extent, of present and future capacity or ability. Either because one likes what he can do well, or because one gives zeal and effort to what he likes, or because interest and ability are both symptoms of some fundamental feature of the individual's original nature, or because of the combined action of all three of these factors, interest and ability are bound very closely together. The bond is so close that either may be used as a symptom for the other almost as well as for itself." [15]

Granted that interests *are* symptomatic of ability, the problem of *identification* of intrinsic interests is by no means a simple one. In the first place, the range of individual interests is so great that the 200 items of the Play Quiz do not provide alone a sampling of interests for every child. For individual diagnosis it is, therefore, necessary to study carefully the items written in the blank spaces that are provided in Part B of the Quiz. Indeed, the activities listed in Part B may prove to be the *most* significant indicators of individual interest and aptitude.

From analyses of the various parts of the Quiz, some intrinsic interests may be identified. It is obvious that other interests, deep-rooted and desirable, result from directed effort with attendant satisfyingness. This fact must be taken into account. It seems reasonable, however, that a careful analysis of the play life of the child will afford the counselor an invaluable tool in effective guidance. The technique described by the writers in Chapter IV is one which obtains quickly and efficiently extensive data regarding the play life of the child. Careful analyses of data so obtained should form a part of every well-ordered guidance program. Through such analyses, interests and perhaps abilities also will be revealed.

A single example will suffice to show the value of such a program. Through the use of the index of social participation, it is a relatively easy matter to identify children who avoid social contacts in their play life; children who manifest an actual distaste for activities involving social intercourse.

Repeated administration of the Quiz is necessary to identify with certainty such children. It will be desirable to plan remedial measures providing many and diverse social contacts for some of these children. However, it may be that some healthy and well-balanced children are characterized by a tendency to withdraw persistently from social contacts. They may possess also superior mental capacity and aptitude for certain solitary activities. Obviously, such children should be directed into occupational channels for which their abilities and interests are best adapted, occupations in which they will be happy and through which they can contribute their maximum to social welfare.

The values of such a program are many. Unfortunate indeed is he who is obliged to follow an occupation in which he is little interested. Aside from the unhappiness attendant upon such functioning, there is, of course, the problem of efficiency. It is a demonstrable fact that satisfyingness has a favorable influence upon efficiency even if efficiency be considered only in terms of the quantity and quality of output per unit of time.

Although it is true that satisfyingness adds to the quantity and quality of work done, there are numerous instances in which output is kept up to the maximum through vast expenditure of effort attended by sickening boredom or disgust. The measurement of efficiency therefore should recognize the emotional products of work.

"The satisfaction which one gets while working is another thing which may be taken into account. This is especially true because other criteria of efficiency, such as speed and accuracy, do not show a direct correspondence with what Professor Thorndike has called the 'satisfyingness' of work. The long and continuous performance of most types of work leads to a falling off in accuracy or speed, but satisfyingness generally decreases at a more rapid rate than these other two. It is possible for a worker to become utterly bored and disgusted without an appreciable loss in the accuracy or speed of his performance. Still, it is important to know of the development of that boredom or disgust, because it may indicate a coming collapse or revolt which may be of far more importance than an early loss in accuracy or speed." [16]

Measurement of efficiency which fails to take into account the long-run effect of an activity is short-sighted indeed. Fielding maintains that lack of interest in one's work sometimes gives rise to "nerves" and that intrinsic interest in one's work is a cure for "nerves."

"There is one essential requirement in making arduous work nerve-proof, and that is it must be interesting. This does not make it consume any less energy, but it means that work then becomes a source of satisfaction to the ego. As the ego is a factor of our primitive personality, we are again brought to the point where we must stress the necessity of coördinating the social and primitive sides of our personality. When the nature of our work is such that it accomplishes this result, there is no danger of nervous collapse from overwork.

"Comparatively few people, however, are so fortunate as to have this kind of 'job.' With the rapid specialization of industry and business, the opportunities for expression of the personality and gratification of the ego at one's work are becoming more rare. The exceptions are to be found mostly in those fields that are devoted to experimentation and development, or that offer free play to the individual's initiative." [17]

Those who have chosen their occupation in accord with their abilities and interests afford evidence of the increased joy in living that comes from finding one's "work."

"We all have our work, our set tasks and duties; but those of us who get the most out of life are they whose work would be their preferred play, quite apart from its pursuit as a means of livelihood." [18]

The writers have indicated previously that the problem of vocational guidance is a complex one. To perform intelligent guidance the counselor needs rare insight and specific training. He must be able to discover the traits necessary for success in certain occupations and select tests which will measure these traits. There are at present several tests aiming to guide pupils into highly specialized occupations. However, the counselor in his mathematical diagnosis of ability must not overlook a most important factor in occupational success, i.e., the interest factor. Although there is no single, standardized means for identifying individual interests, the present writers feel that frequent administration of the Lehman Play Quiz with subsequent analyses of results will secure data that wisely used will aid materially in securing maximum occupational success.

REFERENCES

1. Mateer, Florence. *The Unstable Child*. New York. D. Appleton and Company. 1924. Pp. xii-471. (p. 169.)
2. Morgan, John J. B. *The Psychology of the Unadjusted School Child*. New York. The Macmillan Company. 1924. Pp. xi-300. (p. 134.)
3. Lyman, R. L. "The Junior High Schools of Atlanta, Georgia." *The School Review*. Oct. 1925. *33*, Pp. 578-94. (p. 592.)
4. Norsworthy, Naomi, and Whitley, Mary T. *The Psychology of Childhood*. New York. The Macmillan Company. 1922. Pp. xix-375 (221 f.)
5. Bobbitt, Franklin. *How to Make a Curriculum*. Boston, Houghton Mifflin Co. 1924. 292 pp. (p. 8 f.)
6. Bobbitt, Franklin, *op. cit.* (p. 44.)
7. Quoted by Van Denburg, Joseph K., in *The Junior High School Idea*. New York. Henry Holt and Company. 1922. 423 pp. (p. 4.)
8. Dorsey, George A. *Why We Behave Like Human Beings*. New York. Harper Brothers. 1925. Pp. xv-512. (p. 460.)

9. Thorndike, E. L. *Educational Psychology.* (Briefer Course.) New York Teachers College, Columbia University. 1913. Pp. xii-442. (p. 330.)

10. Thorndike, E. L. *op. cit.* (p. 325.)

11. Thorndike, E. L. *op. cit.* (p. 318.)

12. Thorndike, E. L. *Educational Psychology.* In Three Volumes. New York. Teachers College, Columbia University. 1913. Vol. III. p. 128.

13. Dewey, John. *Interest and Effort in Education.* Boston, Houghton Mifflin Co. 1913. Pp. ix-101. (p. 7.)

14. Burk, Caroline Frear. "The Collecting Instinct." *Ped. Sem.* July, 1900. 7, p. 180.

15. Thorndike, E. L. "The Permanence of Interests and Their Relation to Abilities." *Popular Science Monthly.* 1912, *81,* p. 456.

16. Robinson, E. S. "Factors Affecting Human Efficiency." *Annals of The American Academy of Political and Social Science* 1923. CX, Philadelphia. Pp. 94-105. (p. 97.)

17. Fielding, William J. *The Caveman Within Us.* New York. E. P. Dutton and Co. 1922. Pp. xv-372. (p. 162.)

18. Seashore, Carl. *Introduction to Psychology.* New York. The Macmillan Co. 1923. Pp. xviii-427. (p. 280.)

INDEX OF AUTHORS AND NAMES

INDEX OF TOPICS

THE END

STUDIES IN PLAY AND GAMES

An Arno Press Collection

Appleton, Lilla Estelle. **A Comparative Study of the Play Activities of Adult Savages and Civilized Children.** 1910

Barker, Roger, Tamara Dembo and Kurt Lewin. **Frustration and Regression: An Experiment With Young Children.** 1941

Brewster, Paul G., editor. **Children's Games and Rhymes.** 1952

Buytendijk, F[rederick] J[acobus] J[ohannes]. **Wesen und Sinn des Spiels.** 1933

Culin, Stewart. **Chess and Playing-Cards.** 1898

Daiken, Leslie. **Children's Games Throughout the Year.** 1949

[Froebel, Friedrich]. **Mother's Songs, Games and Stories.** 1914

Glassford, Robert Gerald. **Application of a Theory of Games to the Transitional Eskimo Culture.** 1976

Gomme, Alice B. and Cecil J. Sharp, editors. **Children's Singing Games.** 1909/1912

Groos, Karl. **The Play of Animals.** 1898

Groos, Karl. **The Play of Man.** 1901

Lehman, Harvey C. and Paul A. Witty. **The Psychology of Play Activities.** 1927

MacLagan, Robert Craig, compiler. **The Games and Diversions of Argyleshire.** 1901

Markey, Frances V. **Imaginative Behavior of Preschool Children.** 1935

Roth, Walter E[dmund]. **Games, Sports and Amusements.** 1902

Sutton-Smith, Brian, editor. **A Children's Games Anthology.** 1976

Sutton-Smith, Brian, editor. **The Games of the Americas,** Parts I and II. 1976

Sutton-Smith, Brian, editor. **The Psychology of Play.** 1976

Van Alstyne, Dorothy. **Play Behavior and Choice of Play Materials of Pre-School Children.** 1932

Wells, H[erbert] G[eorge]. **Floor Games.** 1912

Wolford, Leah Jackson. **The Play-Party in Indiana.** 1959